Cinema before Cinema
The Origins of Scientific Cinematography

Virgilio Tosi

Translated by Sergio Angelini

British Universities Film & Video Council

British Universities Film & Video Council
77 Wells Street, London W1T 3QJ
Tel: 020 7393 1500 Fax: 020 7393 1555
E-mail: ask@bufvc.ac.uk   www.bufvc.ac.uk

ISBN 0 901 299 75 8

Original Italian edition © 1984 ERI Edizioni Rai Radiotelevisione Italiana
Second edition © 1993 Universidad Nacional Autónoma de Mexico

Cover pictures
Detail from *Saut de l'homme au canotier* by Étienne-Jules Marey (c.1887),
Cinémathèque Française.

Typesetting and layout by Gem Graphics, Trenance, Nr. Newquay, Cornwall TR8 4BY.
Printed in Great Britain by Print Solutions Partnership, 88 Sandy Lane South,
South Wallington, Surrey SM6 9RQ

Contents

Foreword

For more than twenty years *Il cinema prima di Lumière* has been one of my most enduring points of scholarly reference, an ongoing source of inspiration and a constant reminder that the history of the moving image goes back way before the Grand Café screening of 28 December 1895. Since the first publication of the book in Italian, much has been published in the domain of the so-called 'pre-cinema', and the names of hitherto obscure pioneers have been brought to the attention of specialists in the field. Still, the process leading to the birth of photographic moving images as a tool for scientific discovery has not yet received the attention it deserves. A great deal of progress has been witnessed in France and other countries under the impulse of a new generation of researchers; however, if one looks for a comprehensive history of the origins of scientific film and the quest for its practical applications, Virgilio Tosi's work still stands out as the truly indispensable work on the subject.

Given the flurry of studies in early cinema published during the past two decades, it is surprising that a seminal work such as *Il cinema prima di Lumière* had not yet found a publisher in English until today. This translation does more than fill a major gap: it reveals the scope and depth of Virgilio Tosi's scholarship and commitment to cinema as a means to explain cinema itself, as exemplified by his outstanding documentary THE ORIGINS OF SCIENTIFIC CINEMATOGRAPHY, the most impressive corpus of audiovisual documentation on the kind of moving images we often read about but rarely, if ever, have a chance to see on the screen. The book and the film complement each other so well that an entire academic course could easily be devoted to these two extraordinary works. I am so used to thinking of them as two facets of a unified vision of cinematic history that I have often found myself incessantly shifting from one to another as if I were looking at one and the same opus.

Another lesson I draw from Virgilio Tosi's work has to do with the language he adopts to convey his impressive knowledge to the non-specialised reader. I am always amazed at his ability to present an admittedly complex set of issues with the understated assurance that derives from a long-standing acquaintance with the subject. In my view, the fact that the author never steals the scene from the people he is talking about is a testimony to the kind of scholarship which endures the test of time, the ultimate trademark of a classic. It is my hope that a much larger community of readers will benefit from this book as much as I did. More importantly, I am confident that the author's sheer enthusiasm for his subject matter will affect those who are eager to question the boundaries between moving image as a technology and as an aesthetic experience. From an academic perspective, Virgilio Tosi is one of the masters who have shaped our view of the discipline; from a human standpoint, his painstaking exploration of this fascinating domain is the living demonstration that curiosity and a sense of wonder are the key ingredients of true creativity.

Paolo Cherchi Usai
Ramingining, May 2005

Introduction to English edition

With considerable pride the British Universities Film & Video Council (BUFVC) has been able to translate and publish in English this version of *Il cinema prima di Lumière* – some twenty years after its first appearance in Italian. The underlying work in the original book and the related compilation films was the result of dogged determination by the author Virgilio Tosi. He was among the first to recognise fully the historical significance of the moving image recording pioneers and their use of time-based media for scientific exploration.

The pioneers of the recorded moving image sought to find out more about the world. The development of the medium of film arose as a direct result of their need to record, slow down, speed up and analyse natural phenomena. In 1984 Virgilio Tosi brought together important historical information on the pioneers and subsequently made arrangements to re-copy examples of their original works to film to document and demonstrate the chronology and process of this vigorous development throughout Europe in the late 19th and early 20th centuries.

Through Sergio Angelini, our Library and Database Manager, who is a practised translator and a knowledgeable film historian, we have finally been able to fulfil our long-held promise to Virgilio Tosi to make his book available to English-speaking audiences. Thanks are also due to Luke McKernan and Joanna Yates for their work in preparing the work for publication. The book comes with an additional chapter, bringing his research up-to-date.

The BUFVC, which promotes the broadest appreciation of film and related media as scholarly resource, was first involved in preparing the English version of the accompanying film compilation series – THE ORIGINS OF SCIENTIFIC CINEMATOGRAPHY – which was produced by Virgilio Tosi in a co-production between the Institut für den Wissenschaftlichen Film (Gottingen), Istituto Luce (Rome) and Centre National de la Recherche Scientifique (Paris). This series has now been made available on DVD.

Cinema Before Cinema (as we have retitled the book) and THE ORIGINS OF SCIENTIFIC CINEMATOGRAPHY demonstrate that the recorded moving image was developed primarily as a medium of discovery and a powerful communicator of ideas. This is also the foundation for the continuing importance of moving pictures in higher education and research.

Murray Weston
Director
British Universities Film & Video Council
September 2005

Translator's note

Umberto Eco, in his book on translation, comments that those undertaking the activity should, if possible, have 'both the experience of translating and that of being translated', but also goes on to state that 'when one has a text to question, it is irrelevant to ask the author.' In my experience with this project it has been my pleasure to experience the value of the former and the inaccuracy of the latter. Professor Tosi displayed considerable patience and awe-inspiring energy in sitting down with me and going through every single line of the first draft of this English language translation of his book *Il cinema prima di Lumière*. I am grateful to him for his generous help and for this most valuable experience.

Paul Auster has likened translating to coal digging, concluding that, 'each lump is a word and each shovelful is a sentence'. You certainly cannot do it without friendship and support, and I particularly wish to express my sincere gratitude to my parents Janet and Giuseppe Angelini of G&J Translators, who provided me with unstinting support and expertise and who went well beyond the call of duty on numerous occasions.

While considerable effort has been made to find appropriate equivalences for the intricacies of the original, any linguistic inadequacies, foibles and opacities that have resulted in this English version are solely the responsibility of the translator.

Sergio Angelini

Acknowledgements

Original edition

The author must thank the many people and institutions that, during the ten years in which the historical research and writing of the text was undertaken, have in various ways helped him in his work. Apologies are due for the inevitable omissions.

Special thanks go to Jean Painlevé; Susanne Duval at the International Scientific Film Association; Noëlle Giret and Pierre Bracquemond at the Cinémathèque Française; Henri Savonnet, secretary of the Association des Amis de Marey, Beaune; Hans-Karl Galle, director, and Werner Grosse at the Institut für den Wissenschaftlichen Film, Göttingen; Manfred Gerbing at the Hochschüle fur Film und Fernsehen, Potsdam-Babelsberg; Nat Taylor at the Open University; Ion Bostan at the Sahia film studio in Bucharest; Edgardo Macorini, for his encouragement which helped the author complete the writing of the text; Alberto Angelini, for his contribution to the bibliographic research for the first part of the book.

Among the libraries, museums and film archives which, beyond their institutional functions, exhibited true collaborative spirit, the author would like to thank Lucia Fanelli, director, and Angelo Urban at the library of the Centro Sperimentale di Cinematografia, Rome; Maria Adriana Prolo, director, and Roberto Radicati, librarian, at the Museo Nazionale del Cinema, Turin; F. Schmitt, curator of the Archives du Film, Bois d'Arcy; Mlle Alexandre at the library of the Paris Observatoire; Mrs Baker at the Library and Museum at Kingston-upon-Thames. Additional thanks also go to Gerlof Van der Veen, University of Utrecht; Robert Dickson, University of California; Walter Url, University of Vienna; Aleksandr Zguridi in Moscow; Jan Jacoby and Z. Czeczot-Gawrak in Warsaw; Dominique Negel and Véronique Godard in Paris; Marie-Pierre Romand, director of the Musée Marey, Beaune; Etienne-Noël Bouton in Chagny-en-Bourgogne; Christine Delangle at the Archives du Collège de France.

Finally, a thank you that serves as a dedication, to my wife Alena, and my daughters Barbara and Giulia who – without feeling too exploited – helped with translations from various languages, transcriptions and revisions of the text.

English edition

For this English edition my thanks go in particular to Murray Weston, Director of the British Universities Film & Video Council, who, for decades, has shared with me in the most active period of the International Scientific Film Association. I thank him now, with the publication of this book, for the tenacity with which for years he has pursued the objective of making it available in English. My thanks go to Sergio Angelini, a valuable collaborator, for the care he took in undertaking the translation and for the attention to detail he brought to clearing up points that could have lent themselves to misunderstandings. Last, but certainly not least, my thanks also to Luke McKernan for the help he provided in the delicate role of editor of the book, accomplished with the spirit of a passionate scholar of the book's subject matter.

Editor's note

Further thanks are due to Stephen Herbert, for his careful reading of the text and his suggested amendments in the light of recent scholarship; and to Jo Yates, BUFVC Publications Officer, for adroitly seeing the book through to publication.

Images come from the Archives du Collège de France (Paris), British Film Institute (London), Cinémathèque Française (Paris), Institut für den Wissenschaftlichen Film (Göttingen), Kingston Museum and Heritage Service (Kingston-upon-Thames), Musée Marey (Beaune), Národní technické museum (Prague), the Photographic History Collection, National Museum of American History, Smithsonian Institution (Lucien Bull image), Science Museum (London), and the author's collection.

Introduction and thesis

As the twentieth century came to its close, the cinema, meaning cinematographic exhibition, celebrated its centenary. Traditionally this has meant the inaugural public screening for paying customers of the Lumière brothers' Cinématographe on 28 December 1895.

It appears that the lively debates, with their nationalistic bias, have died down, debates which for decades saw the four great western powers all claiming to have come first in the race to invent the greatest and most popular entertainment in the world. Facing each other were France; the USA with Thomas Edison (the first Kinetoscope parlour opened in New York on 14 April 1894, where individual paying customers viewed short films which started being made in 1893); Germany with Ottomar Anschütz (who projected photographic motion pictures of very short duration to paying customers from 25 November 1894) and the Skladanowsky brothers (who began a series of regular public showings from 1 November 1895 as part of the variety show at the Berlin's Wintergarten); Great Britain with William Friese-Greene (who claimed to have filmed and projected actual short films from 1889). Even Italy could have claimed a candidate with its Kinetografo patent (lodged on 11 November 1895) by Filoteo Alberini, who had designed a machine that could shoot, print and project film. After the Lumière success, Alberini immediately gave up his role of inventor and, having set up Italy's first company for cinematographic production, he became an important film producer.

The print campaigns supporting these diverse claims between the nineteenth and twentieth centuries were not however made just out of nationalistic pride. At the same time, in the world of business, industry and commerce, a series of hard battles were taking place in what cinema historians now refer to as the 'patent war.'

Then for a few decades these polemics kept cropping up, predominantly for chauvinistic reasons. At its most intense, entire volumes were written, some even with documentation and annotations that had been doctored, to give credence to deformed and partisan views of history. This nationalistic ardour made otherwise serious academics into ugly and shabby figures.

In the end good sense and historical reality prevailed: in their most recent work, various researchers have tended to align themselves to a view of the invention of the cinema as a gradual and multiform phenomenon, and therefore attributable to neither a single individual nor country. Nevertheless, the conventional view remains which takes as the historical reference point the projection in Paris at the Salon Indien of the Grand Café on the Boulevard des Capucines.

As was predictable, the great celebrations and exhibitions in honour of the centenary of the birth of cinema took place in and around 1995, with all of the attendant publicity that one might have expected.

But what has it become, what weight will cinema exhibition have in everyday life now that we are faced with a new century? Having been for a few decades the greatest and most popular entertainment in the world, with the advent of television a process has begun – one which is still ongoing – a transformation of social habits, of structural and economic crisis in the filmmaking industry, of reassessment and transformation of the creative work itself.

So is 28 December 1895 still a date of historical significance? Did 1995 mark an important centenary from a socio-artistic-cultural standpoint, on a global scale? Or should 1995 have seen only a ribbon of surviving cinema exhibitors unveiling a plaque full of regrets on a Paris street? This book was not intended, in its original form, to anticipate the centenary celebrations for the Cinématographe Lumière. If anything, it arrived late to try and fill a gap – that of a centenary that had already passed without having been celebrated. It tried – and it still tries – to re-establish a significant historical point: the true birth of cinema, which is to be found with roots different from those of entertainment.

Thesis

1. The real birth of cinema is not to be found in the invention and development of the cinematic spectacle.
2. The cinematograph, as we have come to know it in the glorious decades of the silent era, later sound and eventually colour, in other words the traditional cinema spectacle, might even vanish or anyway be reduced to a marginal phenomenon, replaced by new, more global methods of audio-visual mass communication.
3. The real birth of cinema was determined in the nineteenth century by the needs of scientific research, by the need (and the gradually increasing technical possibilities) to record physical reality in its dynamic quality for the purposes of analysis, discovery and therefore understanding.
4. Scientific cinema, born many years earlier than cinema as spectacle, constitutes the historical basis for the language of moving images. It represents a new and underestimated dimension in man's ability to perceive and to communicate by way of a code that expands on those already in use (gestural, verbal, written, plastic, representational).

Part One

How Histories Give Birth to the Cinema

To get to grips with the bibliographic documentation relating to the birth of the cinema, not just the part that relates to the thesis of this book, but the whole history, it has been necessary to consult several dozen texts published in several languages over almost a century. The object of this research has been to make a comparative analysis of how the histories of the cinema tell the story of the birth of the cinema. To sum up the work that has been undertaken, the existing literature has been divided into groups:

a) general histories of the cinema;

b) histories of the cinema that give emphasis to the birth of cinema and works that are entirely dedicated to the latter;

c) works that deal specifically with scientific cinema.

Obviously the first group is the largest, but it is possible to synthesise the general trends common to most of the authors and then gather and organise these by their main approaches.

1. Hunting for ancestors

It is immediately clear that historians have, almost in unison, attempted to give the origins of the cinema a sort of hinterland, ancestors in the history of human culture, as if they were afraid simply to present the phenomenon of cinema as a technological accomplishment. In other words, they attempt to ennoble it and so redeem the origins of cinema exhibition that by and large first took place in cafés and fairs and circus tents. It is easy to recall the camera obscura created by G.B. Della Porta, the design by Leonardo da Vinci which preceded it, the studies by Leon Battista Alberti, to conjure up the marvels of the magic lantern demonstrated by Kircher the Jesuit, even if all these attractive mementoes from the past have actually very little to do with cinema. There are those that think that they have hit the bull's-eye with the ancient tradition of Chinese shadows. Then there are those who are even braver and who reach much further back, citing the frescos by Giotto, the bas-relief of the Trajan's column, the figures on Grecian urns, even the hieroglyphics in Egyptian papyri, as evidence of a need for cinema being expressed with the limited methods then available.

Then there are the ideologues, those who go looking in ancient texts for the poetic expression, the prefiguring, of cinema. Thus we find citations featuring Lucretius and Plato: the former from *De Rerum Natura*, book IV (768–773), the latter from book VII of the *Republic*, both of which are supposed to have described the cinema-going experience many centuries ago. In some histories it is claimed that perhaps someone in Ancient Greece or Rome had in fact already invented cinema and that subsequently it had mysteriously disappeared. Those wishing to look up the texts by Lucretius and Plato can easily do so. It would be out of place here, even though one historian has defined Plato as the 'theoretical inventor of cinema.'[1]

Then there are the 'altamirans'; in other words, those that believe that humanity's obsessive need to create cinema goes as far back to prehistoric time, when an unknown artist carved and painted onto the ceiling of a cave in Altamira, Spain, a running quadruped, representing it with eight legs so as to suggest, albeit in an approximate way, the dynamics of movement.

One historian, a Spanish one interestingly, refers to 'man's millennial aspiration towards the invention of cinema, which guided the hand of the Altamira artist.' According to him, everything from the graffiti in the cave to comic book stories, bears witness to the persistence of this aspiration throughout the centuries, but which 'could not transform itself into a complete reality until the progress of science had reached a point at which it could cross the gap between myth and invention.'[2] In view of the fact that many film historians have used the Altamira example, an attempt has been made to get to the bottom of this, despite a deep-rooted suspicion that the origins of the true birth of cinema would not be found in the prehistoric caves of Northern Spain. In fact, on the ceiling of the so-called bison cave, the lateral view of the eight-legged boar is today barely visible, decipherable only if one looks extremely carefully with the aid of powerful lights. According to many sources it has been like this for quite some time; the person who discovered these rock paintings and who described them and sketched them in 1880 did not even take note of this animal. There is just a squat shadow, a blot of colour in the place of a body without signs of any legs; the animals around it, however, have been copied in detail.[3]

What is clear, however, is that from the time that this figure of a boar was more clearly described as such, with all the fuss made over an intuition of the cinema made in this so-called Sistine Chapel of prehistoric art, various colour reproductions and touched-up photographs became commercially available. In these images, one could see all that one wished to see. The fact remains that fifty years ago the two scientists of high international reputation who dealt with this case clearly stated their position; in their opinion the image is of one figure painted over another, at different periods. The position of the body is the same, but not that of the legs.[4]

A film historian, again from Spain, dedicates a whole chapter to this myth-making: 'Glory and fame of the Altamira boar – the emotion of movement.'[5] Even though forced to cite the specific scientific opinion that denies that it is an attempt to represent movement by duplicating the legs, the historian still will not give in. Instead he concludes that science simply lacks imagination, his only rebuttal being to question why then, if they were painted at separate times, would the second artist have so carefully painted over the original image. One could point out that the majority of the images in the cave (there are over thirty in all) use the contours and irregular planes of the rocky ceiling to give shape and depth to these superb primitive images. But it is hard to ask for even the shadow of a doubt from one that considers 'these miraculous drawings from Altamira, incorruptible examples of spiritual flights …'[6] But one never ceases to be amazed, such as with an American film historian who defines the painter of Altamira as an 'antediluvian Disney.'[7]

2. The nationalism of the invention

Another pernicious category is those over-the-top nationalistic writers that will subordinate empirical fact to prove their thesis for the invention of cinema (assuming that they are not simply texts written on commission to support a particular point of view). Such was the case with Terry Ramsaye's *A Million and One Nights*, a work that had a certain success some eighty years ago, and which for a long time was considered to be a serious reference work.[8] The author, a well-known figure in the Hollywood film industry, was the editor of the *Motion Picture Herald*, a film industry journal. The eulogistic preface was by Thomas A. Edison. Inevitably the book 'proved' that the true and sole inventor of cinema was Edison. To do this it demolished anything and anyone that might have in any way cast a shadow on the glory of Edison, even some who had never even thought of putting themselves forward as a potential candidate as the inventor of the cinematic experience. Ramsaye's book was even taken as reliable by such well-known scholars as the French historian Georges Sadoul. He, however, had the excuse that he was writing during the Second World War and therefore did not have direct access to American sources or the possibility to double check some of the information that Ramsaye passed off as fact. Only in the last few years has it been possible for researchers to pull down the house of cards built by the brilliant journalist, clearly with his own agenda, to the greater glory of Edison.[9]

Unfortunately there are many examples of this kind of chauvinistic alteration of the history of the birth of cinema, and they include many different countries. Whether it is the British who claim that the true inventor is Friese-Greene or the Americans who use the strangest ways to insist that the birth of cinema was in the USA, the examples are really too many to cite here.[10] There is even one writer who says, seemingly without fear of rhetoric and partiality of information, that 'the Italians were the first to address scientifically the problems of projecting images.' This, we are told, is because 'the analytic description of the so-called "camera obscura" by the immortal author of the *Mona Lisa* is the starting point of the long journey that after four centuries of hopeful research will bring the decisive discovery by the Lumières.'[11]

The literature from France is clearly very rich and presents a number of cases which border on the paradoxical, when its historians, not content simply to sing the praises of the Lumières to foreigners, end up attacking each other over other possible candidates, albeit still French ones. We shall return to this aspect later on. For now, let us limit ourselves to a quote from an author who entitled his book's chapter 'Du Soleil à Lumières' claiming that 'science and history march side by side certifying the French invention', and who closed his book with the fateful words: 'it is incontestable and not contested that *photography and the cinematographe are and will for ever remain glorious sons of the French nation ...*'[12]

3. The mythology of the cinematic spectacle

Among the various histories under consideration, one can extrapolate a group that, with respect to the issue of the birth or invention of cinema, represents a legitimate diversion: those that maintain an interest not in the birth of cinema as a mechanical fact, but as the birth of the art of film. A typical example of Anglo-Saxon pragmatism comes from an American historian who writes:

> The art of film, depending on the instrument, had to wait for the invention of the device. The machine, however, wasn't invented to make art possible, it was created essentially as a device to record and illustrate movement.[13]

The exaggerated idealism of many Europeans can be represented by the Italian writer who states (with reference to Chinese shadows), that 'cinematic expression certainly preceded the relative technical means.'[14] It can also be seen in the work of the famous French critic André Bazin who wrote:

> The cinema is an idealistic phenomenon. The idea that men had of it was already well established in their brains like the Platonic sky, and what is noteworthy is the way that the material resisted the idea, rather than the technical influence on the imagination of the inventor. Similarly, the cinema owes next to nothing to the scientific spirit. Its fathers are not scientists...[15]

A more down to earth writer, a Belgian who taught film history in Italy, has made a few interesting admissions:

> Originally, the cinema was an experiment by a few researchers motivated, predominantly, by scientific reasons. At that time they could not have foreseen the unique impact that their discoveries, with the passage of time, would have had on the analysis and synthesis of movement, born from an imperfection in the human eye ... For ourselves we have addressed studies from the point of view of the formation and evolution of film as a wholly original form of artistic expression.[16]

The same author, in a subsequent chapter, writes that the cinema is 'the natural result of a series of studies, discoveries, of various kinds of experiences: scientific, optical, chemical, mechanical.' At no point does he even remotely ask the question as to why these studies, experiences and discoveries were made; for him the cinema is just the *natural* consequence of all this. With the traditional attitude of the sufficiency of idealistic culture, he concludes: 'One will not be amazed, therefore, if we have reduced to its base essentials our look at the origins, which belong first of all in the technical arena.'[17]

Another scholar, referring to the eighteenth century physicist-aeronaut in Paris who terrified audiences with his phantasmagorias, writes:

> Robertson is the real ancestor of the cinematic art, the Méliès of the 1700s, and even if after him and before the inventions of the Lumière brothers, studies in movement led to more important scientific discoveries, his figure looms large in the history of cinema, inasmuch as he was the first instinctively to lay down the elements of a new aesthetic sensibility. In the same way as Robertson can be seen as the direct precursor of the more fantastical and expressive elements in cinema, so Plateau should be considered the forefather of its mechanical dimension.[18]

Many historians try to bypass the whole issue of the scientific origins of cinema by taking refuge behind a phrase attributed to Louis Lumière while he was speaking to Georges Méliès. Trying to dissuade him from buying one of their camera-projectors, Lumière is reported to have said that his invention would only have curiosity value for a while and that its commercial prospects were negligible. Whether it was said in good faith or not, the phrase is of no real help in addressing the issues of the true significance of the birth of cinema.

In a few isolated cases some authors, whether by chance or by a fortunate combination of words, although without the necessary historical documentation, have managed to get to the heart of the matter. One such author is Arthur Knight, who stated: 'If subsequently the cinema has been accepted as one of the recognised arts, it cannot be denied that it remains a child of science.' Another is the English author Eric Rhode, who refers to the development of the cinema as a phenomenon that grew out of the industrial revolution, in which the interests of the showmen played a secondary role since the cinematic spectacle in essence developed as a by-product of more important interests, as represented by scientific research. Even the British writer and documentary filmmaker Basil Wright, in a book not actually about the history of cinema, defines the cinema itself as 'son of the laboratory and the machine', pointing out that the research and experiments that led to its development came from the work of scientists who were analysing movement.[19]

4. The historiography of the origins

The following will consider histories of cinema that give particular emphasis to its origins and those few texts that have concentrated exclusively on this particular topic.

Shortly after the initial international success of the first Cinématographe screenings, books started to appear which attempted to describe the process by which cinema came into being, some even in a serious, methodical and well-documented fashion. In 1899 Hopwood, an Englishman, published a book some chapters of which it is still possible to read with great interest.[20] Being so close to the time of the events, he is able to bring a broad range of information, details and anecdotal episodes to some of the issues surrounding the studies of the persistence of vision that took place in the first half of the nineteenth century. He describes Muybridge's method (i.e. taking a series of stills with a number of cameras) as one that 'was not successful in its fight for survival' against the other techniques that followed it, while still appreciating its scientific value.[21] In the final chapter, he underlines again the importance that scientific uses of the cinematograph will have, though when dealing with the potential fathers of the invention, he is an early victim of those who limit themselves by only considering those that contributed significantly to cinema spectacle.

In the 1920s two important works were published in France, although both seem affected by a distinctly nationalistic spirit. The first is a history of the cinema 'from the origins to the present day' (1925) by G.-Michel Coissac, at the time well known in cinema circles, but also a journalist on scientific issues. Unfortunately, the importance of the information and documents assembled is occasionally undermined by its rather chauvinistic stance.[22]

The other book looks exclusively at the origins. Its author, Georges Potonniée, was a unique source of information as he was for many years the librarian of the Société Française de Photographie, an organisation that, as we shall see, was an important presence throughout the decades which saw the development of scientific cinema and the cinematic spectacle.[23] Potonniée is above all a historian of photography and Georges Sadoul (who states that he is in his debt for many details) considers him 'one of the best historians on the invention of cinema.'[24] It has to be said that Potonniée's book does contain some interesting historical points on the precursors of cinema. With regards to his self-confessed pro-Lumière stance it is worth recalling something he said during the debates in 1924 on the invention of cinema: Potonniée 'expresses in the end the fear that the United States, the United Kingdom and Germany, all of which claim to have invented cinematography, will take advantage of our disagreements to deny our country the credit for this discovery and suggest one of their own instead. It is to be hoped that we in France will reach an agreement and come to a shared opinion.'[25]

As for Coissac, it should be noted that his work is a notable and detailed treatise that also considers the scientific aspects of the preliminary research which led to the invention of cinema. Naturally, since the premise of the book is the establishment of Lumière as the *sole* inventor, there is a constant effort to establish the limits of the other contributors. Coissac, however, also gives great emphasis to the role of cinema in teaching and dedicates the last section of the book to this. It is therefore jarring the insistence with which, right from the rhetoric in the introduction, he claims that the credit for giving humanity this invention be given to France, just as it seems frankly excessive that in another book Coissac tries to pass off as mere Nazi propaganda the work of the German pioneer Skladanowsky, whom he insists on referring to as Kladanowsky.[26]

In the years immediately after the Second World War, Georges Sadoul, whom we have already mentioned, came to dominate the bibliographic history of the cinema. His work, as a 'full time' film historian, has appeared internationally in many publications, which have been published over the years in new editions and in new versions aimed at a broad range of readers. His two main works are the already mentioned *Histoire générale*, a multi-volume specialist work, the first volume of which was entirely dedicated to the invention of cinema (1837–1897); and the *Histoire du cinéma mondial des origines à nous jours*, aimed at a broader readership.[27] Sadoul, like many others, started with the intention of writing a history of the arts and of the cinema, but his Marxist orientation lead him to give particular weight to the economic and instrumental aspects of the cinema phenomenon. As far as it concerns us, Sadoul can be seen as the first general historian of the cinema to look at the issues surrounding its invention in terms of a social process and technological development. Shrinking from the mythologising of the lone inventor, the shadow of which hangs over all others, he tried to maintain, so to speak, a certain international spirit to underline the variety of its contributors.

Particularly significant is the final phrase of the first volume of the *Histoire générale*:

> Plateau and Stampfer, therefore, established the principles, Muybridge undertook the first filming, Marey invented the first film camera, Reynaud gave life to the first shows of animated projections, Edison perfected the first film, about ten inventors tried to project it on a screen and Louis Lumière was more successful at it than all the others. Shortly after Méliès, adapting films to the way of theatre, transformed cinema, which before him had been a scientific curiosity, into a true entertainment.[28]

Here one finds brought together the positive results, albeit somewhat schematic and not entirely correct, of the historical research of Sadoul, and at the same time its limits. Even he does not address the main question of why these scientists and technicians, from many different countries and of differing orientations, thought to construct and make functional machines that could record and reproduce the phases and dynamics of movement. Referring to Stampfer, Sadoul uses a phrase which would not be followed up in the formulation of subsequent developments: 'First stuttering of scientific cinema applied to teaching.'[29] Let us not forget that he was referring to experiments and demonstrations that took place in 1832. Photography had barely been invented (if we accept Niépce as its inventor) and was still largely unknown.

Briefly to leave behind the French language bibliography (which is undoubtedly the richest), let us look at an important German contribution (although it contains a few errors) on the reconstruction of the period of the origins of cinema. F. von Zglinicki's *Der Weg des Films* is particularly valuable for its precise information on the activities of German pioneers and for its attempt to provide a detailed international bibliography.[30]

The basic layout remains a traditional one, however, and the same can be said for a subsequent work by Jacques Deslandes that forms part of an ambitious if slightly pretentious *Histoire comparée du cinéma*, which after the publication of the second volume remained unfinished. The first volume (*De la cinématique au cinémato-graphe, 1826–1896*) looks at the history of the origins starting from a basically scientific premise, looking at optical illusions and the illusion of movement that lies at the heart of the dynamic effect of cinema. The author provides details and clarifications that were the result of original research, much of it in-depth. Given the comparative character of the work, Deslandes in many cases tried to establish a synoptic view in relation to questions of priority. Deslandes, however, was motivated by a highly polemical perspective on Sadoul's earlier works, and although he was able to dispute some of his facts and opinions, the often bitter tone and personal attacks have the effect of diminishing the perspective on the subject under consideration. On the other hand, even he, both in his premise and in his conclusions, repeatedly makes the point that his chronicle of the history of cinema is only meant to function as an introduction to the history of the Art, with a capital a. He almost apologises for the fact that the first volume 'will deal much more with machines than with films, more with mechanics than with aesthetics.'[31] He gives great weight to the disputes among the various inventors, but he does not ask himself the reason behind so many inventions.

Remaining in the French language and in the 1960s, there was another multi-volume work, this time by Jean Mitry, a university lecturer in film history, which despite its stated period (1895–1914) looked in broad terms at the preceding period, even casting its net as far back as prehistoric caves.[32] The treatment is the traditional one and states that it will not look at *how* cinema came into being. The treatment is fairly precise, if somewhat didactic, and in it there are a number of accurate acknowledgements such as the comment that Marey had conceived of his instrument 'to facilitate the study of locomotion in men and animals, *to analyse movement*.' However, a few lines, later he is taken to task over it for having 'ignored the fundamental role that it could have played in the history of cinema', because he had not resolved the issue of projection, despite the fact that this really did not actually interest Marey.[33] It is certainly a curious overturning of the methodology of historical analysis!

In any event, nearly ten years after publishing his history of the cinema, Mitry did return to the topic, with an issue of a journal edited under his supervision by his students at the Sorbonne.[34] The text did not stray too far from the traditional course, but the publication did include a number of interesting contributions and references to a number of rare texts, as well as a bibliography of publications from the period of the origins.

Rather different were the efforts of the English writer and critic Roger Manvell, who collected a series of essays from different countries in *Experiment in the Film*.[35] Despite some interesting sections, nothing is added to the historiography of the origins of cinema, not even in the text by John Maddison (one of the co-founders of the Scientific Film Association in 1947), which under the title 'Experiment in the Scientific Film' quickly and superficially dismisses the historical theme, concentrating instead on recent developments in scientific cinematography. Some original ideas can be found, amid much second-hand material derived mainly from Sadoul, in a book by Kenneth MacGowan.[36] The author was an unusual figure in the American cinema: starting off as a film critic during the First World War, he then became a film producer in Hollywood during the early sound years, and after the Second World War he dedicated himself to setting up the film studies programme at UCLA and to the study of film history. Among the book's illustrations is a reproduction of a flier announcing that on 22 February 1895 there would be the screening of 'Le Roy's Marvellous Cinematographe' in a theatre in Clinton, New Jersey (which later turned out to be non existent). MacGowan describes how, following research by Gordon Hendricks, one of the best-known scholars on the origins of American cinema, it was established that the flier was in fact a fake created many years later by independent producers to try and protect themselves against Edison's lawyers during the patent wars. This episode is indicative of how, for political reasons and due to economic interests, some reached the point of manipulating and even inventing events during the origins of cinema, and of how much work still remains to be done in the field of historical research.[37]

To conclude this review of the literature on the subject we need to look at four very different, but particularly important, publications. Foremost among them is *Eine Archäologie des Kinos* (*Archaeology of the Cinema*) by C.W. Ceram, which was dedicated to our subject matter at hand and which was widely distributed throughout the world.[38] This popular and extremely readable volume only deals in part with the origins of cinema and for the most part treats it accurately. However, there are a few notable omissions (for example it ignores the contribution made by the astronomer Janssen), and it presents itself always in the context of an industry that will give birth to the most popular entertainment medium in the world. The book is none the less extremely interesting for its iconographic documentation that dominates the text proper.[39]

The second publication is a small German book, *Als Man Anfing zu Filmen*, that can only have had a limited distribution but which must have in large part influenced Ceram's work. The publishing and educational branch of the famous UFA production company published this semi-educational book by Hans Traub.[40] The author had already published a pamphlet by the same title in 1935 but in this new publication he emphasises what he claims to be the fundamental importance of the historical work by Liesegang, to whom we will return later. Traub's book comes close to a scientific look at the issues surrounding the birth of cinema. He starts by looking at how images were used to study behaviour and then presents the development of sequential images, combining Muybridge, Marey and in part Anschütz with the Skladanowsky brothers. He concludes with a section on moving images (*Das Laufbild*) and the contributions made by Le Prince, Demeny, Lumière, Messter, Edison and Reynaud, presenting them in a rather odd order of appearance.

The third publication is a pamphlet from the Science Museum in London cataloguing their collection of documents and devices on the origins of cinema.[41] The author (the curator of that part of the museum) produced 'an introductory booklet on the prehistory of cinema.' Despite a slight tendency to privilege Edison and some British inventors, it provides a useful historical survey within the context of providing a broad look at the basis for what is not simply a type of entertainment but also a form of art, an educational tool and a scientific instrument.

Finally, Jean Vivié, a historian and lecturer on cinematic technique, in the first volume of his treatise compiled a sadly little known but none the less notable summary on the birth of cinema seen from the point of view of the development of technical equipment.[42] The occasional lapse or omission takes nothing away from the importance of this general and comparative look that is constructed with both precision and clarity. His exposition, given the technical character of his treatise, has a fairly rigorous methodological basis, even though the text is rather a condensed one.

Initially it might seem strange, even contradictory, that Vivié should place his description of the historical developments relating to the synthesis of movement ahead of those relating to its analysis. One must not forget, though, that his fundamental perspective remains that of a historian studying the birth and development of the techniques of the film entertainment industry. Thus a comment made by Vivié can be considered as a specific indication and starting point for the work we are undertaking here: 'cinematographic recording was born from the requirements of scientific research.'[43]

5. What caused the birth of cinema?

All that remains now is to review those few works, the most specialist in nature, which deal directly with scientific cinema and which relate to the birth of cinema itself. Beyond the small number of these texts one also bemoans, with the odd exception, the only limited interest shown in the fact that scientific cinema clearly predates entertainment cinema. This can be explained by the power of the wide acceptance of the ideology behind the cinema as the most popular entertainment in the world. This myth requires the removal of anything that might tend to contradict it, especially if it precedes it. Georges Mareschal, in his preface to one of the first books dedicated to scientific cinema, was the amazed interpreter of this point of view:

> It is rather curious to note how the cinematographic machine, created to assist in the study of movement, becomes an object of curiosity when used in this way on the screen.[44]

Jacques Ducom, the author of this practical treatise on cinematography, first published in 1911, was the assistant projectionist for the first public screenings of the Cinématographe Lumière in Paris. His duties were to regulate the lamp in the machine and to rewind the film back on the spools; later on he worked, still as a technician, in Gaumont's first workshop in Paris. His book is thoroughly mediocre and written in the style of a second-rate pot-boiler. The main section of the first chapter consists for the most part of the full text of a conference held by Georges Demeny on 1 February 1909 at the Ligue Française de l'Enseignement, on the 'origins of the cinematograph.' We will consider Demeny's own contributions later on and will therefore discuss this conference at that point. Ducom limits himself to commenting that the inventors of cinema were basically good and simple scientists who did not concern themselves with 'the moral responsibility that they were assuming in giving to the world this machine for reproducing external manifestations which so successfully interpreted the innermost emotions of that organised and thinking being that we are.' He bizarrely concludes the chapter thus:

> The universal cinematograph will become, we hope, the most powerful machine invented by man, to help him fight against barbarity and ignorance ... Happy those that will be able to profit from it financially.[45]

The book published and partly written by Franz Paul Liesegang in 1920 is of a much higher order.[46] He was a physicist specialising in photography and projection techniques; the actual scientific treatise which he co-authored is mainly a re-write of his manual of practical cinematography first published in 1907 and which had gone through six editions. For this major work, Liesegang asked the noted German photo-chemist K. Kieser to contribute a chapter on positive and negative film, but for the most part he collaborated with Professor Polimanti, director of the Institute of Physiology at the University of Perugia. He wrote approximately a third of the text, on the use of film in the natural sciences, medicine and in teaching, a general historical introduction and introductions to each of the sectors to which it applied, plus a very rich, specialised bibliography. Right from the preface, Liesegang specified that Polimanti was 'representative of a branch of science that for the first time used film as a technical instrument, that used this research method in the most successful way and which drew the most benefit from it.' He points out the ways in which the Italian scientist used cinematographic methods in his research, thus making him particularly qualified to wrote on the scientific applications of cinema.[47]

Liesegang does not deal directly in the text with the origins of cinema, but on the other hand, with the rigorous approach befitting a manual, he takes as his sole object the study of film as a technical process and its scientific applications. Those that brought cinema as entertainment into being, from Lumière and Edison to Skladanowsky and others are referred to with reference to particular discoveries and the technical innovations of their equipment. A number of chapters look not only at the more specific aspects of scientific cinema (micro and high-speed photography, X-ray photography), but also at projection systems, issues of colour and stereoscopic cinema; throughout the whole book there appears to be no mention of fiction films. In its detailed description of camera technique one finds allusions to the final objective in shooting film: according to Liesegang (and most modern writers on scientific cinema) this can be for research purposes, teaching and popular dissemination.[48] Naturally within the individual chapters the author traces the history leading up to the latest developments, and in this regard his technical documentation as well as his descriptions of the tools and results of early film pioneers is particularly valuable. Among those mentioned most frequently by him is Marey, the French physiologist.[49]

In his historical introductions, Polimanti also avoids the questions over the origins of scientific cinema, taking them as a given. In his brief summary on the main contributors, he mentions in passing the Lumière brothers who 'popularised luminous living images' (*die lebenden Lichtbilder*), then moves on to detailed descriptions of those that pioneered the use of film in various aspects of scientific research.[50]

In the 1920s a disciple of Marey named Lucien Bull (to whom we will return later for his pioneering efforts) published what one might call the French equivalent of Liesegang's book.[51] The book was grounded as a scientific treatise on the subject, dealing with such topics as the origins of cinema through the graphic description of movement; chronophotography and the synthesis of movement; the technical description of equipment and materials; a discussion of the issues surrounding cinematic 'illusions'; colour and relief; the application of cinema to scientific research and documentation. In the final chapter there is a reconstruction of the invention of cinema. In the preface, Bull claimed that 'cinema was born in the still of the laboratory', admitting that he only wrote the last chapter following the various arguments that had arisen. This, he said, was not to deny where credit was due (a comment that implicitly refers to the Lumières), but because it would have been unfair 'not to give at least equal recognition to those that did the preliminary work before its creation.' In any event, in this serious and detailed work, Bull presents without undue emphasis the view that current cinematic equipment derived from Marey's prototypes, while at the same time acknowledging the imperfections of the latter. In his conclusion, he claims that the astronomer Janssen was the first to undertake 'expériences ayant un caractère cinématographique', with Marey and Muybridge later developing a true scientific cinema without considering its potential as an entertainment medium, since their primary concern was with the study of movement.[52]

Among the few publications that have dealt with the birth of cinema as a scientific phenomenon, there is *Cinematografia e medicina*, a monograph published as an issue of a medical journal by a multinational pharmaceutical company.[53] The text was almost entirely the work of a doctor from Zurich, Dr Nicholas Kaufmann, apart from a brief chapter provided by a biologist working for the company itself. Although principally aimed at those in the medical profession, this brief work is notable for its very effective summary and a fairly rich documentation. Kaufmann writes that, 'the birth of cinema is closely tied to physiological research. This is demonstrated by the very definition of "chronophotography" by the International Congress of Photography (Paris, 1889), which called it a combination of the scientific study of human and quadruped movement, the flight of birds and insects and the movement of fish, not to mention the fall and vibration of inanimate objects.'[54] In his enthusiasm he pushes at the edges of historical reality, claiming that 'Marey handed over the results of his research to the Lumière brothers', trying to make this sound more persuasive by emphasising that Auguste Lumière was a physician.[55]

Le cinéma scientifique français is dedicated to French scientific cinema and its history and remains an important book in many respects, but is nonetheless disappointing from our point of view.[56] One would have thought that such a specialist work would state, and then show, how scientific cinema, especially in France, had been born and subsequently been developed well before the establishment of cinema as entertainment. The authors begin with the sacrosanct claim that 'the analytical study of rapid movement is, historically, the objective of the first cinematographic research'; proving themselves to be unaffected by nationalistic pride, they write at length about Muybridge as a precursor to Marey.[57] When faced with the controversies, which pitted supporters of the Lumière brothers against those of Marey, they state that they find themselves unable to come to a firm conclusion on the matter, claiming instead that the debate is outside the stated parameters of their work. In the end they conclude that Marey, like Muybridge 'was already making films without knowing it.'[58] In this context, such a statement is extraordinary and incomprehensible, and cannot be excused by the haste with which the book was written.

A volume of documents on scientific cinema published in the Federal Republic of Germany (as it then was) by the government in Bonn and edited by the director of the IWF of Göttingen (one of the most important international centres for the production of specialised scientific films) is also just as disappointing in its, albeit brief, look at the origins of film. In it one finds the following phrase: 'One parent comes from the sciences; the other, it cannot be denied, from the carnival booths.' It then goes on to insist on a marriage between the analyser and the illusionist.

Finally let us look at *Research Films in Biology, Anthropology, Psychology and Medicine*, an important work by Anthony R. Michaelis, a British academic.[59] The author dedicated the book to the memory of Marey, 'the originator of the research film', and to the many scientists that have 'ennobled the cinema.' In the text he restates that, 'it is too often one forgets that cinematography for scientific research purposes originated with the great French physiologist Marey.'[60] For so specialised a book, it is surprising that the brief look at the origins of cinema is so broad and so full of errors, relying as it does on some questionable general texts, the limits of some of which we have already questioned.

This therefore is the state of the literature based on our research and knowledge on our main theme: how histories give birth to the cinema.[61] We have seen that what is missing, above all else, is an answer to the question as to why the cinema was born. On the historiographic plane we note that previous attempts by numerous writers, from many countries and backgrounds, faithfully to recreate from objective sources the true events that led to the birth of the cinema phenomenon were frequently led astray, sometimes without even realising it, by the dominant ideologies of the entertainment cinema.

We shall now attempt to go down the route of the true birth of cinema once again, thanking those that came before us, even if on occasion we have criticised them harshly, for their contributions and for the stimulus they have provided for our own work.

Part II
The pre-history of scientific cinema

The term 'pre-history', as generally understood, refers to the period that precedes history proper; what we term 'history' is the period defined and dated from when accounts of actual events are, to one degree or another, documented. Pre-history therefore has a certain indeterminate quality to it, a sense of looking back with hindsight, one which may have to be undertaken with evidence that is not always strictly historiographic, but which may however be able to provide the details and the direction for historical interpretation. It is in this direction that we wish to take this chapter.

The pre-history of scientific cinema therefore means that we will be looking for the events and the people who instigated, discovered, interpreted, hypothesised and created it. They constitute the necessary first indication, even if not a conscious one at the time, of what will later develop into the historical process of the birth and development of scientific cinema.

This section will not give the description of specific events, dates or persons to indicate that these were the *first*, even if they are the true prehistoric progenitors of scientific cinema, as so many others have endeavoured to do before. One must not give in to the temptation to go too far back in the past or to try and categorically fix the precise year and day of the *beginning*.[62] Rather, it is important to identify the historical moment and the cultural conditions under which the necessary elements, human and material, came together, in addition to that element of chance (which is often found but whose importance is difficult to determine), which mark a qualitative leap and a significant step forwards in relation to later developments.

The historical moment is poised somewhere between 1820 and 1840. There is a beautiful passage by Georges Sadoul, which frames it:

> The first locomotives chug along the railroads. In capitals the night is illuminated by trembling flames of gas, recently discovered. By the light of gauzed Davy lamps, miners descend to underground depths. Steam engines set in motion weaving and spinning mills. For twenty years paddle boats have been ploughing the Atlantic Ocean. In chimney stacks coal is replacing wood.
>
> In England the number of mechanical weavers is approaching that of manual ones. British cotton and coal dominate the world. In France factories are mutliplying, and are being built in Germany and the USA. In the suburbs of Lyons and London unknown forces have their first tremors, while electricity and

chemistry, in the first laboratory stages, are not yet industries. The telegraph uses Chappe's optical signalling with mobile arms while its electrification is still in experimental phase. The first sulphur matches – and the first cigarettes – are considered curioisities like the arc lamp, liquid gas, the anaesthetic properties of nitrous oxide, the tottering ancestors of the bicycle or the motor car. Nevertheless, so sudden and rapid, more or less everywhere, is this technical evolution that there is already talk of an unlimited progress destined to ensure total dominion over nature, the world, mankind.[63]

6. London, c.1820

In London, around this time, there was a concentration of scientific minds, albeit from differing backgrounds, all of whom were pragmatically devoted to the scientific method of experimentation. A few names here will suffice for our historic, or rather pre-historic, reconstruction: Peter Mark Roget (1779–1869), physician and mathematician, as well as author of the thesaurus; Sir John Herschel (1792–1871), astronomer and son of the celebrated astronomer William Herschel; Sir Charles Wheatstone (1802–1875), physicist and inventor; William Henry Fitton (1780–1861), physician and physicist; John Ayrton Paris (1785–1856), physician and physicist.

At the beginning of the 1820s, one of the most important areas of research and exploration for scientists (due not only to a certain amount of chance but because it responded to the needs of the time – the Industrial Revolution was in full swing) was that of visual perception and the persistence of vision on the retina as related to dynamic phenomena.

On 9 December 1824 Roget gave a lecture at the Royal Academy the mere title of which was significant: 'Explanation of an optical deception in the appearance of the spokes of a wheel seen through vertical apertures.'

A curious optical deception takes place when a carriage wheel, rolling along the ground, is viewed through the intervals of a series of vertical bars, such as those of a palisade, or of a Venetian window-blind. Under these circumstances the spokes of the wheel, instead of appearing straight, as they would naturally do if no bars intervened, seem to have a considerable degree of curvature. The distinctness of this appearance is influenced by several circumstances presently to be noticed; but when every thing concurs to favour it, the illusion is irresistible, and, from the difficulty of detecting its real cause, is exceedingly striking.

The degree of curvature in each spoke varies according to the situation it occupies for the moment with respect to the perpendicular. The two spokes which arrive at the vertical position, above and below the axle, are seen of their natural shape, that is, without any curvature. Those on each side of the upper one appear slightly curved; those more remote, still more so; and the curvature of the spokes increases as we follow them downwards on each side till we arrive at the lowest spoke, which, like the first, again appears straight.

The most remarkable circumstance relating to this visual deception is, that the convexity of these curved images of the spokes is always turned downwards, on both sides of the wheel; and that this direction of their curvature is precisely the same, whether the wheel be moving to the right or to the left of the spectator.[64]

A footnote on this phenomenon had in fact already appeared in an English periodical some years before.[65] If one were to look for other evidence, one need look no further than the observations of the way that a flaming coal, when moved rapidly in circles, will appear as a lighted circle; more significantly, one should also keep in mind the classic example offered by Newton's disc, the segments of which reproduce the spectrum of the sun and which, when rotated rapidly, blend together to appear white.

One might also recall that in 1765 at the Académie des Sciences of Paris, the chevalier d'Arcy had measured to 13/100ths of a second the length of the persistence on the retina of the image of a flaming coal fixed to a rotating wheel at a known speed. There are, needless to say, many other similar examples.[66]

Roget's observations, however, mark a qualitative leap, for two reasons: not only because they probably constitute the first experimental attempt to explain the phenomena, but also because they began a process of development and a deepening of efforts to understand the phenomena themselves, which as we shall see will bear important results. Roget, in an attempt to explain and analyse his observations, recreated the circumstances under scientific conditions. Probably by chance, he controlled the limits and conditions in an experiment, studied it and drew conclusions (even of a mathematical nature) based on the various images that appeared as the result of variables introduced into play. It is clear from his conclusions that 'a more detailed examination of the conditions in which these optical illusions are created, may be able to provide new methods to measure the length of the impressions of light on the retina.'[67]

The years that followed would agree with him. It is interesting to note the analogical methodology used by Roget to study the phenomena:

He wanted to repeat the experiment in the laboratory and replaced the fence with a mobile strip of black paper, intersected by equidistant slits, and moved it with a cardboard disc rotating round a fixed axis. In the disc, to more or less resemble a carriage wheel, slits in the shape of cake slices were opened, in the direction of the spokes.[68]

The importance of Roget's lecture to the Royal Society is underlined by the fact that, at around the same time (1826), a toy called the Thaumatrope was making inroads, first in England then in other countries.

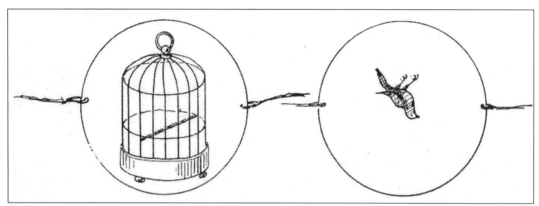

The Thaumatrope.

It was based on the illusion of superimposition of two images drawn on two sides of a disc created when the disc is rapidly rotated using either a short piece of string or an elastic band.[69] A propos of this toy, which every now and then turns up again, it has been said that it is a precursor of the cinematograph. As pointed out by Ceram, 'the thaumatrope does not in fact present any kind of movement, but instead transforms two separate images into a new one thanks to an illusory process of identification.'[70] Even Deslandes correctly agrees with this point of view, and yet both continue to devote time to illustration and comments on this toy, so providing for, albeit at one stage removed, the continuing argument over whether the inventor was Dr Paris or Dr Fitton.[71]

In this climate of general interest surrounding visual perception in relation to movement, which was not just limited to scientific circles, in the years following Roget's experiment came a series of other scientific works which would themselves lead to further discoveries and applications.[72]

Faraday, although mainly interested in the areas of electromagnetism and chemistry, did not ignore this field of study. On optical matters he mainly collaborated with Sir John Herschel, but in physics manuals the so-called Faraday's Wheel appears under his name only.[73] This series of experiments and observations focuses on the use of one or two cogwheels moving at great speed. If one observes the cogwheels in motion in a mirror, looking in the gaps between the teeth, in the mirror the wheel appears to be immobile. Two coaxial cogwheels rotating at high speeds in opposite directions, if viewed from the same axis as the wheels, will appear as one immobile wheel.

Subsequently Faraday twinned the wheel with Newton's disc rotating coaxially, and in the mirror observed that some of the colours did not blend together. Wheatstone made the same discovery by observing Newton's disc in the dark, only illuminating it with intermittent electrical sparks.

Faraday's Wheel.

In other words, what we are dealing with here are the rather primitive early experiments with what will later be termed stroboscopic techniques, but which at the time were only thought of as optical illusions, as no practical purpose for them had as yet been suggested.

In his paper, Faraday described in minute detail all the possible variations of the experiment, and even explained how to construct the machine using wire, pulleys, cork, wood, pieces of copper and cardboard cut-outs, so that anyone could make the same observations. Some of his text refers to the images created as having the effect of a 'continuous impression' provoked in the eye by the succession of individual visual images close up.[74]

7. Brussels, c.1825

If in London we find a number of illustrious scientists all living and working and interacting with each other in the large city, in the small country that would become Belgium we find a single isolated figure, Joseph-Antoine-Ferdinand Plateau (1801–1883), one that is prone to hagiography and around whom one might fasten the glorious halo of a scientist who sacrificed himself for his work and the search for new ideas.

This is how Potonniée begins his book *Les origines du cinématographe*:

There is a precursor of the cinematograph whose name should be written in gold letters on the title page of the history of cinematography, the Belgian professor Joseph Plateau, without whose work neither Lumière nor anybody else would have invented anything at all.

Plateau dedicated the best years of his life, beginning even before he got his degree, to the study of visual perception. Eventually he sacrificed his eyesight, becoming blind at the age of forty-two after spending too much time studying the rays of the sun.[75] Blindness did not stop him from enjoying a long life; he continued to teach at the University of Ghent for many years, eventually becoming the member of many international scientific academies.

His life was spent divided between Brussels, where he was born, the University of Liège where he studied and gained his degree, and the University of Ghent where he taught and continued his research. Unsurprisingly, in 1964 he was made the subject of a documentary by J. Brismée, which celebrated his life and work through the presentation of documents, scientific experiments and historical reconstructions.[76]

In terms of our discussion, Plateau got to the heart of the matter right from his earliest experiments. He started by looking at the results obtained half a century earlier by d'Arcy, who had calculated the length of the persistence of images on the retina. Plateau was dissatisfied by these results and so developed new experiments not only using rotating flaming coals but also coloured discs. Consequently, he was able to get results in which the length of the perception varied depending on the colour and the objects used.[77]

He obtained his doctorate in physics in 1829 with his *Dissertation sur quelques propriétés des impressions produites par la lumière sur l'organe de la vue*. What is particularly interesting here is that, despite being forced to work with extremely limited resources, albeit with a little encouragement from a few Belgian scientists, he was already aware of the results obtained in England by Roget and Faraday, and even described the Thaumatrope in his dissertation. Even more significant is the fact that he was able to look at the problems of perception with a critical eye and tried to see the objective limits of the experiments he was undertaking, indicating the possible outcomes of a greatly refined methodology and trying to answer the questions raised by the limits of the scientific knowledge of that time.

By the end of 1832, Plateau had reached a new and important stage and he described this in various scientific publications in 1833. Here is the first of two extracts from his work:

> The apparatus consists in essence of a cardboard disc with a number of thin radial fissures with figures painted on one of its faces. We rotate the disc in front of a mirror and with one eye look through the fissures: the figures we see reflected in the mirror do not become blurred as they do if we look from another angle, do not seem to follow the rotation of the disc any more, and instead appear animated and to be following their own set of movements.
>
> This illusion is based on a very simple principle. If a number of objects, gradually different as to shape and position are presented to the eye in succession at brief intervals and at sufficient speed, the impression provoked in the retina will link them together without blurring and so will give the illusion of seeing but one object which gradually changes its shape and position.

Sadoul commented on these results by saying: 'In this way Plateau, in 1833, established with admirable lucidity and clarity, the principle of modern cinema, or more precisely the law on which is based the viewing or projection of film.'[78]

On another occasion Sadoul referred to Plateau as 'le grand-père du cinema.' From a scientific point of view however, matters are much more complex and important. We shall shortly examine some of the practical applications (toys which introduce in a minute embryonic form the 'cinematic' experience), which derived from the rotating disc with Plateau's figures. Before that, though, it is worth underlining that these experiments were concluded with the study of periodic movements. Plateau again:

> Given an object with a periodic movement too rapid for the eye to receive a distinct impression of it, the apparatus described by myself will allow us:
> a) to establish the shape of an object by reducing it to apparent immobility;
> b) to observe every characteristic of the movement by seemingly slowing it down whenever desired;
> c) to find, in conclusion, the effective speed of an object or, at least, the duration of a period of movement by means of two observations and of a formula.[79]

Here, perhaps for the first time, is clear expression of the new possibilities for exploration and knowledge offered by the scientific study of movement. Even Plateau was probably not completely aware of this: one of his publications from 1833 has as its title *Des illusions d'optique sur lesquelles se fonde le petit jouet appelé récemment phénakistiscope*.[80] Nonetheless, he had clearly seen the difference between the effect of repetitive movement with stationary effect – as produced by a series of figures that carry out a cyclical movement in the same positions to the small observation slits of the rotating disc – and the effect of perpetual and advancing motion produced, for example, by a series of drawings of a man walking, where there are more drawings than slits.

Plateau believed that the machine he built could be used to study phenomena that it had not been possible to analyse up until that time, such as vibrating objects (he undertook experiments with a vibrating cord, using a disc that rotated at a controlled and variable speed by using a clockwork mechanism). The twirl of a dancer dressed as a pageboy drawn on the disc, reproduced on the diagram that Plateau attached to his paper which described his completed experiments, was only meant to serve as a concrete, easily understood example that would be clear to all.[81] It is worth noting that, even though it was partly by chance, in the first demonstration disc prepared by Plateau there were sixteen figures and slots, just as sixteen frames per second would be chosen at the birth of cinema to give the images fluidity and stability.

Going well beyond his original intentions, Plateau's experimental device entered the public domain with its publication; it is even possible that Plateau himself sent a copy to Faraday in London. Soon opticians and draughtsmen in London, Belgium, Paris and probably other cities were selling these discs with the Hellenised name Phénakistiscope, exhibiting a variety of different images.[82] Frequently, however, the manufacture, reproduction and the placing of the figures were not up to the necessary standard required for a truly successful viewing experience. Outraged, Plateau sent specific instructions to London on the correct way of building of the device to scientific standards, which would eventually come to be sold under the name Fantascope.

8. Vienna, c.1830

At the same time that Plateau was concluding his experiments, in the Austrian capital Simon R. von Stampfer (1792–1864), a professor of applied geometry at the Polytechnic, produced a practically identical mechanism that he called the Stroboscope (continuing the fashion for Greek etymology). Neither was aware of the other's work, but, like Plateau, Stampfer knew of the research and results obtained by Roget, Faraday and others. It was simply a case of contemporaneous discovery and invention in a now mature field following on from developments made, sometimes unconsciously, by earlier researchers. Perhaps inevitably, as a result of his field of study and the environment in which he worked, Stampfer used his stroboscopic disc for the analysis and reconstruction of mechanical movement (for example, gear systems) and for research in physics.

In his proposal he illustrated the characteristics of optical effects of movement and of arrested movement obtained by rotating the disc with the figures in front of a mirror; but also referred to the possibility of substituting the disc with a cylinder in which the drawings are laid out on a strip. He also anticipated equipment that would only be built decades later, postulating a great many images which could then be transferred to strips of paper or cloth joined end to end so as to make a single loop drawn between parallel cylinders.

He also hypothesised the possibility of dispensing with the mirror by using an

Stampfer's Stroboscope discs.

apparatus made up of two discs rotating on the same axis: the first with the slit through which one watched, the second with the series of figures.

To solve the problem of all the figures being seen in motion at the same time, he suggested that a matte be placed between the disc and the mirror allowing for just one image to be viewed, perhaps giving this matte the appearance of a theatre proscenium.

> It is clear that with this technique it will be possible to represent not just the various movements of a man or an animal, but also those of a machine in operation, and even complex actions of a longer duration such as excerpts from plays or the like.[83]

The events that we have been looking at in a few European cities refer in the main to the history of science. Some serious historians have studied them and made them better known so as to locate and give emphasis to the collaboration made by these scientists to the genesis of cinema.

However, in the effort to present these scientists as the technological forefathers of the cinema, often the fundamental direction of their work has been obscured or deliberately ignored. There are either no references, or only incidental ones, to the reasons for and the significance of their research and their experiments.

By highlighting this limitation and by trying to remedy it, by modifying the point of view of the events that occurred and the way that they are interpreted, it seems to us that in this way it may be possible to open up new prospects for study and historiographic research. Sadoul, with his materialistic type of approach, came close to this problem:

> The construction of a phenakistiscope in fact requires simply a disc made of lightweight material, based upon the wheel of a cart, a mirror of an equivalent shape and a series of images that break down the movement.
>
> With regards to the material elements, well, the ancient Egyptians – who knew of the wheel and the mirror, and who made some bas-reliefs which truly are series of drawings on the point of being animated – should not have found any obstacles in the construction of such a machine.[84]

A few lines later, his answer is formally correct, but remains on the wrong side of a perfect answer as to the reasons for the interest of nineteenth century scientists in analysing movement:

> In particular circumstances, furthermore, the material possibilities precede the progress of human culture; while in others, scientists (or a wide range of people) can readily imagine inventions which it is not yet possible to turn into reality through technical limitations.

A little later, at the end of a chapter not by chance entitled 'The prophets of cinema', he adds:

Techniques and economics thus blocked turning animated photographs into reality, even though this had already been clearly envisaged by illustrious forerunners. With their research and patents they had demonstrated that filming was possible, but the delicacy and difficulties of the complicated systems then available would only allow them to be realised as the subsidised research of scientists or the costly pastime of rich amateurs.[85]

As can be seen, Sadoul comes close to what we believe to be the correct interpretation of the true origins of cinema. But instead of finding ourselves among presumed prophets of entertainment cinema, we are actually in the pre-history of scientific cinema.

It is interesting to note how the usual disagreements over procedure and jealousy over citations arise among research academics. Having said that, these are not in the same league as the patent wars that exploded noisily among scientists once commercial interests, either real or perceived, raise their heads. Chronicles of who first thought up and then built the Phenakistiscope or the Stroboscope have already been made and so we would suggest that those interested in developing this argument, which is mainly of slight historical worth, look to these sources, as well as perhaps suggesting a more in-depth motivation behind the research.[86]

As for Roget, who also entered into argument over who was the first to construct machines such as the Phenakistiscope, he claimed to have built some in advance of other claimants and to have shown them to his friends, but not to have published on this owing to his 'more serious activities and interests.'

Returning to the pre-history of cinema, which we left when discussing Stampfer's stroboscopic discs, we now recall an event that confirms that the psychogenetic line of development of thought at that time was essentially that of analysing movement for scientific ends, to visualise the invisible, and still not to reproduce movement artificially for the purposes of entertainment.

In 1832, possibly earlier than Plateau or Stampfer, or else at the same time, there was another scientist inspired by Faraday's experiments to study bodies in motion and analyse their condition in both qualitative and quantitative terms. In that year, the French physicist Savart demonstrated that a fine trickle of water falling is not made up of a stable continuum, but instead comprises a swelling and thinning, rather like drops dragged and linked to one another. The technique behind his experiment was inspired by Faraday and he repeated the trial using the band and ring as used by Roget (but putting white vertical bands on a black background). He even made use of the spark illumination technique as pioneered by Wheatstone.[87] Savart specialised in sound and Savart's Wheel was used as an instrument to measure quantitatively the vibration of a chord emitting sound.

In the years following the invention of Stampfer's Stroboscope there is news of the use of this apparatus to present dynamic demonstrations of various types of work by Professor J. Muller in Freiburg.[88] Historiographic research on the direct scientific application of the instruments and on their didactic use has been overlooked for so long but there is probably still a great deal to be discovered and specified.

Much more widely disseminated, however, have been the imprecise and sometimes contradictory details regarding the applications of the stroboscopic principle of the Phenakistiscope to games (since we cannot yet talk about entertainment).

9. A 'daedaleum' full of inventors

All histories of the cinema include references to William George Horner (1786–1837), also a mathematician by profession, who in 1833, only a few months after the publications by Plateau and Stampfer, constructed an ingenious machine that he named the Daedaleum. Horner describes a series of drawings placed between equidistant slits which were then

> … placed cylindrically round the edge of a revolving disc. Any drawings which are made on the interior surface in the intervals of the apertures will be visible through the opposite apertures, and if executed on the same principle of graduated action, will produce the same surprising play of relative motions as the common *magic disk* does when spun before a mirror. The phenomenon may be displayed with full effect to a numerous audience.[89]

The major advantage of Horner's invention, apart from its use by a number of persons at a time, within certain limits, was that an infinite replaceable series of drawings on sheets of paper could be substituted inside the cylinder. This has led those excitable cinema historians to see in it the foreshadowing of cinema film. In addition, the Daedaleum had the positive feature that, under strict conditions, each observer could see each figure or image in movement, whereas since both the Phenakistiscope and the Stroboscope were normally used with a mirror, in practice these showed all the drawn figures at the same time making the same movements.

We do not know what drove Horner to make this new version of a machine for watching apparent movement on a strip of paper; what we do know is that as a mathematician he was known for his discovery of a method for solving multiple equations.[90]

In the decades that followed, Horner's Daedaleum was discovered by various people, who sold it in many countries under a variety of names from the Zoetrope (perhaps because most of the drawings for it were of animals) to 'magic drums' to the 'wheel of life' – the same thing had already happened with Plateau and Stampfer's machines.

In the 1860s, designers in Europe tried to patent a type of zoetrope, but it was not until 1867 when W.E. Lincoln patented the 'Zoetrope' in America that it really took off. The film historian MacGowan recalls his youthful enthusiasm when, at the end of the nineteenth century, he was given one of them as a Christmas present.[91]

10. The heart beats to a didactic end

To conclude this series of portraits, all of scientists, and all of which in my opinion belong to the pre-history of scientific cinema, it is now necessary to add a name that has, until now, been ignored by international cinematograph historians. It is the noted Bohemian physiologist Jan Evangelista Purkyně (1787–1869), best known today to all doctors that have to study the brain cells and cardiac fibres that still bear his name. Right from his university years he dedicated himself to the study of visual perception and he graduated in 1818 with a thesis on this argument.[92] In 1840 Purkyně perfected Stampfer's Stroboscope, by placing the pictures and the slots onto two separate disks but both on the same axis. From a practical point of view this allowed for a quick and simple substitution of the disk for the images, making it usable for an unlimited number of cycles of movement. It was also, from a technical standpoint, a specific application of the rotating shutter that improved the visual quality of the movement.[93] Purkyně's first machine was named the Phorolyt and it went on sale in the 1840s, mainly in Breslau (now Wroclaw) in Poland, where he was teaching. At a conference he even suggested replacing the drawings with three-dimensional figures, a technique he dubbed 'phorografia.' Some of the first discs that Purkyně, with the help of a painter, made for his Phorolyt, showed the movements of micro-organisms, a butterfly and a lizard. As one can see there is a clear emphasis on the educational/scientific use of the machine, though in toy-shops there were also series of discs showing acrobats, dancers and other optical effects.

Purkyně returned to Bohemia on 1850 to found and direct the Institute of Physiology at the University of Prague. He continued to use his machine for class-room demonstrations. He also developed two important discs on the circulatory system and on the heartbeat. With the help of Durst, an optician from Prague, he continued to develop the Phorolyt, re-naming it the Kinesiskop.

In a contemporary print showing Purkyně in his studio, prominently placed on his desk with his microscope, is his machine for creating animated images.

In the 1860s Purkyně made two more developments which, irrespective of issues of priority which are always difficult to ascertain and which in any event should be related to the quality of the result, are worthy of note. His 'beating heart', presented to the Royal Academy of Science in 1861, was magnified and projected onto a screen, while in 1865, according to the sources, a sensation was caused in Bratislava at a congress of naturalists and doctors when it was shown at a gigantic size, apparently using a clockwork mechanism for the movements of the image.

Purkyně's niece had a Kinesiskop showing a series of images of the scientist

Purkyně's Kinesiskop.

himself while he turned his head. One must of course keep in mind that the techniques of the time (Purkyně died in 1869) meant that sheets of wet collodion were used, so that the nine exposures taken one after the other certainly could not give a very satisfactory result.[93]

11. Optical toys

In the years between 1820 and 1870 we have seen a group of scientists (mathematicians, physicists, doctors, physiologists) from various European countries develop a series of connected, sometimes even contemporaneous, but independent studies and experiments on problems of the visual perception of movement, of persistence of vision on the retina, optical illusions and related phenomena.

The results of this work were already important for the study of the physiology of the eye and for the understanding of the physical and mental process of seeing. But the same experimental methodology allowed for the discovery of the stroboscopic effect, which permits analysis and measure of movements.

Despite the optical toys which derived from this research and the related experimental machines, it seems clear that the historical impetus, the reason for which all this work was brought forward by such varied people in many different countries, should be sought in the scientific importance that the study of movement (physiological and mechanical) came to have contemporaneously to the development of industrialised society.

There was the real promise of new sources of energy (steam and later on electricity), which would emancipate work from human and animal physical effort, and there is the birth of the myth of the machine as an instrument of progress (before that, the problem of its influence on workers' employment). Machines mean movement and, for the scientist, movement means research on movement. This is the key reason why these experiments and studies were begun even decades before the invention and spread of photography.

It may only make sense from a philosophical perspective (in relation to the development of human thought) to ask ourselves why research and experiments that could have taken place hundreds or even thousands of years earlier were only approached and accomplished during the first half of the nineteenth century; the same argument could be made for many other scientific discoveries, but it is not the intention here to propose a mechanistic or deterministic schema of the relationship between science and society.

By the same token, it does not make much sense to project backwards our (in any event rather limited) current knowledge to attribute to scientists that were not in any way so inclined, certain specific moments of 'illumination' for the future of cinema exhibitions.

12. Photography arrives on the scene

As a sort of counter trial, it now remains for us to make a brief examination of what was happening in the same period outside the scientific-academic environment considered so far, and which can be placed in relation to the group of events we have called the pre-history of scientific cinema.

We can take it as given that in the middle of those years photography was invented, in other words an event that would be determinative and essential for the future developments of our argument.[95] This is even if, at the beginning, the low sensitivity of the materials used with the first photographic techniques (Daguerreotypes, Calotypes), requiring endlessly long exposures, prevents us considering these pictures as useful for the purposes of the research on movement and its perception. One should, however, point to the not incidental fact that at least one of the scientists we have been dealing with, even if only marginally (Sir John Herschel), fulfilled just in those years a not negligible role in the birth and development of photographic technique.

Furthermore, in analysing the body of experimental and research activities carried out in the field of photography, it can be seen that – in parallel with the attempt to improve the quality of the procedures and results – a whole series of attempts was developed in the direction of stereoscopy and chromatic reproduction. The dream of instant photography was still so far away that the aim of 'stopping' movement on the plate was not even considered yet, except in a fantasising sort of way. Plateau, already blind, in 1849 explored ways to use paired Daguerreotypes to reproduce some three-dimensional little figures representing the phases of a movement stereoscopically, in an expressly-produced Phenakistiscope.[96]

In the 1850s, some photographers and opticians attempted to create a sequence comprising successive exposures of a simple human movement (the turning of a couple of ballet dancers, the gesture of a seamstress), making the subjects remain immobile for each of the pre-arranged gesture phases. With equipment that was certainly ingenious, if somewhat precarious, they attempted then to have these simple cyclical movements reproduced using normal Zoetropes or strange mergers with stereoscopes and magic lanterns and project these figures in enlarged form. Obviously, some people found it sufficient to use series of drawn images.[97]

In this period, and still more in the 1860s, the strange figures of 'inventors' started to appear, who were no longer satisfied by a communication to an Academy of Sciences, but deposited patent after patent. In some of these we can find descriptions that make us think of what the cinema would be. The Frenchman, Ducos de Hauron (1837–1920) patented in 1864 an 'Appareil destiné à reproduire photographiquement une scène quelconque avec toutes les transformations qu'elle a subies pendant un temps déterminé' [Apparatus intended to reproduce any scene photographically with all the transformations it had undergone during a fixed period of time], and in the accompanying report, he even quotes 'very curious and amusing effects', such as:

a) condense in a few instants a scene that in reality lasted a considerable space of time. For example: the growth of trees, plants, and all phenomena of vegetation; the passing from one season to another; the construction of a building or even of an entire town; the successive ages of the same individual; the growth of a beard, or hair, etc.;

b) then, contrarily, have transformations occur slowly which, because of their speed, the eye often does not perceive;

c) reverse the order in which a scene or a phenomenon takes place, i.e. start with the end and end with the beginning;

d) reproduce the movement of the stars and the changes occurring on their surfaces (lunar phases, sun spots, etc).[98]

It must be added, however, that this apparatus was not constructed; that if it had been it would have worked very badly or even not at all from the mechanical and optical point of view; that no matter how many double lenses it might have had (it was after all stereoscopic!) it would have been able to shoot only very short actions; but, above all, it would have had to wait for the invention of plates or even photographic film of sufficient lightness and sensitivity for it to be used in the conditions set out in its patent.[99]

In 1867, the *Bulletin de la Société Française de Photographie* published this text:

Nothing could be more curious in physics than the perfect combination of stereoscope, phénakistiscope and photography, with which it would be possible to produce the extraordinary phenomenon of moving figures, with all the illusion of natural relief. An art that would be in a position to make objects appear to be *mobile sculptures* would be the most extraordinary and marvellous result that science could ever have created.[100]

As can be seen, we are still with the futuristic imagining of something that is not cinema, neither as art nor as spectacle: it seems, rather, to anticipate, in its terms of expression, some currents in the figurative arts such as the plastic dynamism of the Italian futurists.

More curious, would seem to be the concrete experience described by the American physician and writer (as well as passionate photography enthusiast), Oliver Wendell Holmes (1809–1894), in the May 1863 edition of *The Atlantic Monthly*. He recounts the inestimable assistance he derived from his study of a series of 'instantaneous' photographs, particularly stereographs (truly an avant-garde technique for the time), which reproduced men walking in the streets of cities such as London or Paris. Holmes' problem, as a physician, was designing artificial limbs for soldiers mutilated during the Civil War. Since there was still no possibility of analysing movement with a series of high frequency shots, he collected a large number of pictures and sought to reconstruct the various phases of that almost instinctive movement that is walking, but which – examined from the physiological point of view – is extremely complex. Here emerged the concept that would become a sort of *leitmotif* of the period of the scientific birth of the cinema: a single image that 'stops' a phase of movement normally imperceptible to the eye, revealing – relativistically, if so it can be said – 'incredible' positions that common sense rejects. 'No artist would dare to represent a figure in such poses.'[101]

The Holmes episode can be taken as a further symptom – a tragic symptom if we consider its link with the consequences of a war, but also oriented towards reducing the trauma – of a scientific instrument for investigation and knowledge that would allow movement to be analysed (and reconstructed), indicative of the needs of a society becoming rapidly more technological.

The *Riegruv slovník naucný* by František Rieger, an encyclopaedia published in Prague in 1865, in an entry dedicated to the Kinesiskop and probably edited by Purkyně himself, says:

> It is a physical-physiological instrument by use of which the most varied movements of natural and artificial objects can be represented.

And then, speaking of the future prospects for development of such equipment:

> ... the most diverse movements of natural historical and artistic spectacles can also be presented to a vast public, and it will originate a particular branch of the scientific industry, useful in schools and, in general, for education and amusement. For example, in the field of physics, representation can be made of the movements of waves, of liquids, sounds, light, the most complex machines in their movements; in the field of physiology, the pulses of the heart, the circulation of the blood, the nerve currents, muscular activity; in the natural sciences, movements of various animals on the earth and in the air, the most diverse plays of colour, the physiognomic expressions on the human face, dramatic gestures, the growth of plants and other organic bodies, the volumetric representation of bodies that are otherwise impossible to represent on a surface; in the field of history, the representation of collective human actions, for example, battles, balls, processions, and so on. These representations can take place in reduced dimensions or by optical means with the enlargement desired on a transparent surface. It can be expected that this technique, thanks to the mastery of the artists, will become over time a particular branch of the figurative arts, for which it will no longer be sufficient to create a single moment of action that is taking place, but the entire act, the action in its entirety.

Even if we are reticent with regard to forced *a posteriori* interpretations, one can see, if one wishes, in that final phrase a generic forecast of the cinematographic artistic spectacle, considered as a derivative of the 'scientific industry.' In reality, we are beginning to emerge from the pre-history of scientific cinema.

Part III
Historical background to the birth of scientific cinema

The temptation to fix the birth of the scientific cinema at an exact date, on a name, on an event, is always with us. It becomes more attractive and insidious inasmuch as this would provide a precise statement of priority with respect to the conventional date of birth of the cinema as entertainment; to be able to say, in other words, how many years, five-year periods, decades, it was that scientific cinema had already existed before 28 December 1895.

The appearance of a phenomenon such as scientific cinema can only be seen as a process that developed over a period of time, distinguished by the contributions of several people in different countries through a series of successive events, often, though not always, directly linked to each other. Some historical details, however, can be given. Scientific cinema was born and lived through its first basic developments in the two decades between 1870 and 1890.

13. The retina of the scientist

Pierre-Jules-César Janssen (1824–1907) was a French astronomer of Norwegian origin. Like other scientists already encountered, Janssen took his degree with a dissertation on vision, and the works he published at the start to his career concerned the functioning of the eye and the problems of ophthalmology. Even before making his most significant scientific observations (he was also the founder and director of the new Observatory in Paris, located at Meudon), he gained fame in 1870 because of a news event, which is witness, *inter alia*, to his dedication to research. Having decided to go to southern Africa in order to observe an eclipse of the sun, and finding his way blocked because at that time Paris was under siege, he had no hesitatation in using a hot-air balloon to leave the French capital.

The pioneering contribution Janssen brought to the birth of scientific cinema is closely connected to his work on astronomical research, and took the form of a conscious utilisation of the new possibilities offered by the analysis of movement through a series of photographic images.

Janssen enthusiastically upheld the importance of the discovery of photography and, in particular, its scientific applications. He was to become President of the Société Française de Photographie.[102] A definition of his became famous: 'Photography is the retina of the scientist.'[103] This modern understanding of the application of new techniques to recording images and the knowledge of their intrinsic possibilities, led him to develop a method, with its relative technological instrumentation, that allowed him to investigate, clarify and document a problem relative to his own specific field of research.

The transit of the planet Venus in front of the sun was to be visible from Japan in 1874. From 1873 Janssen prepared to record this event as it occurred, editing it into its various phases at short, regular intervals. In this way, it would be possible to follow the phenomenon in all its dynamic evolution, but above all it would be possible to isolate the basic moments of the passing of a celestial body in front of another, highlighting the importance of the contacts between the disc of Venus and the sun in relation to the revelation and observation of the solar corona. In a communication to the Académie des Sciences, almost six months before the event took place, Janssen set out his scientific aim:

> It is well known that observation of contact will have a primary role in observing the transit of Venus ... It is understandable, however, what great interest there is in fixing these contacts photographically ... I have it in mind to create, from the moment when the contact is about to take place, a series of photographs at very short and regular intervals, so that the photographic image of the moment of contact is necessarily included in the series and, at the same time, gives the precise instant of the phenomenon. I have been able to resolve the problem by using a rotating disk.[104]

Once his mission was completed, Janssen telegraphed from Nagasake: 'Venus observed on corona before contact, demonstrating the existence of the corona!' Camille Flammarion, the famous astronomer and populariser, commenting on the news, wrote:

> This observation of the passing of Venus *in front of the solar corona* that surrounds the day star and is not visible except during full eclipses of the sun, is very important, because it proves definitively that this corona is not due to an effect of refraction in the earthly atmosphere, but belongs precisely to the sun. The ingenious astronomer had been preparing for this demonstration since last year. He has succeeded, and is the only person who has done so.[105]

Janssen had started on the concept, experimentation and constructive design of his 'photographic revolver' in 1873, entrusting its final construction to the Redier technicians, father and son. The curious name of the apparatus, if one thinks that its external appearance is more similar to a cannon or a howitzer than a revolver, referred to the revolving barrel pistol invented by the American, Colt, in 1837. The photographic revolver was described as follows by Janssen himself:

> The apparatus is essentially made up of a plate on which the sensitive sheet is put; the plate is placed in a round box fixed to the focal surface of a lens or of the apparatus giving the real image of the phenomenon to be reproduced. The plate

is cogged and engages with a pinion with isolated teeth, which transmits to it an alternative angular movement of the size of the image to be reproduced. In front of the box, and fixed on the same axis holding the plate, is a disk perforated with small slots (with an adjustable aperture) and which turns continuously; each time one of the slots on the disk passes in front of the one on the cover of the box, an equal portion of the sensitive sheet is uncovered and records an image. It is unnecessary to add that the movements are regulated in such a way that the sensitive sheet stops when a slot, with its passing, determines the production of an image.[106]

The whole was regulated and moved by a clockwork mechanism. The shutter disk made a complete turn in eighteen seconds, while the wheel holding the sheet was geared four-to-one; that is, it completed a full turn in seventy-two seconds, but in fact moved only at intervals, when the shutter was closed and it was necessary to move the section of sheet already recorded to bring a new section to be recorded in front of the slot.[107]

A difficulty Janssen had to resolve must be borne in mind: not only did dry gelatine-bromide plates not exist at that time, it would have been difficult to use even a common wet collodion plate, seeing that the rotating movement of the vertical plate could have caused the running and, therefore, the distortion of the collodion layer. He therefore used Daguerreotype plates, which were less sensitive, but could not be deformed.

The images would not be perfect, but sufficient to document the phenomenon with scientific precision. On his return to Paris, in fact, the images would be reinforced and redesigned. Janssen had placed his apparatus in a room, positioning a wooden telescope in front of the machine, i.e. a large horizontal tube containing the optical system, directed, through a hole in a wall, towards a heliostat; that is, a mirror moved by another clockwork mechanism that followed the movement of the sun. In the images of the Daguerreotype sheet, in fact, can be seen a slice of the sun and its crown and the round mark of Venus in transit.

On the temporal dynamic of the functions of the photographic revolver, there is information that is contradictory and with parts missing. This is a further demonstration of the need to develop historical studies to reconstruct in detail the phases of development of scientific and technological research in the nineteenth century.

The most important discrepancy concerns the duration of the cycle of shots. Janssen, in his scientific communications (to the Académie des Sciences and to the Société Française de Photographie), spoke always in general terms of the need for 'images that must be taken at moments very close to each other' for which 'a special instrument is required, making it possible to take a large number of pictures without changing the plate.' Janssen wrote:

Janssen's 'photographic revolver'.

The photographic revolver I have the honour of presenting, creates the following conditions:

a) the instrument currently gives forty-eight images and this number could probably be doubled or even trebled;

b) the time of an exposure is determined by the same instrument and can be regulated;

c) the interval separating the images can be increased or decreased at will;

d) the instrument is automatic, i.e. it creates the series of images on its own, with no intervention required by the operator;

e) if desired, the instrument can be controlled manually and in this case create the images at those intervals of time that are judged to be appropriate.[108]

However, Flammarion describes Janssen's apparatus in an even more detailed way, adding the technical details of its functioning that we have already given. The Museum of the Conservatoire National des Arts et Métiers (CNAM) in Paris, which exhibits the photographic revolver and one of its plates (gifts of Janssen's daughter), presents the same data, adding that the period of rest of the plate for each shot is one and a half seconds (48 x 1.5 = 72).

Contradicting this information is a passage by Étienne-Jules Marey, who – as we shall see – is to be considered the protagonist of the birth of scientific cinema. Marey, a colleague of Janssen's at the Académie, wrote that the images of the successive positions of the planet Venus in front of the sun were taken 'at intervals of approximately seventy seconds.'[109] Perhaps this is an oversight (repeated twice on the same page), confusing the approximately seventy seconds of a complete rotation of the circular plate with the time that separates one shot from another? Maybe; what is certain is that, following in his tracks, other serious, technically qualified authors would repeat a statement that, *per se*, contradicts all the assumptions for which Janssen had planned, constructed and experimented with his photographic revolver.[110]

Among the authors attesting to the same line of the Marey quotation, there is his assistant, Lucien Bull; another pupil of Marey, Albert Londe; the librarian of the Photographic Society of Paris, Georges Potoniée; and, more recently, the historian of cinematographic technique Jean Vivié. Given these precedents, it is extra-ordinary what inaccuracies some cinema historians, even authoritative historians, have managed to write: they range from those extending the duration of each individual exposure to seventy seconds (for example, D.B. Thomas) to those stating that Janssen's apparatus had to operate on the occasion referred to for over twenty-four hours consecutively (Henri Fescourt).[111]

In his treatise *Wissenschaftliche Kinematographie*, F.P. Liesegang discusses the problem of the basis for the assertion of Marey and – ignoring the essential article by Flammarion – instead quotes another French astronomer, Wolf, of the Académie des Sciences, who affirmed that individual exposures followed each other second by second.[112]

To bring clarity to this controversial matter, we have carried out an in-depth analysis of numerous texts by Janssen and other authors and here summarise the most significant parts.

The design and experimentation work carried out by Janssen between 1873 and 1874, with the help of some technicians, passed through various phases, testing some solutions and then abandoning them. Janssen recounts how he initially tried to use electricity to move the mechanism, but then resolved on the more reliable spring clockwork movement. That way, having tried to have the disk shutter move at different points, he chose the solution of having it turn with continuous motion to avoid the vibrations produced with intermittent movement.[113] At this point, it could be observed that if the shots had to take place at intervals of seventy seconds, the problem of some brief vibrations would not have interfered with effecting the shots themselves, while this is obvious when it is a question of recording a picture approximately every second.

Janssen had more than one prototype constructed and with these carried out tests of artificial transits of Venus. He tested emulsions of wet collodion, but then chose the Daguerreotype plate. The photographic results of the artificial passages taken with the revolver during the preparatory phase for the expedition in Japan, were presented by Janssen to the Académie des Sciences at its session of 6 July 1874.[114]

Several examples were made of the final apparatus used in December of that year. Two originals are kept in Paris at the Museum of the Observatoire and at the already mentioned Museum of CNAM. However, from a declaration made by Janssen, it appears that (still on the occasion of the transit of Venus) 'the English expeditions honoured us by adopting our instrument and they have obtained in various [observation] stations some very beautiful series [of pictures].'[115]

In the bulletin of the Société Française de Photographie, January-February 1977, Gêrard Turpin describes how the English astronomers had the optician J.H. Dallmeyer build more than one Janssen-type apparatus, to make use of it, as in fact they did, in their different observation stations during the transit of Venus in 1874. The departure point seems to have been the theoretical-technical presentation of the principles Janssen expounded publicly at the Académie des Sciences in 1873. The English apparatuses were not automatic like Janssen's revolver and used collodion or albumen plates of different format.[116]

As far as the shots he had taken during the event of 8 December 1874 were concerned, Janssen declared:

In Japan we obtained a plate of the first internal contact of Venus. The weather was a little cloudy, so that these images are weak, but they are quite visible.[117]

Various authors, in fact, pointed out that the original images were then reinforced, re-photographed or re-drawn for print. This explains why Marey and some other texts give a positive facsimile of the 'internal contact', presenting it as 'Janssen's drawing.' Amongst other things, this figure shows only seventeen images, plus those we would call today a flash frame; and it may be thought that this was a summary for demonstration purposes of the original plate of forty-seven images plus the flash frame.[118] In fact Janssen wrote: 'Mr d'Almeida obtained a plate of forty-seven photographs of the solar edge.'[119]

Concluding this analysis of the functionality of Janssen's apparatus, we wish now to quote a document that we believe has not been taken into consideration before now by those who have expressed conflicting statements on the duration of the revolver's cycle of takes. It is a letter that Janssen sent in January 1882 to his *cher confrère* Marey, who had asked him for information on the photographic revolver, since he, in turn, had started the construction of a photographic rifle to record the stages of the flight of birds, needing numerous takes, at least ten, in the space of a second.

Janssen wrote to him: 'Up to now, only the revolver with relatively slow movements taking separate stages of approximately a second is working.' This statement, as far as can be seen, was the first that can be attributed directly to Janssen on the duration of his takes. When he received the letter from Janssen, Marey had already built and was experimenting positively with his photographic rifle of twelve frames a second. With his scientist's calm, he would write in 1893:

> Janssen was the first who, for the purposes of science, thought of taking by automatic means a series of photographic images to represent the successive phases of a phenomenon. The honour is due to him of having inaugurated what is nowadays called chronophotography on a moving plate.[120]

14. The first scientific cine camera

Janssen's photographic revolver was a genuine scientific cine camera in embryo. It had a motor, an optical system, a variable shutter, and sensitive material in movement. It did not yet allow for the dynamic reproduction of movement, but it did permit its analysis, which, in this particular case, was the most important thing. This was an anticipation of so-called time-lapse cinematography by which the condensation of real time is realised, making it possible to assess movements too slow to be appreciated by the human eye. The fact that the Daguerreotype plate and Janssen's apparatus did not allow for the successive projection of recorded images had no influence on the purpose that the research was proposing. Even today, many scientific films are made to be analysed frame by frame, with special equipment and computers, without ever being projected.

Janssen showed that he saw clearly the qualitative difference that existed between results obtained with his apparatus and with Plateau's Phenakistiscope:

> The photographic revolver resolved the opposite problem to the phenakistiscope. Mr Plateau's phenakistiscope was destined to reproduce the illusion of movement through a series of aspects of the movement itself. The photographic revolver, on the contrary, provided the analysis of a phenomenon by reproducing the series of its elementary aspects.[121]

He also had clear ideas on the new prospects for scientific research and documentation that his apparatus would make it possible to consider.

> The revolver's property of being able to provide automatically a series of images that was as numerous and as close as was wanted of a phenomenon that varied rapidly, would allow interesting problems of physiological mechanics concerning de-ambulation, flight and the different movements of animals to be confronted. A series of photographs that analysed the whole cycle of movements relating to a particular function could provide valuable ways of illustrating its mechanism. It would encompass, for example, all the interest, for such an obscure problem as

that of the flight of birds, which a series of photographs would have, representing the different movements of a wing during flight. At the current time, the main difficulty would be with the inertia of our sensitive surfaces with respect to the very brief posing time required in order to obtain these images. But science will certainly eliminate these difficulties.[122]

In addition to trust in technological progress that would be made possible by scientific development, we should like to highlight the exact indication (by an astronomer!) of the sector of human and animal physiology that could draw an immediate, important advantage from using the first technique of scientific 'cinematography' created by his photographic revolver. Just a few years later and precisely in the field indicated by Janssen, the work of Muybridge and, above all, of Marey, appeared, which would broaden and deepen the identification of those great possibilities furnished by scientific cinema in the study of dynamic phenomena.

Twenty years after his astronomical photography in Japan, Janssen was among the guests of honour at one of the preview screenings, as we would say nowadays, of the cinematographer Lumière.

In June 1895 in Lyons (the city where the Lumière firm had its head office), the congress of the French photographic clubs took place. The participants were shown eight short films, including the famous SORTIE DE L'USINE LUMIÈRE and L'ARROSEUR ARROSÉ. Janssen, chair of the meeting, did not fail to emphasise in his speech at the closing banquet that 'the great event of this session has been the result obtained in the photography animated by Messrs Lumière'; he also added to this recognition an affable criticism regarding the need for 'a final perfecting of their method', to have the persistent stuttering of the images disappear. Above all, however, he chose to make a fundamental distinction between scientific 'cinema' and the cinema of spectacle: referring to the screening of the Lumières', he proposed 'calling it *animated photography*, in order to distinguish it from the analytical photography of movements.'[123]

15. The adventurous photographer

Eadweard J. Muybridge (1830–1904) was without doubt a personality in the history of the birth of scientific cinema, but he was also a personality in his own right, with his extravagant and adventurous image. In the first half of the twentieth century, Muybridge was known to a restricted circle of researchers in the field of the history of photography, where he was spoken of as a controversial figure who had even been in prison for the premeditated murder of his wife's lover. For cinema historians, Muybridge was the man who, with a series of photographic machines, had shot the various positions of a galloping horse. And this he had done to meet the terms of a bet of no less than twenty-five thousand dollars between two rich stable owners. As can be seen, there is enough to awaken curiosity and demand attention.

Eadweard Muybridge.

The name Muybridge itself was the result of a series of alterations that reflected the dynamism of the times, from the Industrial Revolution in England to the conquest of the American West. Muybridge, an Englishman by birth, spent most of his life in the USA: as a result, both countries, when they find it convenient, consider him one of their national treasures.

He was born Edward James Muggeridge. However, when he was about twenty years old, the coronation stone of the Saxon kings was discovered in his native town (Kingston-upon-Thames), bearing the name Eadweard. Later in life, around 1880, he would adopt it as his own.

A few years later, he decided to leave for America in search of his fortune. We find him again in San Francisco, a literary agent full of initiative, calling himself Edward

Muygridge. Finally, when he had turned to the profession of photographer, his surname stabilised as Muybridge. Before this, however, he had had other adventures. In 1860, while crossing the United States to embark for London, his carriage overturned in a sunny and wild part of Texas. Muybridge suffered trauma to the cranium causing him pain and double vision, and underwent long care in America and in England. Back in California, he designed *inter alia* a washing machine, and afterwards built a pneumatic clock that could control various dials at a distance; in the meantime, he became involved in the attractive, pioneering profession of photographer, something between artisan and artist, technician and traveller.[124] He joined the US Government's missions exploring the less well-known areas of the country or parts that had most recently been acquired (such as the Yosemite Valley in California) and became their official photographer. Later, on behalf of the War Department, he would photograph the last battles between Indians and the regular forces of the army, the so-called Modoc War.

In the meantime, at forty-one, he married a twenty-year-old woman, and three years later they had a son. Afterwards, Muybridge realised that his wife had a lover and that this was a friend of his, an ex-military man of English origin, now a theatre critic by profession. He sought to bring an end to the affair, but when he came to believe that his son was the son of his wife's lover, he went looking for him in the distant mine where the journalist had moved for reasons of work, and cold-bloodedly shot and killed him. He then gave himself up to the police, was imprisoned and went on trial after less than four months of detention for voluntary and premeditated murder. Muybridge pleaded not guilty. At the trial, in February 1875, he was defended by three lawyers, two of whom were very much in fashion: one of these, Wirt Pendegast, was a friend of the wealthy industrial magnate and ex-Governor of California Leland Stanford, who had asked Muybridge, at the beginning of the 1870s, to experiment with photographing the movement of horses. It may be assumed that it was Stanford who provided him with such a defence team. During the trial, his lawyers first asked that mental infirmity should be recognised for the accused, as a consequence of the carriage accident fifteen years earlier, but in his concluding address, Pendegast asked for full acquittal on the grounds of justifiable homicide. The jury met for thirteen hours and found the accused not guilty. Muybridge appeared shaken by the verdict, for which he had not been prepared, and seemed for a few seconds to lose the self-control that he had demonstrated before, during and after the crime. Such a totally absolute verdict for a murder of that kind was unusual and, so the newspapers reported, a similar one was unlikely to be experienced for many years.

A few days after being freed, Muybridge the personality took up his role again. He left by ship for a long journey, stopping over in Mexico, the various countries of Central America (he was to stay nearly six months in Guatemala) and the isthmus of Panama. It was a good opportunity to take a lot of photographs of verdant countryside and picturesque people, renewing his professional fame, but also letting the comments and polemics on his acquittal die down in the social circles of San Francisco (where Major Larkyns, his victim, had been well known). While Muybridge was travelling, his wife (to whom he had refused a divorce and alimony) died of an illness at only twenty-four years of age.[125]

Back in San Francisco, he made a gift of a splendid album of his exotic photographs to his lawyers (who had recieved no money for their legal representation at his trial), to the widow of Pendegast (who had also died), to Mrs Stanford, and to the magnate's secretary. The Stanfords commissioned another series of photographs of the inside and outside of their new luxurious hill top residence which overlooked the bay of the city. Muybridge, for his part, carried out a complex photographic operation with a series of plates making up a circular panorama of the city of San Francisco. This initiative brought him economic success, while with other photographs of country scenes he obtained an award at an international competition in Vienna. His relationship with Stanford now allowed him to take the initiative and to explore with his rich patron the possibility of carrying out an organic programme of experiments with serial photographs to analyse the movement of horses. It was at this point that Muybridge came on the scene as a personality in scientific cinema.

Before discussing it in detail, we must return to what we were saying at the beginning of this chapter, of the relatively small fame of Muybridge in the first half of the twentieth century. The international resonance that his figure and work had obtained in the last two decades of the nineteenth century, rapidly disappeared after his death in 1904, and it is not difficult to guess the causes in view of a public opinion (including that of specialists) distracted by the invention of the cinematograph as a spectacle, and by the polemics arising over who originated the invention.

Things changed for Muybridge starting in the 1950s. In 1955 and 1957, two of his most significant collections of photographic series, *The Human Figure in Motion* and *Animals in Motion*, which had been difficult to find for over a quarter of a century, were re-published in New York.[126] In 1969, still in New York, the first volume came out (with the series photographs of nude male figures) of what could be considered the *opera omnia* of Muybridge's studies of movement, *Animal Locomotion*.[127] In 1962, with an article and in 1968 with a book, Aaron Scharf analysed the importance these photographic series had had upon the work of numerous painters of the period and today (from Degas to Bacon).[128] In 1972, at the Stanford University Museum of Art at Palo Alto (California), an exhibition entitled, 'Eadweard Muybridge – The Stanford Years, 1872–1882' was organised, of which the valuable and rigorous catalogue, together with its essays and documents, formed a kind of critical re-launch of the work of Muybridge.[129] In the same year, a curious book by Kevin MacDonnell was published, dedicated to *Eadweard Muy-*

bridge, the Man who Invented the Moving Picture (the author was presented as an ex-photo-journalist and ex-British secret agent).[130]

Attractive in presentation, but fragmentary and incomplete in content, this biography was subsequently re-evaluated because of the lack of documentation, and the alterations and inaccuracy of reproduction of the photographs. On the plus side, however, specific attention was given to the technical aspects of Muybridge's work.

In 1975–76 two scientifically rigorous works were published, which now make it possible to give Muybridge the place he is due, with all his light and shade, without running the risk of serious under-valuing or unjustified mythologising. There is still space in the Muybridgean bibliography for scholars who wish to investigate the existing evidence further; however, a general, comprehensive picture was established with the publications of Gordon Hendricks and Robert Bartlett Haas.[131] These two authors had the great advantage, compared to the somewhat discontinuous commitment of MacDonnell, of living in the USA and thus having easy access to the sources still largely unexplored in the Californian and Pennsylvanian archives, as well as the George Eastman House museum at Rochester, where the materials by and on Muybridge were waiting to be researched. Hendricks declares that he dedicated fifteen years to his research on Muybridge and it should be noted that this interest of his must be placed in the larger context of his other, much appreciated works on problems and personalities linked to the birth of cinema.[132] Haas, for his part, goes even further, announcing that he worked twenty years to prepare his book; and he does not hide his privileged position as Director of the Department of Arts at the University of California. Furthermore, his great-grandfather was a friend of Muybridge; and, finally, he had received valuable and unpublished documentation from the daughter of the aforementioned lawyer Pendegast, who had dedicated all her life to re-establishing the accuracy of the information concerning the many twisted Muybridge legends. Haas was also co-author of that important catalogue, mentioned above, of the 1972 exhibition at Stanford University.

At the same time as these biographies, a film was made about him, EADWEARD MUYBRIDGE, ZOOPRAXOGRAPHER, by Thom Andersen, a student at the University of California.[133] The film is a biographical documentary based on documents and photographs, but also contains sequences animating, by means of an optical printer, some of Muybridge's photographic series of the movement of men and animals. The dynamic images resulting from this are so fine that they would convince a non-technician that cinema already existed, when, instead, Muybridge was still photographing with wet collodion plates.

These studies of Muybridge and the re-publication of many of his photographic works re-launched his figure and fame internationally. Quotations and reference to his work have multiplied, a bibliography of little value, often second-hand and with the inaccuracies of hurried and superficial scrutiny. A number of photographic exhibitions have been put on, with original prints (or declared to be such) of the plates in the Muybridge series, and a market for selling these prints is prospering.[134]

We mentioned that too often Muybridge's name is attached to the now almost legendary bet between two horse-trainers, and that his photographic intervention solved the dispute in 1872. Although Muybridge himself fostered belief in the story Haas showed that it was completely untrue.[135] In his subsequent book, Haas took up the question again to settle the matter.[136]

The most credible version of the events is that in Spring 1872 there was the rekindling of an old debate between race enthusiasts and stable owners. As Muybridge himself wrote in later years:

> The principle subject of dispute was the possibility of a horse, while trotting – even at the height of his speed – having all four of his feet, at any portion of his stride, simultaneously free from contact with the ground.[137]

Among those supporters of this theory was Leland Stanford, already Governor of California and president of the powerful Central Pacific Railroad, which in 1869 had laid the rail-line connecting the Atlantic and Pacific coasts. Stanford had an ambition to be a scientific racehorse trainer and his training and breeding techniques, considered revolutionary at the time, were widely adopted.[138] Stanford was joined by Fred MacCrellish, the owner and editor of the *High Californian* newspaper, while the opposing view was taken by the President of the San Francisco Stock Exchange and two important New York newspaper owner/editors.[139] Considering the high profitable nature of the principal participants in the public debate, which was covered in newspapers from coast to coast (horse racing was by far the most popular of sports at the time), one can understand how the rumours of the $25,000 bet arose.

It appears that MacCrellish suggested to Stanford that he contract Muybridge, who was already well known as a photographer, in an attempt to settle this *vexata questio* with a documented proof of scientific worth. It also appears that Muybridge initially hesitated to accept the offer made by Stanford by telegram, not feeling sure that he would be able to resolve the request.[140]

In fact there was much for him to be worried about, considering the very limited sensitivity of the plates at the time. Looking at some of Muybridge's other photographs from that time, such as his beautiful panoramas of Yosemite Valley, we can clearly see that the water of the waterfalls is blurred and undefined; the amount of time needed for a good exposure was still too great. One should remember that a galloping horse can cover eleven metres in less than a second.

Research has not so far unearthed the original photographs that Muybridge claims to have taken in 1872 and which probably consisted of a mere silhouette of a horse exposed on a wet collodion plate. Beyond his claims, there is also an article published on 7 April 1873 in MacCrellish's paper that reported on the various attempts by Muybridge, even giving the technical details of the shooting: an aperture of 1/8th of an inch for 5/100ths of a second. It also says that the spokes of the small gig did not appear to rotate.

In 1873 a colour lithograph was made by a well known equestrian artist that showed the same horse that was apparently photographed, a favourite sporting champion called 'The Californian Wonder.' Pictured in mid-race, the horse has all four legs off the ground at the same time. It has been suggested that the drawing was inspired by Muybridge's plates, but it is certain that these early attempts were not sufficient to show the disagreements over animal locomotion and of the usefulness of photographs as defensive and incontrovertible documentary evidence.

We already know why Muybridge was not able to continue with his experiments. We have to remember though, beyond matters relating to his private life and professional affairs, other elements appeared in the cultural and technical process which influenced developments in the scientific study of movement.

In 1872 the photographer O.G. Rejlander had made a theoretical proposal for the study of animal movement, especially that of horses, fixing the various positions in photographs taken with a series of cameras.[141] A few years earlier in 1869, the astronomer Sir John Herschel wrote of his proposal 'which might seem like a dream', but which he believed to be possible: to create stereoscopic photographs taken in rapid succession at 1/10th of a second to reconstruct the development of the action taken by a Phenakistiscope. 'If they were in colour' he added 'the illusion would be complete.'[142]

Outside of intelligent scientific prediction, one must note the publication in 1873 of E.J. Marey's book *La machine animale* which was published in English the following year. There seems to be little doubt that the results obtained by the French physiologist stimulated the interests of the part-time horse breeder Leland Stanford, who continued in his attempts to obtain photographic evidence of equestrian locomotion.[143]

Muybridge was called again to photograph 'Occident', the favourite thoroughbred of Stanford. It is the summer of 1877. Again, neither a negative, a print on paper, nor a glass plate or even a slide for a magic lantern has yet to be found. Newspapers at the time, however, talked of them as a triumph in the progress of photographic art. Muybridge himself wrote that the photographic exposure was of less but 1/1000th of a second ('I believe [it] to have been more rapidly executed than any ever made hitherto') while the horse was running at an approximate speed of eleven metres per second.

The camera was placed thirteen metres from the racecourse. Sending a positive print of the photograph, he said that it had been touched up 'as is the custom these days for every first class photographer.'[144] In any event the photographic reproduction of a watercolour by John Koch, entitled *The Horse in Motion*, which shows 'Occident' trotting with a gig and driver, was printed. The caption gave 'copyright 1877' to Muybridge and added that the original negative of the 'Automatic Electro-photograph' had been exposed at less than 1/2000th of a second, and that the details had been touched up.[145]

An X-ray examination of Koch's watercolour demonstrated that only the head of the driver of the gig was a photograph, cut out, glued on and printed with the rest of the picture. This probably means that the original photograph lacked good enough definition to be used for the touching-up and colouring. It is possible Muybridge had a magic lantern slide made which was then re-photographed.[146]

Without getting into the issue of the quality of the photograph taken by Muybridge in 1877, one should remember that no other system existed for photographic printing apart from the positive process on sensitive paper, so that every example from a certain point of view becomes an original. For serial reproduction, one had to translate the photographic image either into a hand-drawn picture, a lithographic plate or an engraving. It is worth emphasising the technical classification relating to the 'Automatic Electro-Photograph.' This suggests that Muybridge had already adopted (or was thinking of adopting) an automatic system based on an electrical contact caused by the passing of the horse setting off the mechanical shutter. One should not forget that it was common photographic practice then to expose the plate with a manual exposer, which is to say removing and replacing the cover of the lens after an instant (hence the term 'instantaneous photography'). The results obtained by Muybridge (for which he received a medal at San Francisco's industry fair) convinced Stanford – who in the meantime had purchased large plots of land in Palo

Muybridge's track and camera shed at Palo Alto, 1879.

Alto with a farm, stables, race and training course – to develop and complete his attempts to gain photographic representation of equestrian movement.

16. Twenty-four cameras for a horse

In the summer of 1878 there was open talk of a project to document photographically a theory on the position of the legs of a running horse which ran contrary to popular opinion. Muybridge was authorised to set up a battery of

Camera and shutters used by Muybridge at Palo Alto.

cameras placed one after another, taking exposures in rapid succession. He had at his disposal a racetrack in Palo Alto, where a wooden structure was erected to house the photographic equipment and for the preparation of the plates, while on the other side of the track a white wall was erected. The walls, placed directly in the field of vision of the cameras, were marked with graduated vertical lines and numbers so as to provide exact points of reference for the position of the horse in successive photographs. Twelve stereoscopic cameras were purchased from Scovill of New York and a series of lenses, among the most luminous then available, ordered from the English lens manufacturer Dallmeyer.

The most delicate part of the whole set-up was the shutter. Muybridge had devised a system with a double shutter curtain with a vertical movement that allowed for extremely fast exposures, and which worked for both of the lenses of each camera. For the shutter technique it was necessary to ensure perfect synchronisation in the opening and closing of each exposure as the horse went by each camera.

Muybridge's first idea was to use a mechanism that would be started manually on the horse's departure and which would then continue based on prior calculation of the horse's speed. This was an ingenious piece of equipment, something between a clock and a musical box, but it proved too hard to keep synchronised. Stanford then put Muybridge in contact with his technicians at the Central Pacific Railways, among whom was John Isaacs. With their help, an electro-mechanical system was devised so that the passage of the horse in front of the camera would close the circuit and set off the shutter.[147] In practice, it was the metallic rim of the gig drawn by the trotting horse that made contact with the wires on the track, which corresponded to the cameras placed fifty centimetres apart. The problem of how to photograph a racing horse mounted by a rider (and so without the gig) was solved by keeping the fine wires drawn across the track at the height of the horse's chest, which then ran through them: this also served to close the electrical contact.[148]

By June 1878 the whole experimental apparatus was ready; journalists and guests were allowed to assist on the first series of exposures. The guests, wrote one newspaper, were allowed to watch as the negatives were developed a mere twenty minutes after the experiment. In the same month, Muybridge took along his documents to patent his 'method and equipment for photographing moving objects.' At the same time he published six cards of prints from wet collodion negatives using the title *The Horse in Motion*, but differently from the previous year, each print featured a series of photographs (between six and twelve) almost all 'untouched', reproducing the phases of the entire cycle of movement (trotting, strolling, galloping etc).

The stated interval between one photograph and the next was 1/25th of a second, each exposure having been taken at 1/2000th of a second. Accompanying each still was an analytical description of the position of the horse in each phase of its run.

The cover of *Scientific American*, 19 October 1878.

One newspaper, writing about the success of the experiments, divided equally its plaudits 'since it is hard to say who deserves the greater acknowledgement' between Stanford, who had the original idea and who financed the experiment, and Muybridge, the photographer and artist of rare genius, who invented the procedure which overcame all the scientific, chemical and mechanical obstacles.[149]

The quality of the photographs is reasonably good, far superior to the modest silhouettes that the old and prejudiced detractors go back to. They allow one to see that which the human eye unaided cannot. News of Muybridge's results aroused great interest not only in sporting and equestrian circles but also in the artistic and scientific world. The first authoritative articles on this appeared in two prestigious scientific publications: *The Scientific American* (a news item appeared on 27 July 1878; an article and a series of cover photographs then followed on 19 October) and *La Nature* (14 December 1878).[150] Muybridge started to sell the series of six prints by subscription at $15 each and received orders from all around the world.

Marey, whose physiological studies of the movement of horses were probably what started Stanford's interest in the first place, wrote to Gaston Tissander, a friend as well as the editor of *La Nature*, after seeing Muybridge's plates: 'I am impressed by the instantaneous photographs by Mr Muybridge which you have published … could you put me in contact with the author.' In the same letter, he mentioned that Muybridge might supply some good images for use in a Zoetrope and pointed out that for artists this was truly revolutionary as many would have at their disposal real positions from movement, for which a model could never pose.

The Scientific American, which also suggested that Muybridge's work could be used in a Zoetrope, returned to the argument of these instantaneous photographs.[151] It pointed out that they appeared to be 'a physical demonstration of the truth which mathematics establishes' and therefore 'the first visible demonstration of the much disputed fact that the top of a wagon wheel, when running along the ground, moves faster than the bottom.' The evidence was deduced from the clarity of the photographic image in which the one third of the lower part of the wheel seemed to be immobile while the upper part was clearly in motion.[152]

That same year Muybridge started to exploit his first successful results financially, with a series of paid lectures in which he showed slides using two magic lanterns simultaneously. One was used to show close-ups, almost life-size enlargements of particular positions of the horses; or else placed next to photographs of sculptures and other types of graphical representation to show viewers the artistic interpretation as compared to the scientific value of his work.

On a wave of interest and success, Muybridge continued to develop his experiments. Always at Stanford's expense, the series of cameras reached twenty-four in number.[153] The photographs were not limited to horses, but extended to domestic animals, as well as athletes from a San Francisco club, shown in various sporting activities. It is interesting to note, however, what Muybridge wrote on 7 May 1879 to Thomas Eakins, partner and teacher at the Academy of Arts in Philadelphia, who was also directly interested in the study of movement through chronophotography. Describing his current experiments, he assured Eakins that after every photographic session a map of the course was made to mark the prints of the horse's hooves to corroborate the photograph, as if to say that it was good to have faith but it was even better to have proof.

In fact, one of the aspects that gained most attention from both the public and specialists (scientists, artists, sportsmen), was the implausibility and apparent absurdity of some of the positions shown by photographs taken at a 1/1000th of a second. The important and widely distributed French periodical *L'Illustration*, in its edition of 25 January 1879, included a long article on Muybridge by Colonel Duhousset, a noted equestrian expert. The text, illustrated by a number of 'facsimiles' taken from the original photographs, pointed out that those images showed 'nature captured in the act' and that documents of such importance 'constitute for artists a precious complement to the interesting works of graphic physiology on locomotion by Marey.'

Muybridge's photograph, 'Leland Stanford Jr on his Pony', Palo Alto, May 1879.

The periodical returned to this argument on 19 April, pointing out that the photographs were taken 'according to nature', but that 'some movements seem so unlikely that we thought it would be interesting to *prove* their accuracy.' In short, they provided as a special offer to their subscribers paper strips showing the phases of the trot and at the gallop (taken from Muybridge). With these, via a Zoetrope, offered at the special price of ten francs, 'one *sees* the horse *gallop*, which is the absolute proof of the accuracy of our *silhouettes*.'

While in Europe people still contented themselves with tracing by hand for the cylinder of the 'animator' (or Zoetrope), or the disc of the old Phenakistiscope, Muybridge perfected a new machine, based on pre-existing models and principles. After various attempts (with a variety of names given to the succession of machines) he presented the Zoöpraxiscope in the autumn of 1879 to a specially invited group at the house of his sponsor, Stanford. The Zoöpraxiscope used both the properties of optical toys and the magic lantern.[154] Practically speaking, it was made up of a magic lantern projector in which, between the light source and the lens, two concentric discs were placed which turned in opposite directions. One of the discs, metallic and equipped with small slits, functioned as a shutter, while the other one, made of glass, carried the source of images which went through a complete cycle in a single rotation. As we can see, even at an embryonic level and within the limits of which its author envisaged, the Zoöpraxiscope really did prefigure the modern film projector.

In 1898 Muybridge wrote:

> It is the first apparatus ever used, or constructed, for synthetically demonstrating movements analytically photographed from life, and in its resulting effects is the prototype of all the various instruments which, under a variety of names, are used for a similar purpose at the present day.[155]

Muybridge himself described what happened at Stanford's home at the first public screening by invitation.[156] Muybridge told the master of the house and the guests that, as the Zoöpraxiscope started working, they were now watching the horse Hawthorn galloping. A few seconds later however Stanford exclaimed, 'I think you must make a mistake in the name of the animal; that is certainly not the gait of Hawthorn, but that of Anderson.' Muybridge checked his notes and insisted on his version but Stanford remained unconvinced. The following day the trainer revealed that it actually was Hawthorn and not Anderson. Muybridge concluded:

> At the moment he felt more disappointed at the inaccuracy of his registry than gratified with the perfect manner in which the Zoöpraxiscope had performed its duties.[157]

One should also keep in mind that the images being projected were not of the photographic originals, but drawings (a later series was coloured), copied onto the glass of the disc from the photographs. According to Muybridge, after many experiments he sought to dilate the figures horizontally to correct the seeming vertical lengthening of the animals provoked by the fact that they were viewed through the narrow slits of the shutter disc.

The Zoöpraxiscope was not patented. This might seem strange if we consider that Muybridge had so completely taken on board the American view that 'business is business', that when he had sought the patent for his system for photography in series he had included the backdrop with its vertical and horizontal co-ordinates and reference numbers, as if they were his own innovation. In the use of the projection equipment, however, it was clear that its various elements were made up of parts already known and in use. It was rather a case of a new way of using them all together, which did not warrant a patent. Despite this, according to Hendricks, Muybridge did try to get one and was helped, without success, by Stanford's lawyers.[158]

Theirs was an unlikely partnership, where one (the rich patron) was happy for his idea to be realised vicariously, putting up large amounts of money and using his influence to get what was needed, while the other (the adventurous photographer) was happy to work just for the greater glory – in the sense that apart from exposure, he received no salary from Stanford.[159] Nevertheless, it laid the foundation for a discrete business since, with the tacit approval of the patron, he placed his copyright on all the photographs sold, patented the photographic technique, and commercially exploited the results of his efforts as a photographer, making personal appearances at conferences, an activity he would continue to exploit for almost twenty years, accompanied of course by his projection equipment.[160]

In 1881, the Stanford-Muybridge partnership reached its apex with the conclusion of a cycle of experiments, the results of which are written into the first pages of the history of scientific cinema. The following year saw the end of the relationship between those two very different men, and as is so often the case, it ended in acrimony, with lawyers and disagreements. The two events that marked that year were the publication of Muybridge's album *The Attitudes of Animals in Motion* and the trip to Europe undertaken by Stanford and Muybridge.

The album (of which fewer than twenty copies are known to exist) can be seen in effect as a kind of final report on the research undertaken. After the title, it reads:

A Series of Photographs Illustrating the Consecutive Positions Assumed by Animals in Performing Various Movements executed at Palo Alto, California, in 1878 and 1879, copyright 1881, by Muybridge.

It was made up of 203 prints in albumen of approximately 17 x 24 centimetres, from wet collodion negative plates. Each copy was made up of original positives printed by Muybridge and some copies included an introduction by him and an index of the illustrations. The photographs bore only the copyright details, while the introduction included the captions from the first photographs, which showed, just as is done in the case of a research report, the experimental equipment, from the panoramic view of the Palo Alto ranch, to details of the 'electro-shutters', and the techniques used. In the first line it says that the photographs were taken 'by instructions of Governor Leland Stanford.' In the copy that Muybridge gave to his patron, it bears a handwritten note that more or less repeats this acknowledgement. Perhaps Stanford was expecting (or even deserved?) something more.[161]

The album collects series photographs of various horses running and walking, as well as of other animals and athletes. A plate entitled *Athlete swinging a pick* shows Muybridge himself, nude, with a pipe in his mouth.

There are various examples of shots taken at an angle and in perspective, denoting the simultaneity of the cameras in the experimental track and with other mobile equipment.

The European trip of the two men was not directly linked to the publication of these materials, but it increased their importance and would have serious and definitive consequences for their relationship. Many of the details relating to the events that followed still remain unclear and so make it harder to explain the true significance of their trip to Europe or the origin of the disagreement that eventually would bring them to court.

'Athlete swinging a pick' (Muybridge himself), from *Attitudes of Animals in Motion*.

Stanford was already in Europe with his family by the summer of 1881. It is said that he had the intention of personally presenting the results of the Palo Alto experiments to a number of scientific and artistic circles.[162] One of the specific reasons for the trip to Europe (a common one for rich Americans of the period) was to get his portrait painted by a famous French artist, something that he had already arranged for his wife a few years earlier. Since 1879 he had wanted to be immortalised on canvas by the hand of Meissonnier, the official painter renowned for his great historical paintings, one of which shows Napoleon on his horse. However, the French painter initially refused.

Stanford eventually managed to get the portrait after discovering that the painter was interested in studies on animal locomotion.[163] They entered into discussion on the matter and Stanford showed him the first photographs of 'Occident', with the result that the portrait incorporated a perspective view of Muybridge's *The Attitudes of Animals in Motion*, which Stanford must have brought with him to Paris. It is possible that it was during the lengthy sittings for the portrait (for which he paid $10,000) that Meissonnier persuaded him into asking Muybridge to come to Europe to expound on the results of his photographs of animals in motion.[164]

By the time the ex-governor left for Europe, the experiments at Palo Alto had come to an end. The equipment had been dismantled and handed over to Muybridge. Obviously there had been an initial agreement or a unilateral decision on Stanford's part to give the equipment to him. In practice this was a kind of settlement of their affairs. In a photograph from 1915 which shows the remains of the wooden construction that in 1878–79 had housed the battery of cameras, one can see the remains of the rest of the equipment, including at least one of the famous 'electro-shutters' and a few of what were probably the baths for developing the plates.[165] Still on Stanford's instructions, Muybridge was paid the lump sum of $2,000. Was this payment for services rendered, an act of generosity, or money towards travel expenses to Europe? Not even the punctilious acts of pique and reciprocal objections that the two would raise against each other in court shortly afterwards helped to find the true facts.

Muybridge crossed the Atlantic and, after a brief stay in England, arrived in Paris. On the evening of 26 September 1881, Marey invited many famous people to his new home at the Trocadéro to meet Muybridge and to see his photographs. Stanford was not there. Among the invitees, celebrated guests included scientists such as Helmholtz and Bjerknes, Professor Govi of the University of Naples, professors from the Sorbonne and the College de France, Colonel Duhousset and Gaston Tissandier (the latter were of course the first in Europe to present Muybridge's work) and the photographer Nadar.

The next day, the newspaper *Le Globe* dedicated a long article to the event under the headline 'La photographie instantanée', and presented Muybridge as an

American scientist.[166] The soirée was a great success and led to another event two months later in the great study of Meissonnier (who had also just completed Stanford's portrait) at boulevard Malesherbes, with a select group of invited guests including painters, sculptors and writers.[167] Once again, Stanford was absent, although he was in Paris by then. That same day he left with his family for Liverpool to return to the United States. From one of Muybridge's letters we know that Stanford was not in good health.

Once again, all the celebrations were in Muybridge's honour. Among the 200 guests was Alexandre Dumas *fils*. On both of these two occasions, images were projected by both a magic lantern and the Zoöpraxiscope, using both the instantaneous photographs and the discs that reproduced movement. First Muybridge showed images of the experimental installation, then explained the techniques behind the photography, and then showed the results, analysing individual photographs and reconstructing movement via images. It appears that the effect provided by the Zoöpraxiscope was extraordinary. *Le Temps* wrote:

> The American inventor manages, through a series of instantaneous photographs, to fix the movements of a man walking, of a horse running, and, with the help of a rotary movement, to project with electric light the moving images of the man and of the horse.[168]

Gaston Tissandier, in an article illustrated with images from a greyhound race and from the experimental track in California, said of the Zoetrope for projection that Muybridge, 'the able physicist from San Francisco' had used:

> The effect is extraordinary: it is real movement caught live; for the physiologist, from a scientific standpoint, and for the painter, from an artistic point of view, innumerable avenues of study spring up. For everyone there is material of teaching value and of general interest.[169]

The article refers to Marey's 'photographic gun', to the generous patronage of the ultra-rich Stanford who made the Palo Alto experiments possible and, in conclusion, hoped that Muybridge's work would be made generally available and published *in toto* so that all could profit 'from one of the finest results of modern photography.'

Muybridge, variously referred to as 'inventor', 'scientist', 'chemist', 'physicist' and 'photographic critic', stayed in Paris for about six months. One can imagine what his plans were from letters that he wrote to Frank Shay, Stanford's secretary.[170] Less clear is the situation regarding his relationship with his ex-financier. Nothing has emerged as to the exchanges that must have taken place in Paris. Muybridge said that he awaited in vain 'for dispositions to arrive on behalf of the governor' and that in the meantime he collected information on the movement of animals in works of art from the Assyrians to modern artists; that he was proposing to resume his experiments and had talked with Marey and Meissonnier about joint efforts which would be financed by 'a capitalist', whom he does not mention by name, but from which he would not want to exclude Stanford.[171]

It is all very vague, and it is unclear if this was to take place in France or England. He asked Shay in a mellifluous but insistent tone, as if trying to regain a friend lost, for a complete list of the sums paid by Stanford in funding the Palo Alto experiments (acquisition of equipment, photographic materials, construction costs, wages for assistants, monies paid to Muybridge for personal use excluding the two thousand dollars given to him by the governor); all of this was requested so that he could make a budget for his new plan. There is also a reference to the large sums Muybridge would be paid if he were to assign to Meissonnier (who wanted to run the new company) his copyright in the techniques used in Palo Alto in this new company between Muybridge, and the 'capitalist friend.' Muybridge was also looking to be paid for the time spent setting them up beyond his usual quotation for his work in California.

One gets the impression of rather vague manoeuvres, with the use of phrases such as 'happily I have strong nerves, or I should have blushed with the lavishness of their praises'; or with such reckless comments such as

> ... if in the course of your travels you should next summer find yourself in Paris, make me a visit to my Electro-Photo studio in the Bois de Boulogne and I will give you a welcome ...

without specifying that it was simply a plan to go and work in Marey's new institute.[172]

Shay did not apparently pay much attention to Muybridge's requests, who in any event, after his great scientific, artistic as well as social successes, seemed quickly to lack any really concrete possibilities for the projects. In fact, by the beginning of March 1882 he had already left the French capital for London.

The successes that he had in Paris were again repeated here for the 'American' Muybridge, whose English heritage seems to have been obscured or ignored. On 13 March he was at the Royal Institution, three days later at the Royal Academy of Arts, and subsequently at many other important bodies including the South Kensington Museum (now the Science Museum) and even the Liverpool Arts Club where he held a conference with projected images before boarding ship and returning to the USA. Among the most interested and enthusiastic supporters at his presentations were the Prince of Wales, the Duke of Edinburgh, the poet Alfred Tennyson as well as Professors Tindall, Gladstone and Huxley.

The London correspondent of the San Francisco *Morning Call* wrote in exalted tones of Muybridge's 'American courage' in addressing his lofty audiences and of the pride the journalist himself felt in watching 'a countryman of mine installed as an instructor within the sacred walls of this great temple of fine arts.'[173]

It is worth noting that in his Parisian presentation, Muybridge included slides of classical and modern works of art showing horses in motion to point out errors when compared with his photographs.[174] The London journal *Photographic News*, in response to the projection of moving images (which for the occasion was dubbed the 'zoepracticoscope'), wrote that 'a new world of spectacles and marvels has truly opened with photography, and it is nonetheless amazing for being simply true.'

The already cited writer of the *Morning Call* also wrote:

> I believe if he were to 'hire a hall' and give exhibitions twice a day at a shilling entrance fee, Mr. Muybridge would clear enough money during the coming Summer to greatly assist him in the in the pursuance of the researches in the field where he has already made such curious and unexpected discoveries.

Despite these optimistic opinions, the success in London was not followed by any concrete development, and nothing followed from the initial agreements made with Marey and Meissonnier.[175] What did occur instead was the disagreement between Stanford and Muybridge, with the latter potentially involved in a scandal branding him as a blaggard for having presented as 'his', results of research that were either not his or in which he was only involved in a marginal technical role. Stanford, in line with his ambitions to become a modern patron with intellectual prestige had certainly not become interested in the movement of horses because of a bet.[176] Rather, it had been with the slightly confused intention of establishing new technical principles of racehorse training and breeding on a scientific basis. Seeing the results of Muybridge's photographic experiments, he had conceived of a book which would develop his theory of equestrian locomotion in anatomical and physiological terms. To write the text he turned to an old friend, J.B. Stillman, who had a degree in medicine and therefore an academic title. Stillman had a skeleton of a horse sent over from Chicago which Muybridge then photographed in various poses.[177] However, right from the beginning a strong rivalry existed between the two.

Muybridge had been asked to provide a text on the phases of the photographic research, but Stillman practically refused it, saying it was 'ungrammatical, redundant, full of hyperbole, which would make the thing ridiculous.'[178] For his part, Muybridge had complained that his job of putting the book together had gone to Stillman. It was tacitly understood, though, that the eventual book would bear Stillman's name as author of the text and that of Muybridge of the illustrations. In fact he was expecting payment for the rights to them since he owned the copyright.[179] One may assume that the publication of Muybridge's *The Attitudes of Animals in Motion*, albeit in such small numbers, must have pricked Stanford's vanity (he is hardly mentioned or thanked) and interfered with the project with Stillman. Thus, while Muybridge was in Europe, Stillman, with the full backing of Stanford and his private secretary, brought forward the date and published the book.[180] The book, full of errors, clearly on account of the speed with which it was

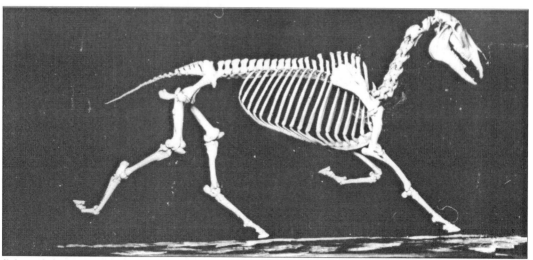

Skeleton of a horse, from *Attitudes of Animals in Motion*.

written, ignores Muybridge in its title page, despite the reference in its title to 'instantaneous photographs' and to the 'revelations of the camera'; in fact, he is really only mentioned in Stanford's preface, who refers to him as an employee, albeit an expert in photography.[181] The illustrations are almost all heliotypic transcriptions taken from Muybridge's plates, hence losing the documentary validity of the originals. Only five of the original photographs were reproduced directly.

The arrival of copies of the book in London in April 1882 resulted in the president of the Royal Society contesting Muybridge's right to publish in the Society's proceedings until he could prove himself to be the true author of the photographic research now contained in Stillman's book, which gave him so little mention. Muybridge claimed to have been greatly damaged by the manifest injustice committed by Stanford and Stillman; so much so in fact that he was forced to sell some of the copies of his album to be able to secure funds to return to the United States.

Arriving in New York in the summer of 1882, Muybridge sued the publisher of the book, who declined all responsibility, as did the fearful Stillman, who asked for the cancellation of the copyright he had asked to be in his name, loading everything on to Stanford's shoulders. Muybridge therefore went to trial against his powerful ex-patron.

The lawsuit dragged on while the preliminary inquiries collected evidence on the relationship between Stanford and Muybridge, going as far back as 1872. A Boston journalist wrote that:

> The case will be interesting as casting some light on the question whether a poor scientific investigator has any rights that our plutocracy is bound to respect.[182]

A week later, however, the paper was obliged to publish an unsigned letter which not only accused it of taking Muybridge's side, but which insisted that it was Stanford who first had the idea of using photographs, and that Muybridge was simply employed to carry them out; that Stanford paid for everything, and therefore had the right to ask other 'competent talents to interpret the resulting photographs, and to harmonise them with the anatomy and physiology of horses.'[183] This would prove to be the argument that eventually won the case for the ex-governor. Muybridge did not get the $50,000 in damages that he was seeking. On the other hand, Stillman's book was a total failure for which Stanford had to pay the expenses. The publishers removed it from their catalogue and sold off the leftover copies cheaply.

It seems certain that if the suit had been brought against Stillman, then Muybridge would have won. Despite the way the trial was going, Muybridge continued to make a living charging for his personal appearances.[184] In October 1882 he lectured at the prestigious Massachusetts Institute of Technology in Boston. Looking at the dates, this event can be seen as influencing the initial position by the newspaper quoted above. In February 1883 Muybridge took part in a conference in Philadelphia at the Academy of Fine Arts. A new chapter was beginning in the adventurous life of the Anglo-American photographer.

17. To study locomotion

It was in the capital of Pennsylvania that Muybridge was able to accomplish his most important work, that for which he deserves to be remembered in the history of scientific cinematography. Philadelphia, despite its proximity to New York, but perhaps precisely because of it, was often the focus for independent initiatives, not just in the economic field, but in artistic and cultural circles as well. At the beginning of the 1880s we find in this city a number of interesting figures that had a direct bearing on the history we are relating.

First among them was Thomas Eakins, still considered to be one of the most important American painters of the nineteenth century.[185] He was also a devotee of photography. He had been corresponding with Muybridge for a number of years and was taking his own photographic series to study the phases of movement. For the purposes of study he had transcribed some of Muybridge's first series of stills of a moving horse, using Marey's graphic method, from whom he had also taken some chronophotographic techniques. He also became the subject of discussion in a curious episode that provides a sense of the period. Eakins taught at the Academy of Fine Arts and was a firm believer in studying and drawing nudes, including male ones. This, however, created problems: two female students fainted at the sight of a naked male model. A petition was drawn up against him and, after many arguments, he was forced to leave.

Fairman Rogers, a wealthy racehorse owner, was Eakins's friend, patron and fellow photography enthusiast, and was, of course, also interested in equestrian locomotion. There were significant differences between patrons on the East and West Coasts, typical of the different pace of development in American society. Stanford always wanted to overdo things in all senses, to assert his power. He was convinced that the research photographs were his and that he could do what he liked with them, simply because he paid for them. He got his portrait painted in Paris and had a villa with a 'Pompeian room' in San Francisco because it was the fashion among the rich. But he was not an intellectual and did not wish to be one. It was only a family bereavement that led to his name being tied to a famous academic institution: Stanford University. It was created in 1885 to commemorate the death of his fifteen-year-old son, the campus emerging in the Palo Alto estate where Muybridge had made his first experiments.[186] Fairman Rogers, although having at his disposal a large fortune left to him by his father, became professor of civil engineering at the University, wrote scientific articles and books, was the author of a widely respected coaching manual, spoke out against racial discrimination in the administration of the Academy of Fine Arts, and ran artistic and musical institutions. When he commissioned a painting from his friend, he asked for what was a practically impossible undertaking: the representation of movement.

In 1879, immediately after seeing the first successful serial plates published by Muybridge, Rogers commissioned from Eakins a picture in which he (Rogers) and his family would appear, as well as servants, on board a moving coach. The challenge was to show the sixteen legs of the coach and four as fitting in with the photographic studies on movement. Eakins set to work with great commitment, studying not only Muybridge's photographs, but taking his own, making a great many sketches and drawings, even going so far as to make models of racing horses.

The result was a painting that became famous, so much so that he subsequently painted another. The 1879 original, which was supposed to be entitled *A May Morning in the Park*, but which was later changed to *The Fairman Rogers Four-in-hand*, can be found at the Philadelphia Museum of Art. The painting soon found itself at the centre of heated debates, references to which could still be found twelve years later in a presentation by the American painter Joseph Pennell at the London Camera Club on the relationship between photography and painting:

> Their legs had been studied and painted in the most marvellous manner. He then put on the drag. He drew every spoke in the wheels, and the whole affair looked as if it had been instantaneously petrified or arrested. There was no action in it. He then blurred the spokes, giving the drag the appearance of motion. The result was that it seemed to be on the point of running right over the horses, which were standing still.[187]

In an article by Fairman Rogers, aside from its appreciation of Muybridge's first results and Eakins' studies, we find a reference that – if we want to be fanatical in our search for the new pioneers of cinema – might mark him as a forerunner of sound cinema.[188] He wrote, independently of Stanford and Muybridge, who had also considered it, of putting silhouettes of horses racing in a Zoetrope and thereby creating a synthesis of movement, 'to determine whether the photographic analysis was correct.' He did not take particular credit for this, though he did go on to say that he built a large metallic Zoetrope, with various features making it neither a toy nor a drawing room entertainment, but a scientific instrument. He then added:

> An addition to the zootrope is now being made by which, at the moment at which each foot appears to the eye to strike the ground, a sharp tap of a small hammer will be made by the instrument, and the cadence of the step will be made manifest to the ear, and will aid materially in the study of the motion.

A third figure of interest was a notable Philadelphian, Professor William Pepper, who for fifteen years was the provost of the University of Pennsylvania. He strikes us as something of a cross between an industrial entrepreneur and a patron. He never hesitated to invest his own money in scientific research, but he was particularly adept at getting wealthy people to donate funds to the university, which during his time there went through a period of considerable development and expansion. New subjects included veterinary science, while university clinics were expanded and new courses in philosophy, natural science and palaeontology were introduced. Not least among his initiatives was allowing women to study there, even if only in a special department.

It was in this environment that Muybridge was fortunate enough to find the opportunity for which he had long been searching. His personal appearances and visual presentations helped to make ends meet, but also allowed him to develop ideas for new photographic experiments on locomotion, not just with horses, but many others animals as well as people. His proposal to study human beings (not so much from a physiological standpoint but as documentation for artists) had been suggested to him by Thomas Eakins. After the failure of his European travels, Muybridge was still on the look out for a new source of finance; this might include a small group of investors, in the form of subscribers, who would pay in advance for a series of photographs, with explanatory notes on the results of the research: a kind of corporation aimed at scientific experimentation.

In April 1883 Muybridge sent out on the headed notepaper of the Scovill Manufacturing Company (Publishing Department) of New York, a 'Prospectus of a New and Elaborate Work upon the Attitudes of Man, the Horse, and other Animals in Motion.'[189] The text referred to the earlier experiments, and to 'zoopraxiography' as the art of illustrating the movements of animals in movement by means of electro-automatic photography. It hinted at the possibility of obtaining perfect photographs at 1/10,000th of a second, and drew the attention of scientists, artists, and the owners and trainers of horses to the benefits they might gain from the results of this new research.[190] Assurances were made that the results would be provided on permanent positive prints derived from photographic negatives, not lithographic reproductions 'absolutely worthless for scientific or artistic purposes, and of little value or interest for general use.'[191] Various types of subject were announced, including images of performing actors, women dancing and playing tennis, men – clothed and nude – undertaking various activities both military and sporting. It suggested that they would include research on the propulsion methods of marine birds and seals, the continuation of works of aerial locomotion, and 'some experiments will be made for photographically recording the successive phases of the Heart and Lungs while in action, with an apparatus I have invented for this purpose'. All of this was promised if at least two hundred subscribers were willing to pay one hundred dollars each. Muybridge offered to the 'shareholders' one hundred original serial photographs (each containing between eight and twenty-four phases of movement), to be chosen from the total number realised and which would include numerous reproductions of modern and ancient works of art featuring men and horses. He stated that this selection would be made with 'the devoted assistance and invaluable advice' of the painter Meissonnier, that it would include an essay on zoopraxiology by Professor Marey, and that the analysis of the works of art in the light of the photographic discoveries would be undertaken by Walter Armstrong, the art critic of the *London Art Journal.*

As we can see, Muybridge's promotional leaflet promised much from a fire that had yet to be lit, though it was already producing a lot of smoke. However, the interest in this project led to concrete results in the summer of 1883. Eakins and Rogers convinced Pepper to patronise this initiative within the university. Although Muybridge had initially thought that $20,000 would be needed, he agreed, or pretended to, that $5,000 would be enough, at least to start with. A board of financiers (from outside the university) and a scientific board made up of professors (of anatomy, physics, veterinary science, biology, engineers and from the Academy of Fine Arts) was established to supervise the work of the 'researcher.' Muybridge was given a courtyard and some rooms in the new veterinary department where the labs would be set up and an experimental stage (which would be locked off at the sides with canvas as there was to be some nude photography). The businessmen that advanced the money were offered an interest with a guarantee that all costs would be covered by sales of the photographs, and that all the optical equipment would be handed over once it was no longer required.

Work was scheduled to take place in the spring and summer of 1884. A new prospectus was issued by the university, in which the future publication of the photographs was entitled *Animal Locomotion,* and even before the experiments began, there were subscriptions amounting to around $15,000 (although by then the overall budget had risen to $30,000).

The typically American undertaking therefore got off to a good start. While in Europe, Muybridge had had the chance to experiment with the new type of dry

Front and back of the camera series used by Muybridge for diagonal photography at the University of Pennsylvania.

plates, which did not need to have wet collodion spread on them as soon as prepared. These instead were relatively stable, produced industrially with the sensitive emulsion made up of a silver bromide gelatine fixed to the glass support. By the time the experiments began, these plates were being already produced and sold in America: in addition they had the great advantage of being much faster than the earlier ones, which is to say that even a really brief exposure could result in a good quality negative.

For his part, Muybridge had perfected a new and improved shooting technique, both with regard to the structure of the new cameras and the command and timing of the shutters. The cameras were already a step in the direction of the movie camera and a shift away from traditional still cameras. The battery had thirteen lenses, twelve for shooting in series, one for focusing and to act as viewfinder. The shutters were no longer controlled remotely by the passing of the horse, but instead worked on the basis of a timer that Muybridge regulated depending on the needs of each individual shoot.

At the request of the university, which wanted scientific guarantees of the precision of the technical information derived from Muybridge's results, a system of calibration and control was set in place. The vibrations of a tuning fork, connected to the circuit, were used to give a trace on blackened paper, indicating the exposure time of each shot, and the intervals between exposures. To check the interval time between exposures precisely, a white dot on a black disc revolving at a set speed was photographed in series, and the results corresponded with those of the tuning fork trace. For photographs taken laterally or diagonally, Muybridge, for reasons of economy, used strips taken from a normal plate, thus generating very small negatives, close to the modern format of 24 x 36 millimetres.[192]

Between spring 1884 and early 1886, over 20,000 negatives were exposed. Muybridge in the first instance dedicated himself almost entirely to human subjects as well as repeating some sessions with horses, using the 'studio' set up in the triangular courtyard in the university's Veterinary Science Institute. He then moved onto the zoological gardens where he recorded the movements of many different animals and where he tried to photograph birds in flight, using subjects tied down with a rope long enough to allow them to take off.

On these occasions the equipment proved itself reasonably flexible, as Muybridge moved it from one part of the zoo to another, even though the resulting photographs were not always of the best. There were some technical limitations that took a great deal of patience to overcome; for instance, white backing was required in the lion cage, for lighting reasons, which the lions frequently tore as it blocked access to the internal part of the enclosure. Next came the hippodrome to complete a series on horses galloping at high speeds. Finally, fulfilling an obligation to some of the university professors who had gone out of their way to ensure the success of the project, Muybridge produced series dedicated to pathological or unusual clinical cases, as well as disabled and paraplegic people. During the lengthy shooting period, the student newspaper as well as some local papers covered the experiments. Muybridge seemed unwilling to give any in-depth interviews, but a journalist gave what is probably the first 'on set' report of shooting a scene: a simple action lasting only a few seconds in which a woman sits down, crosses her legs and cools

Animal Locomotion, plate 758, 'Cockatoo: flying'.

herself with a fan. Later on we will see that these were not in fact the very first shots of a person in motion.

Muybridge had some difficulties when it came to choosing his models, as he called them. Some of the men were students or teachers at the university, while others were athletes, or sports trainers. Some of the women were artists' models, but there was also a prima ballerina from a theatre, as well as some ladies of high society; Muybridge thought that they would exhibit more spontaneous movements than a trained artist's model. Inevitably, problems arose over the nude sessions, especially in the case of the men. Despite the artistic/scientific aspirations, it appears that it was very difficult to persuade an ironmonger or a soldier that for scientific reasons they should allow themselves to be photographed naked while hammering an anvil or marching with a rifle.

One can also imagine the problems of photographing non-domesticated animals: in the case of sudden movements (such as a bird lifting off) it was necessary to start the clicking of the shutter mechanism automatically.

With the end of the shooting, the process of printing the results began. With the help of some full-time assistants that had already helped set up the facility for taking the photographs, Muybridge spent the winter of 1885 and the following spring studying, cataloguing, analysing and selecting the most important series of images.

Eventually some 781 assemblies were selected: of those, ninety-five showed horses, 124 other animals and 562, more than two thirds of the total, were dedicated to human movement. At this point the organisation's scientific board decided to open up the subscriptions for those that might want a partial or complete set of the collotype plates. Compiled into eleven volumes, the complete set was priced at 600 dollars. Complete sets were bought by some of the more prestigious scientific institutions in the USA and Europe (including Princeton, Yale, Cornell, Oxford, Cambridge, etc) as well as some very rich individuals (such as the emperor of China and the Khedive of Egypt).

Most of the subscribers, however, took advantage of a special offer comprising 100 plates of their choosing, bound in a leather portfolio. To pick the plates, it was possible to make use of a prospectus with analytical descriptions or to view the complete series, copies of which had been deposited in cities such as New York, Washington DC, Boston and London, in addition to Philadelphia. The subscribers included such celebrated artists and scientists as Alma-Tadema, Gérôme, Meissonnier, Rodin, Helmholtz, Mach, Marey, Mosso, Mantegazza, Pasteur and Righi. The *Prospectus and Catalogue of Plates*, published in 1887 to advertise the work, included a detailed listing of each of the 781 plates with reference to the movement it showed, the identification number for the model it used, the type of clothing or nudity, the number of images for each angle, and the gaps between the individual images from the various phases of movement. The catalogue was preceded by a number of short introductory chapters, in which Muybridge explained the various ways in which the plates were assembled, describing in great detail the techniques used for the project, even managing to continue, in a section entitled 'Retrospective', the polemics regarding his treatment over the publication of *The Horse in Motion*.

In 1891 the prospectus was reprinted with a greatly modified and updated text and with a slightly changed front page – instead of *Animal Locomotion* the title now read *The Science of Animal Locomotion (Zoopraxography)*. The detailed catalogue was replaced with a more general description divided into subjects, inviting subscribers to select their specific interests and then let the author pick the individual plates. Apart from the reference to the University of Pennsylvania, it also gave Muybridge's London address as he had now moved back to England. In the text one finds reference to a 'debt of gratitude' to Meissonnier (who had died in the intervening years) and a long list, meticulously divided into categories, of the previous subscribers. In the final miscellany one finds reference to the Archbishop of York, Field Marshal Count von Moltke, the Duke of Portland and Count Wharncliffe.

The university board had to make a decision on the publication of so many nude studies: they finally let them pass because of the scientific and artistic value of the work and because those that chose the plates did so with complete knowledge of its content.

The official title of the work when published was: *Animal Locomotion, An Electro-Photographic Investigation of Consecutive Phases of Animal Movements* by Eadweard Muybridge (1872–1885), published under the auspices of the University of Pennsylvania.

Muybridge finally had something with which to feel truly satisfied, also because the above dates included his first, not entirely successful, efforts in Palo Alto. This gave him his due recognition as author and pioneer, which had been obscured after the unpleasant legal disputes with Stillman and Stanford.

The 136-page monograph which accompanied the publication of the plates, entitled *Animal Locomotion: The Muybridge Work at the University of Pennsylvania – The Method and the Result* made no reference at all to the painter Thomas Eakins, who had worked so hard to get the board of the university to fund Muybridge's research. Aaron Scharf claims that the two had disagreed over the technique of experimental photography.[193] Eakins followed the research path taken by Marey, in which only one camera was used with a mobile plate, with the images being successively exposed on to the same plate. He had experimented with this himself and had demonstrated the results at conferences and presentations. Muybridge had clearly disliked this competition and had tried to ignore it and get others to sideline the work of his former supporter. Despite this it appears that Muybridge, following a suggestion from Eakins before their disagreement, had experimented with using a 'wheel' camera, based on the model made by Marey.[194]

In 1887, as the first complete set of plates was being prepared, Muybridge began a series of conference-demonstrations in the United States, partly with the intention – expressly agreed by the university – of finding new subscribers. In fact, at that point only half of the cost of the enterprise had so far been recovered, leaving the remainder (a minimum of $20,000) still owed to the financiers.

18. A century on

The importance of Muybridge's research and photographic documentation while at the University of Pennsylvania is clear even today, for the richness of the observation that can be drawn from the study of his plates. The data he collected ranges so widely as to make it a resource that is always open to fresh in-depth analysis. One should remember that Muybridge did not have a scientific background, but rather that he was a self-taught person who, in technological terms, tried to master both physiology and aesthetics. As to the value of his work for artists, it is enough to refer to the relevant chapters in Aaron Scharf's *Art and Photography*.

What should be emphasised, though, is the revolutionary nature of Muybridge's approach and the sheer number of analytical and comparative elements offered by the plates to those studying physiology, zoology, comparative anatomy and medical and veterinary science. It was no coincidence that the three professors who provided the commentary on the plates were: an engineer for the presentation of the methodology of the photographic research, a psychologist, and a doctor of nervous disorders.

An examination of a number of the plates dedicated to animal movement makes it clear just how much was achieved solely or exclusively thanks to his work. One need only think of the possibilities they offered to compare the locomotive characteristics of various different quadrupeds analytically and all the influence that this has had in the fields of physiology, comparative anatomy and the then new behavioural sciences.

Leafing through Muybridge's work one hundred years later, even given the advances in scientific cinematography made since then, in analysing and studying movement, a number of observations spring to mind. Although seemingly marginal, they still seem worth considering for the way they illuminate both the man and his work, while at the same time highlighting its limitations.

We begin with the part dedicated to animals. Among the plates of horses there are some that seem repetitive, gratuitous, even redundant: for example, a horse strolling while being ridden by a horsewoman or a naked man, a horse walking while carrying a bucket in its teeth. In fact the documentation is extremely interesting, when one looks at not just the side view but the posterior and diagonal perspectives as well. These different angles enrich the observable data. One can still appreciate the amazement of artists when looking for the first time at instantaneous shots of horses trotting, galloping or jumping in positions which were thought impossible or seemingly ridiculous to portray accurately in a painting.[195]

With regard to the notorious bet which allegedly motivated the experiments in California in the early 1870s, there is considerable photographic documentation showing the horse with all four legs off the ground, as well as shots of horses about to leave the ground or placing the weight on only one leg.

The plates dedicated to other animals, such as dogs, cats, camels, elephants, lions, baboons, gazelles, bison, kangaroos etc and birds (pigeons, eagles etc) betray an uneven interest and, owing to some technical difficulties, the photographic quality is less good. Muybridge claimed that the shortest time for a single test exposure was 1/6000th of a second, and that the interval between exposures was variable starting from a minimum of 1/100th of a second. To achieve such extraordinary speed, before every shot he had to calculate the exposure time and the most appropriate intervals to obtain the photographic quality and the effect desired. He then regulated the electro-mechanical device that would automatically set the three synchronised cameras in action. Muybridge himself (or an assistant) set off the first camera and then the equipment worked on its own. A string wound over a drum would unwind at differing speeds, depending on the setting of a counter-weight, through a ring of hard rubber with platinum contacts inserted. Cog wheels and a brush rotating with other contacts, connected to an electric battery, would open and close each successive shutter.

The limited interest of some of the animal plates is more than made up for by those that studied the movement of animals such as the camel for the first time, initiating research that could only be confirmed and deepened decades later using with film cameras under scientific conditions.[196]

Even among the few plates of birds taking flight there are some highly significant examples. The speed of Muybridge's mechanism meant that it was possible to shoot birds and cats at a speed of twenty images in 1/3rd of a second. This provides a very high coefficient for the analysis of single phases of movement.[197]

The last of 781 plates selected for publication was entitled *Chickens, scared by torpedo*. If, as claimed by Aaron Scharf, the detonation also served as a start of the filming mechanism, then we are dealing with a very modern experiment, both in terms of its starting point and its methodology.[198]

Moving on to over 500 plates dedicated to humans, one instinctively feels that the primary interest was the generation of material for artistic ends (i.e. as models for painters and sculptors). Only a minority of the plates have strictly scientific aims, often demonstrating a clinical interest in pathological cases. Overall, one gets the impression that Muybridge had a more eclectic approach when compared with the more rigorous and narrow approach of Marey.

Of particular interest are the movements photographed simultaneously from different viewpoints. Many positions would be far less clear, and much more difficult to interpret, if seen only from one point of view. In some cases the choice of angles appears like a series of frames from a modern movie tracking shot. Many of the photographed movements are of sporting activities, as well as a whole series of basic types of movement: walking, running, jumping, climbing, descending, climbing stairs etc. There are also work and military actions. Women are photographed not only in some of these elementary activities, but a considerable amount of space is given over to recording domestic, futile or humorous activities, such as ironing, dressing and undressing, serving tea, pouring water on oneself, spanking a child and smoking a cigarette. Whereas many of the male models were nude, the women range from complete nudity to fully clothed, with some intermediate (fairly suggestive) stages featuring partially transparent clothing.

Animal Locomotion, Plate 465, 'Child bringing a bouquet to a woman'.

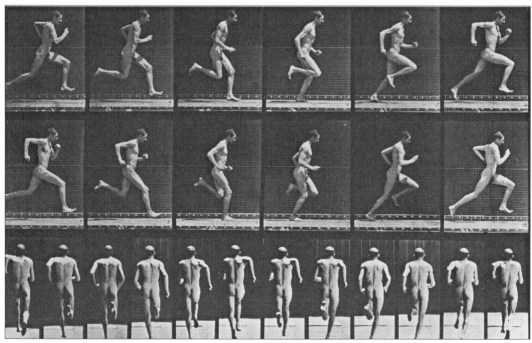

Animal Locomotion, Plate 62, 'Running at full speed'.

Inevitably some of the activities can appear ridiculous on account of the model's nakedness (which may be emphasised by the presence of accessories such as a cartridge box for a man holding a rifle, or a fan). There are also marvellous

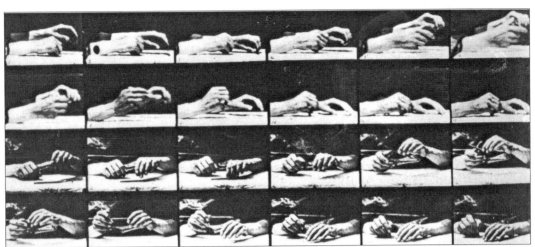

'Movement of the hand', from *Animal Locomotion*, plate 533.

photographic images of water frozen in mid-air in various phases, such as when a woman is shown washing or pouring a bucket of water over another. An extraordinary series of twelve images shows a man doing a complete somersault, balancing himself with his hands on the ground. In the foreground a pigeon enters the shot and then flies up when startled by the man. Unfortunately many of the plates do not have timings, and when they do they are only for the interval between two clicks. Long and complex actions are condensed into only a few photographs, making them less useful for scientific analysis, but certainly valuable to artists.

Particular mention should be made of the plates dedicated to the movement of pathological subjects, like the child without legs that climbs up and down a chair, a woman suffering from cerebal palsy walking with the aid of a nurse, the paralytic boy walking on all fours (one of which served as the inspiration for a well-known painting by Francis Bacon produced in 1961).[199] In addition one should draw attention to the five shots of 'close-ups' (as we would now call them) of hands in movement: one hand handling a ball, two hands shaking, one apparently beating time etc.[200] Once again one is forced to point to the strong way these foreshadows subsequent developments of film language.

A less well-known incident, recounted by L.F. Rondinella who as a student worked with Muybridge between 1884 and 1885 as chief-assistant of his technical crew, gives some indication of the vast and eclectic approaches he applied to his research:

During one of the earlier two summers of Muybridge's experiments we devised a carriage to which a large snapping turtle was strapped on its back, the under shell removed, the heart was exposed, and as its carriage was drawn under one of the portable batteries of twelve cameras pointed downward, we made successful series of twelve photographs each, analysing the heart beats.[201]

Once again, the heart (not by chance the symbol of life and hence the emblem of movement) was the subject of investigation for those creating basic techniques for a new medium for expression and communication based on images.

19. Speaker by necessity

From the period in Philadelphia there are some first hand accounts attesting to Muybridge's solitary temperament and introverted personality, and to his eccentric and extravagant behaviour. He was particularly criticised for his shabby clothes: even the rector of the university pointed out that the rags he wore could diminish the standing of the work he had been given to do.[202] After all his efforts and the results obtained with the thousands of plates, Muybridge's spirit and self-confidence were restored. On 27 February 1888, as he later recalled, after having thought of ways to improve the Zoöpraxiscope, he met with Thomas Edison to discuss the possibility of using his equipment; he foresaw that 'the combination of such an instrument with the phonograph … will … reproduce visible actions simultaneously with audible words.'[203]

Edison was too busy trying to develop and market his own inventions properly to consider Muybridge's proposal for what was a forerunner of sound cinema. It would be unfair to Edison's intelligence, however, to suggest that this meeting did not have an impact. Some six years later, Edison launched the Kinetoscope, the first commercially available machine for the viewing of short films.

The need to sell copies of *Animal Locomotion* and so cover the large deficit accumulated in completing the project, meant that Muybridge was forced to become a full-time professional speaker.

After travelling across the Eastern states, he returned to Europe for a long tour through England, Scotland and Ireland. His visual presentation was entitled 'The Science of Animal Locomotion in its Relation to Design in Art.' It included images of art works showing animals in motion from prehistoric times onwards up to the present day.

With his personal prestige restored, he returned to speak at the Royal Institution and the Royal Society. *The Illustrated London News* put him on the cover of the issue for 25 May 1889, showing Muybridge with his long flowing white beard, in full lecturer mode, standing before the projected image of a horse ridden by a jockey.

In 1891 his series of lectures took him to many European countries. Universities subscribing to a selection of plates included Berlin, Jena, Copenhagen, Monaco, Bonn, Heidelberg, Vienna, Innsbruck, Prague, Budapest, Geneva, Basel, Florence, Padua, Naples, and others. Muybridge presented his work to the International

Illustrated London News cover showing Muybridge lecturing at the Royal Institution, 1889.

Artistic Society in Rome and to the French Académie, both of which purchased a copy.

Despite these successes, the project stayed at a deficit, although on a personal basis Muybridge managed to go on thanks to his expenses being reimbursed, payment of fees and commissions on the plates he sold. It was clear that he would not be able to mount any new experiments as the New York parties were still owed money.

It was at this time that Muybridge approached the president of the newly-founded Leland Stanford Jr University at Palo Alto. Making reference to his earlier experiments there, he proposed a new research project photographing insects, explaining that he had developed a machine that would take twelve photographs of a single beat of a wing, even at a speed of 500 beats to the second. In his letter he wrote that scientists such as Helmholtz and Edison had expressed an interest in his new research. However, the men of the ailing but still powerful Stanford (now a state senator in Washington) did not even answer.

After Europe, and while preparing to leave for Japan, he returned to California for the first time in many years. He tried again to get in touch with Stanford University offering to give a lecture. Once again he did not receive an answer.

A manuscript has been found of a long letter Muybridge wrote on 2 May 1892 to Stanford directly, in which, with objectivity and great attention to detail, he went over their twenty-year long relationship, ignoring the trial and trying instead for reconciliation. No evidence exists of an answer to it, and in any event Stanford died the following year.

Instead of going to the Orient, Muybridge was officially invited to the World's Columbian Exposition in Chicago in 1893, celebrating the 400th anniversary of the discovery of America.[204] He had his own pavilion, which had a front of fake stonework with neo-classical columns, solemnly entitled 'The Zoopraxographical Hall.' Unfortunately, in the general confusion and hubbub of the exposition this popularising initiative was not much of a success. Despite this, from a purely theoretical standpoint, one could claim that his Hall was the first (fee paying) public cinema, though it showed illustrated lectures rather than entertainment films, which is to say that it was perhaps the first film club rather than the first public cinema. For the occasion of this series of cultural events (which took place under the aegis of the US Ministry of Education), Muybridge wrote a booklet entitled *Descriptive Zoopraxography* with which he launched the neologism of the new science of zoopraxography, or as stated in the book's subtitle, 'the science of animal locomotion made popular.'[205]

With the Exposition not a particular success for him, Muybridge returned to England. It was as if he had decided to retire, shortly after his sixtieth birthday. He seemed to have given up on any new undertakings and instead planned to live off what he had already accomplished. For a few years he continued to work as a lecturer, work which was both gratifying and remunerative, and which kept him so busy that he took on some assistants for the projections.

In 1896 he was forced to return to the USA to protect the negatives made during his experiments at the University of Pennsylvania. The Photogravure Company (which had 33,000 unsold copies of the printed plates in its warehouse) had threatened to destroy everything if it was not paid. In addition to this, the financiers that had advanced the money were still awaiting the return of thousands of dollars. At the last minute, when everything seemed lost, Dr Pepper, who was no longer the rector of the University, intervened. It seems that he felt in some way personally responsible for the undertaking, which had taken place under his patronage, and so out of his own funds, he bought the plates corresponding to about forty complete copies of the huge *Animal Locomotion* and ensured the continued availability of the negatives, the copyright of which remained with Muybridge.

Muybridge returned to live at Kingston-upon-Thames, and in the final years of the century dedicated himself solely to completing two books, which in effect stand as the summarisation of all his research.

The first, *Animals in Motion* was published in 1899, the second *The Human Figure in Motion*, courtesy of the same London publisher, in 1901. In putting together these large summary works on his technical-scientific efforts, Muybridge had two main objectives: to disseminate more widely the meaning and value of his research, and to make more accessible his materials which were frequently talked about, but only available to a select few. By organising the material so that part of it was aimed at zoology and the other part to artists and physiology, and by using a cheaper form of printing (photographic engraving had only recently been introduced in publishing), the two books seem to have met their aims. Without courting controversy but with the dignity and wisdom that came with age after an often tumultuous life, these two works for Muybridge acted as an opportunity to set the record straight and to provide the dates and documentation to back up his work. This had become increasingly important at a time which saw the establishment of film entertainment and the surrounding controversies over its inventors, whether they be Lumière, Edison or any of the other pretenders to the throne.

Muybridge however demonstrated a certain detachment, remaining above personal claims, instead establishing himself as a scholar of movement, a scientist of animal locomotion, and a zoopraxographer.

This is demonstrated in particular by the substantial introductory text to *Animals in Motion* in which he occasionally made use of a scientific tone to which he was not completely suited. Making use of the research gathered for his innumerable conferences and for his work published for the Chicago Exposition, he began by quoting Aristotle, Alfonso Borelli and the physiologists Weber, Marey and Pettigrew. He then went on to describe the methodology and technique behind the experiments in Philadelphia. The text however is hardly a model of clarity and, for the Dover reprint, was replaced with one of his earlier pieces.[206] Passing on to the 'analysis of animal locomotion', one can clearly see the characteristic touches, and limitations, of the basis for Muybridge's work.

Lacking a background in anatomy and physiology, he instead turned his attention to the issues surrounding the artistic representation of animals in motion. Here and there, as if to try and reclaim them, he inserted the photographs he had taken of a horse's skeleton when preparing the book commissioned by Stanford from Dr Stillman, albeit without much comment.

The most interesting parts of the text are those dealing with the systematic analysis of the different types of animal movement (walking pace, trot, gallop, jumping etc) from a comparison of three animal groups that have the same dynamic in the arts. In addition to which we see the comparisons he makes between a quadruped and a child walking on all fours, a paralytic case having to do the same, and a man standing upright whose arm movements are compared with the anterior joints of an animal.

As previously mentioned, Muybridge devoted most space to looking at works of art that sought to represent movement, starting with the Assyrians and the ancient Egyptians. Among others he studied the statue of Marcus Aurelius on a horse in Rome, damningly commenting on 'the failure of a sculptor to express his obvious intention', inasmuch as the solemn demeanour and posture of the emperor denoted that he was participating in a slow procession, while the horse's legs were shown in the act of trotting at a speed of fifteen to eighteen kilometres per hour. Praise was reserved instead for the bronze horses at San Marco in Venice, those by Donatello and Verrocchio.

In his analysis of the gallop he dedicated some pages to what he considered to be the three phases of the artist's representation of that type of running. He gave numerous quotations, sometimes of quite a disparate nature, demonstrating deep study and a considerable search for sources.

At the end of the long introductory essay, Muybridge dedicated a few pages to the flight of birds, mainly to express his relinquishing of any attempt to explain the issues of flight, leaving them 'to the attention of future investigators.'[207] He mentions that he had a crane dissected to put forward a hypothesis on the voluntary movement of certain types of feathers. In the last chapter, bemoaning the limits of his research and the fact that he was not able to photograph animals in their natural habitat and therefore with complete freedom of movement, he makes reference to a number of naturalists (including Darwin) who had described the movement of animals from personal observation, even referring to his own notes on the movement of reptiles and birds. In these pages Muybridge writes about the importance of photographic documentation of wild animals running, such as a rhinoceros or a hippopotamus, in view of their possible extinction.

With the publication of those two books, which were reviewed positively and which sold well, Muybridge considered his work complete. In the brief introduction to the second book he limited himself to providing empirical data on his recording, analysis and reproduction of movement. He made a point of emphasising that the plates in the book had been produced some fifteen years earlier and that researchers should not use them as a substitute for first-hand observation. He also admonished readers not to view the photographs in isolation, their true value lying in their representation of the combined phases of movement, their analysis and synthesis.

In 1904, after the second editions of both books had been published, Muybridge died in Kingston, his native town, at the age of seventy-four. In his garden he had been digging a scale model of the great lakes in the United States, his second home. On both his tombstone and on the register of the crematorium, his name is variously misspelled, as it had been so many times before in his lifetime.

20. Muybridge afterwards

After Muybridge's death, Benjamin Carter, Librarian at Kingston-upon-Thames, tried to see him credited as the 'inventor of cinema.' A devoted friend in his final years, Carter had copious documentation on his side as Muybridge had willed to the local library his Zoöpraxiscope, many discs and projection plates, negatives and original prints, a collection of his publications and a valuable volume of clippings documenting episodes of his life and work. However, there were many in England, especially those working in the film industry, who wanted to back more obviously British candidates as the 'inventor of cinema', since Muybridge had spent almost all his life in the USA. Preferred figures included Robert W. Paul and especially William Friese-Greene, though with the passing of the years their roles were either be forgotten or radically reassessed.

It is also worth adding that Muybridge had behaved, as we have already noted, with discretion (and modesty). Carter himself, in an article published in 1913 entitled 'The Genesis of the Motion Picture', had to acknowledge that during the preparation of his final two books, Muybridge had resisted his urging that he enter into the debate over the invention of cinema 'even if only for the sake of historical accuracy.' He also confirmed that Muybridge wanted to be remembered for his research into animal locomotion.[208]

In 1926 came Terry Ramsaye's *A Million and One Nights*, which among its secondary objectives, had the intention of changing the perception of Muybridge at any cost, even on a personal basis, to the extent of giving John D. Isaacs all the credit, so as to eliminate Muybridge entirely from the process. To do this, however, he had to dedicate an entire chapter to him. Almost as a correction to this, in 1929 the Hollywood community through the Academy of Motion Picture Arts and Science and Louis B. Mayer (then head of MGM), celebrated the fiftieth anniversary of the 'Motion Picture Research' undertaken by Leland Stanford, together with

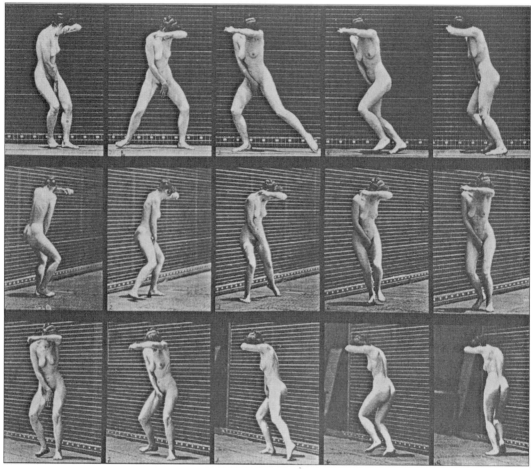

Animal Locomotion, plate 73, 'Turning around in surprise and running away'.

Muybridge, Isaacs and J.D. Stillman. One should not be surprised by the rather odd attribution of roles and the mixture of people, since the event was sponsored by Stanford University.

Many decades would pass before the university, with its 1972 exhibition and the catalogue that accompanied it, would re-establish many historical truths, and return to Muybridge a reputation that which could no longer be denied him.

In the interim, such historians of photography as Beaumont Newhall, Josef Maria Eder, and the Gernsheims, or of the cinema such as James Card, were able to make contributions that brought some light to the life and work of Muybridge. Newhall, as director of historical collections at George Eastman House, was able to do much in this regard, collecting many materials including negatives, prints, equipments and a microfilm copy of all the materials held at Kingston-upon-Thames.

In 1931 a bronze plaque bearing his portrait was placed in the library at Kingston on which he was honoured as 'scientific investigator of animal locomotion', but which also stated that he had been producing 'moving pictures' since 1880, concluding that 'from these inventions the modern cinematograph has been evolved.'

In 1929, L.F. Rondinella, who assisted him in Philadelphia and was now a Professor at the University of Pennsylvania, had written that there was '**ample** justification for declaring Eadweard Muybridge the inventor of motion pictures.'[209] The first book on Muybridge was entitled *The Man Who Invented The Moving Picture*, and when Gordon Hendricks published his essential work he entitled it *Eadweard Muybridge: The Father of the Motion Picture*; Arthur Knight dubbed him 'the man who made pictures move', while Beaumont Newhall wrote that Muybridge 'bridges still and motion-picture photography' and that he should be considered 'as a pioneer who anticipated the moving picture.' Even Robert Bartlett Haas, whom we have quoted as a scrupulous biographer of Muybridge, and who in the title of his work did not compromise (*Muybridge, Man in Motion*), ends by concluding in his text that

> … he may justly be considered the father of the modern motion picture and of the later industry which sprang up to develop the idea for mass markets.[210]

To conclude, one most re-state once again that we are not interested if and to what extent he can be termed the father, godfather, pioneer or inventor of cinema as entertainment. His work, original and unique, even if not always without some methodological failings, must be considered in relation to that other great protagonist in the development of scientific cinema: Étienne-Jules Marey.

21. Marey and movement

A cheetah can reach speeds of over sixty miles per hour in the pursuit of its prey. Today on our television screens, we can see this framed by a powerful zoom lens, filmed with a high-speed camera which shows us in ultra-slow motion the marvellous bone and muscle dynamics of this perfect physiological machine, bringing all its details to the fore.

And there is the Space Shuttle, a flying vehicle we have likewise seen take off on a rocket, fly beyond the planet, then re-enter the atmosphere, overcoming without damage extremely high temperatures, finally glide and then land like an ordinary aircraft.

These two events, and their enjoyment by hundreds of millions of people, now constitute a normality that skirts on the edge of the banal. 'Just another animal documentary' is a phrase that may be mumbled by a television viewer reduced to an addict of episodic programmes; the ratings for live broadcasts of space launches get lower every year, as there is no longer any sense of adventure or wonder for these gigantic technological undertakings which, in fact, we may instead find frightening for the implied link to escalation in the military-industrial complex.

Only a century has passed since Marey, the lead character in the birth of the scientific cinema, pondered research problems at the heart of the two events referred to above. In 1881 the fifty-year-old French physiologist Étienne-Jules Marey was studying human and animal movement. He was also interested in bird flight, though his was not simply the specialised interest of a physiologist, as he was attracted to a fascinating problem: human flight.

Little more than a century ago, when Marey lived his life as an academic and experimental researcher, the world was so different that we can end up thinking that far more than 120 years have passed since then.

A Euro-centric society with, increasingly, a young North American tail end. The rest, with a work-force to exploit and riches to plunder, was an easy place to conquer for the powers of the period, which had just defined a *modus vivendi* at the Berlin congress (1878): one that had sanctioned some peace for the old continent, and given a free hand to the more agile among them to divide the zones of influence in the colonial world. France after the fall of the Second Empire, the tragic blood bath of the Commune and the subsequent repression, was quickly re-gaining its world ranking with the Republic of Thiers. The Paris Exposition of 1878 was the most grandiose event thus far celebrating the glories and conquests of the working world. Silhouetted at the entrance was the gigantic iron head of the Statue of Liberty, bound for New York.

Étienne-Jules Marey.

The streets of the French capital had only recently been illuminated with electric lights. Steam ships were starting to travel the oceans while there were still great fleets made up of sailing ships. Railways were slowly constituting a net of modern transportation, although the horse drawn carriage was still the preferred mode of transport. The Morse telegraph, which connected the continents after the laying of undersea cables, gave a sense of progress, of the arrival of a new era for humanity. Communication, news, information, were no longer tied to the messenger, to the postal courier, but instead flew on the wings of electricity. The first telephones were the privilege of the very few.[211] A few methods for printing photographs typographically had been tried out, but for decades to come the majority of illustrations in books and periodicals remained drawings and figures reproduced with the traditional engraving and lithograph methods. Automobiles were still a thing of the future, except in the minds and laboratories of a few pioneering engineers. The dream of human flight was still tied to the myth of Icarus. After the daredevil activities of those Frenchmen who in 1870 escaped the Prussians' siege of Paris in a balloon, there were discussions as to whether the future would be 'lighter' or 'heavier' than air.

The medical doctor Étienne-Jules Marey, who since 1884 had been president of the Société de Navigation Aérienne, in 1894 became the president of the Société Française de Photographie, the following year of the Académie des Sciences (of which time he had long been vice-president); he would only become president of the Académie de Médecine in 1900.

The study and analysis of movement constituted the central axis of all his research – we can even say without falling into rhetoric that it was the fundamental purpose of his life. In 1868 he published *Du mouvement dans les fonctions de la vie*, in 1873 *La machine animale, locomotion terrestre et aérienne*. His last book was *Le mouvement* in 1894. In 1878 he wrote:

> Science has two obstacles to overcome in its advancement; first of all the defects of our senses in uncovering truth, and in addition the limitations of our language to express properly and communicate what it is that has been acquired.[212]

It is in this phrase that we find the key to why it was that a physiologist of the nineteenth century became the prime protagonist of the method and technique of scientific cinema: to overcome the defects of our senses and the insufficiency of traditional language.

22. More engineer than doctor

Étienne-Jules Marey (1830–1904), curiously, was born and died in the same years as Muybridge, but the similarities end there. We have already seen that they had met on occasions and had exchanged information without collaborating, and we shall touch on this further on. There was mutual admiration and acknowledgement of the other's work, with perhaps some appropriation and use of Marey's name and prestige on Muybridge's behalf. They were two profoundly different and unequal figures, yet both incomparable.

Marey was born in Beaune, Borgougne, where his father was the commercial director of a wine company. He wanted his son to study medicine in Paris and then return to Beaune where he might add to the family name by working at the local hospital. His mother wanted him to enter the priesthood. The young Marey, however, aspired instead to study engineering at the Polytechnic. In those days the will of the father was law and even one as determined as Étienne-Jules was unable to overcome it. He did go to Paris to study medicine and complete his internship at a hospital, but did not practice the profession for even a single day. Although he failed to practice medicine at the Beaune hospital, his hometown would later dedicate to him one of its main thoroughfares, a monument and a museum. Already, in studying medicine, he had been able to satisfy his original vocation by the study, planning and construction of machines and systems.

While preparing his thesis on the circulatory system, he constructed small machines to record heartbeats. Camille Flammarion tells of how, to try them out, and obviously to entertain himself, Marey would invite his female friends to let him take their pulse.[213] His spirit as a researcher led him to document the fluctuation in heart rate of some of his female visitors under, let us say, particular experimental situations.

What is certain is that in 1860 Marey presented to the Académie des Sciences his Sphygmograph, an apparatus that had great success abroad once researchers had had the chance to test its results and reliability. For a few more years Marey's interest in engineering remained very close to his medical studies. In 1863 he published a work on the circulation of the blood, based on the beating of the heart and the pulse, with reference to illnesses of the circulatory system.[214] The following year, to prove his research, he set up his own laboratory in the house where he lived, which at one time had been the home of the Comédie Française, a short walk from the École de Médecine.[215] A few years later, with his work veering increasingly towards the area of experimental physiology, interest in his work took him to the Collège de France, initially as a substitute teacher, with access to a laboratory, then as a full-time lecturer.[216] By 1869 (aged only thirty-nine), he took over the chair of Natural History of Organised Bodies from his teacher, the neurophysiologist Professor Pierre Flourens.

The contrast between his father's wish to see him as a doctor and his own aspirations can be seen by looking at the list of publications outlining his experiments which first appeared via the Académie des Science but also (between 1875 and 1880) as collections of Marey's laboratory work.[217] There are fewer and fewer references to medical or clinical matters as time goes on (despite his having been called to the Académie in 1872), but rather a series of notes pointing towards what today would be termed 'bio-engineering': *Détermination expérimentale des mouvements de l'aile dans le vol* (1868), *Reproduction mécanique du vol des insects* (1869), *Du moyen d'utiliser le travail moteur de l'homme et des animaux* (1875), *Expériences sur la résistance de l'air, pur servir à la physiologie du vol des oiseaux* (1875), *Moteurs animés, experiences de physiologie graphique* (1878).[218]

With the publication in 1863 and 1873 of the books already cited, Marey's research interests became clearer and defined themselves as the analytical and comparative study of movement, especially in its physiological aspects of both human and animal, but with constant reference to the physical laws of mechanics: the title of the second book, *La machine animale*, is particularly indicative. The rigorously experimental character of his work method led him to emphasize the need for instruments which could effectively analyse phenomena, record them and break them down, for the comparison of various analogous demonstrations, extrapolating values and constants.

Marey's preoccupation with the limits and defects of our senses in the study of dynamic processes here finds a precise focus, as does the difficulty in finding a language to define and represent them effectively. It was to resolve these issues that he would invent a series of small machines and tools, exploiting a wide range of techniques made possible by progress in the physical sciences and by the developments in industrialised society. Today, much of his equipment seems both complicated and simplistic, as unnecessarily complex toys. But then, just over 100 years ago, they were the *non plus ultra* of technological modernity, representing the highest level of functionality and precision.

The success of Marey's research and the interest it generated extends beyond the study of physiology to constitute a general methodology of experimental research. The title of Marey's 1878 book says it all: *La méthode graphique dans les sciences expérimentales.*[219]

The interdisciplinary character of this treatise and its results placed its author in the top rank in the history of science in the second half of the nineteenth century, independently of his discoveries in the physiological field. In the introductory pages, Marey defined his position: 'every movement is the product of two factors: time and space.'[220] Later on, he enthusiastically wrote:

When a movement changes every instant; when, assuming at every fraction of a second a different deportment, it challenges the eye that wishes to follow it, the mind that wishes to analyse it, will it escape the physicist? Not at all! Here is it recorded by a machine and fixed on paper. It must submit itself to the slide-rule and compass. Shortly before it flew, and now, a prisoner, it reveals itself the rules that govern it. It can be understood![221]

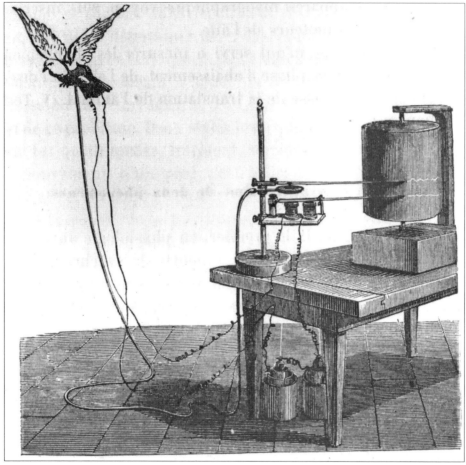

Bird in flight with harness, connected to electro-pneumatic recording equipment.

The first four sections of Marey's treatise look in detail, with various historical references, at the graphic representation of phenomena through devices recording movements, forces and their variations, up to multiple recording. The latter means, for example, simultaneous recordings of the same phenomenon produced in different locations, or of different phenomena which occur in the same location, or in different ones. The fifth part deals exclusively with techniques; it discusses the value, construction detail and the functioning of various machines:

> I have tried to gather all the information necessary so as to allow the reader to repeat the experiences which the book deals with and to apply the graphic method to new subjects.[222]

In his text we even find the fossilised footprints of prehistoric animals used as a reference point for the locomotion of similar animals alive today. The most impor-

Runner with recording apparatus and pneumatic system inserted in his shoe.

tant part of the work, however, is that contributed by the systems of retrieval, transmission and recording of any type of movement (or force) by pneumatic means. For retrieval he built various types of 'exploratory drum', in essence a small metal box closed by a thin rubber membrane; the sensitive apparatus containing air, transmitting every slightest movement it underwent or undertook at the point where applied since the same air was pushed by a fine rubber tube acting as a transmitter for signals. At the end of this tube another drum received the air stimuli and recorded them with a small pen on a strip or cylinder of paper covered with lampblack and animated by isochronic movement, thereby having every signal's precise temporal and spatial references recorded. Naturally, Marey did not ignore electricity and underlined its potential importance for signals transmitted through electrical relays.[223] One must not forget, however, that at this time, lying between mica sheet switches and electro-magnets, we were still at the primitive stage of using simple voltaic batteries in laboratories.

Among the many experimental applications of the machines described by Marey, we can recall the 'determination of the frequency of a bird's wing movements and the relative duration of the phases of its rise and fall' by the simultaneous use of an electro-magnetic signal and pneumatic recording.

> The eye cannot follow these movements which, in small bird species, are repeated eight or ten times a second ... the animal is linked, one might say, telegraphically with some recording equipment.[224]

With this technique, Marey was able to obtain fairly precise timings which allowed him to measure the duration of the flapping of a wing, which were 11.66 hundredths of a second for a duck and 12.5 hundredths of a second for a pigeon, also showing the differences during rising and falling movements.

Marey conducted many such experiments in human and animal locomotion. For humans he perfected the Odograph, an apparatus until then used to measure the routes of vehicles and trains and which Marey produced in an ambulatory version using a wheel pushed by a walker.

He had his pneumatic system inserted into special 'explorer' shoes, where the recording of the signals took place on a cylinder with a clockwork motor carried in the hand by the subject. For years horses had been one of the preferred subjects for study and documentation. Applying four air cushions to the hooves, the rider could hold the recording equipment which bore four small pens giving all the spatio-temporal data necessary to analyse and measure the phases of the movement of a quadruped.

In the history of the birth of scientific cinema, Marey's studies on equine loco-motion are only a beginning. The results of the research based on the graphic method brought much that was new to light and provided a mass of precise and comparable data. In scientific as well as sporting circles, and for horse trainers in particular, these results were met with interest, curiosity and even with amazement. The first edition of *La machine animale* came out in 1873 and by the following year English translations had appeared in London and New York (it was even translated into Russian). In 1874 Colonel Duhousset published *Le cheval dans la nature et dans l'art*, in which the positions of the race horse's hooves in the illustrations were drawn with reference to the data of the graphic method.

For his part, Marey had no idea how great the influence of his work would be on the research being undertaken on the racetrack at Palo Alto by Muybridge, and his sequential cameras.[225]

With *La machine animale* Marey appears to have felt that his experiments in the movement of quadrupeds from the physiological standpoint, the aspect which mainly concerned him, were now at an end.

> When we have concluded the analysis of a phenomenon and believe that we know all of its details, we look at the synthesis for a sort of confirmation ... Repro-

ducing, under artificial conditions, the movements … we have in the past been able to demonstrate the correctness of our theories …

It is here that Marey refers to Plateau and to his ingenious optical instrument, the Phenakistiscope, and the fact that although it was mainly used to entertain children, it could actually be used (as could the Zoetrope) to 'faithfully reproduce the successive positions of the body during a march, a race etc.' He also refers to M. Duval, professor of anatomy at the School of Fine Arts, who together with the scientist Carlet wrote of:

> … sixteen successive positions for each step of the different ways humans walk. Each figure is carefully drawn following the details obtained with the graphic method. Animated by the correct speed of rotation, the instrument simulates, with perfect precision, the various movements of marching or running. Its main virtue however is that, making them move slowly, one achieves a significant slowing down of the movements represented, so that the eye can capture with greater ease those actions the succession of which is not perceptible in normal marching.[226]

Also in *La machine animale* Marey wrote (as he would in greater detail in his 1894 book *Le mouvement*):

> In 1867 [note the date], we made use of the zootrope to represent the movements of a horse in motion … But, at that time, we could not turn to instantaneous photography, so we made do with simple drawings …[227]

Marey is describing an ingenious system, the credit for which went to Mathias Duval (who in the meantime had become a professor of medicine), to represent all the various steps of a horse from the amble to the trot, with just two strips of drawings superimposed. In effect this was an intelligent prefiguring of a technique that would later be developed with animated drawings. Once Marey had discovered and then proved that the fundamental variations in the steps of a horse are constituted by the different relations between the passing of the posterior and the anterior legs, Marey and Duval laid out a Zoetrope strip with drawings showing the various phases of just the body and the anterior legs. In place of the posterior ones two empty squares, or rather two windows were cut out. Beneath was another strip on which, corresponding to the windows, the posterior legs were drawn in the various phases of movement. By moving the strip below one could observe the various steps of the horse.

When towards the end of 1878 *La Nature* published the first of Muybridge's serial photographs, as we have already seen, Marey was very excited by the results and wrote to the editor to get in touch with the photographer in America. The interest and admiration were mostly reserved for the 'valuable method of M. Muybridge of San Francisco' and for the importance such photography would have as an instrument for research and documentation. With regards to the issues over the phases of the movement of horses, Marey subsequently let it be known that the photographic results only really served to confirm what he had already discovered and documented years earlier with his graphical method.

> Effectively, our recording instruments inform us only of the succession and the duration of the supports of each limb, leaving indeterminate the position of the raised limbs.

He added a detailed and analytical comparison between the images drawn with the graphic method and Muybridge's photographs, noting the substantial cross-over between the two sets of positions, and underlining how some of the poses of the horse which he had found and which has been contested for being aesthetically unappealing, were found to be reproduced exactly in the photographs.[228]

In getting in touch with Muybridge, through Gaston Tissandier's journal, Marey had a specific goal: to move ahead with the research that now interested him the most – the flight of birds. Clearly the graphic method in this case had some limitations: the need for a connecting rubber tube and/or electrical wire between the subject and the recording equipment. After seeing Muybridge's brilliant results with horses at high speeds, the photographic method seemed promising, even exciting. So he sent a message to Muybridge in order that

> ... he could bring his contribution to the solution of some physiological problems so hard to resolve by other means ... It is clear that for Mr Muybridge it is an easy experiment to undertake.[229]

Marey was to remain disappointed. In his answer, Muybridge seems to back away, claiming to be worried by the difficulties ahead, ignoring Marey's proposal for a photographic rifle, saying that he would try to photograph birds with a series of cameras using a clockwork mechanism since electrical signals or the broken wires used for horses would not work.[230] Yet from the letter it is also clear that Muybridge wanted his method to be more widely known and would even have liked Marey to help him improve his multi-camera technique. 1881, the year in which they met, would be an important one for both of them: a crucial but controversial one for Muybridge, a brilliant one for Marey, who began the 1880s with a series of events both in the scientific arena and on the social scene.

The Paris municipality put at his disposal some land at Parc des Princes, on the border between the city and Bois de Boulogne, for the creation, on behalf of the Collège de France, of a large experimental laboratory to further his studies on human and animal movement, the Station Physiologique. Marey himself moved to a building, with the top floor turned into a laboratory, in the upper class and modern quarter of Passy, a few steps from the Trocadéro.

It was to this new house that Marey invited Muybridge on 26 September 1881, also inviting for the occasion a number of famous scientists who were in France for the International Congress on Electricity, then the cutting edge topic for pure research as well as for its technological applications. In the newspaper *Le Globe* it was reported that Mr Muybridge's curious experiences had a commentary to accompany every image, delivered by Mr Marey with 'charmante bonhomie.'

For about ten years he had also at his disposal a villa at Posillipo, one of the most beautiful quarters of Naples, and had taken to spending his winters there. A biographical note claimed that 'his private life rarely interfered with his scientific research, except for his trips to Naples.'[231] In fact, Marey had a daughter who was born in Naples in 1871, though this was passed off as an adoption.[232] However, apart from these personal issues, his time in Naples was not wasted as it was here that he developed his photographic gun.

23. The photographic gun

Answering to a request made by Marey in 1878, Muybridge brought with him to Paris the meagre results from his attempts to photograph birds in flight. These consisted of a few plates of pigeons in flight taken at 1/500th of a second. Each plate showed a different phase of flight and Marey was able to see that they were very similar to the predictions made using his graphic method.

> However, apart from the sharpness of those images, they lacked that which instead makes them so interesting, as are those by Muybridge himself of the movement of horses, given that the serial arrangement shows the successive positions of the animal. It is not in fact possible to apply to the free flight of birds the method used for horses, which consists in the breaking by the same animal the electric wires laid out in its path, so as to activate a series of cameras. I made plans therefore to construct a machine in the shape of a gun which would allow one to take aim and follow in space a bird in flight, while a rotating plate recorded a series of images which showed the successive positions of the wings.[233]

This is how Marey recounted his decision to construct the photographic gun, without mentioning that he had already suggested it in 1878 to Muybridge, who had rejected it out of hand.[234] It was from this moment that Marey clearly decided to go it alone, although he would continue in his writings to stress the importance of Muybridge's method, the value of its results and its pride of place in photographing animal movement in sequence. Marey's idea was to take advantage of new photographic processes to integrate images so obtained with the methodology and techniques of his previous research. The essence of the 'graphic method' consisted in placing scientifically the spatio-temporal coordinates of predominantly physiological movement in relation to each other, but likewise those of inanimate objects where he wanted to discover and analyse their mechanics. At this point his experimental techniques – which he called 'chronographic' – would be known as 'photochronographic.' Subsequently, the definitive name to be used would be 'chronophotography.'[235]

At a conference in 1899 Marey said:

To continue more comfortably and with greater economy those experiments which I had asked Muybridge to undertake on the flight of birds, I had to create a new method and it is here, to be exact, that comes my personal role in the invention of chronophotography.[236]

In nearly all histories of the cinema one finds the claim that Marey's photographic gun was directly derived from Janssen's photographic revolver.

Marey himself, in presenting and describing his apparatus, said that it was 'analogous' to that of his colleague (they were both members of the Académie). In addition to which, Marey wrote:

Janssen was the first to have planned, for scientific ends, to take automatically a series of photographic images representing the successive phases of a phenomenon.[237]

In truth, the basis for the photographic gun had been around for years, from both a technical and commercial standpoint, well before Janssen's machine. This developed with the introduction of dry plates which allowed for shorter exposures. The photographic revolver allowed one to point the lens at a target and capture the desired image.

Janssen's great merit lies in having realised the potentially great scientific value of series photography and in the use of a clockwork mechanism to move the plate and the shutter. The photographic revolvers that were commercially available were simple machines more or less in the shape of a gun with multiple plates or with a single plate which could be rotated to obtain four exposures. Even Marey, in inventing his photographic gun, went through the stages involved in using an actual rifle with ammunition, in which one would insert the 'bullet' (a small photographic plate in a metal container), the 'shot' would be taken, the casing would be expelled, and so on. He was able however to grasp the originality of Janssen's method and technique and conceive of how to obtain material of much higher quality, something that Janssen had foreseen.

The revolver of the Parisian astronomer and Marey's gun did not look at all alike from the outside, seemingly having nothing in common. What is more, Janssen's machine was so far removed in appearance from the usual image of a revolver that some called it a 'photographic cannon.' Accepting the relationship between the two machines, it should be pointed out that Marey had practically to create the entire shooting mechanism from scratch. Janssen really only used photographs

Marey's photographic gun, demonstrated by his assistant Otto Lund.

at intervals, while Marey needed to capture rapid movements, requiring not less than ten images per second so as to analyse the results using Plateau's Phenakistiscope.

The technical structure of the photographic gun was attained in the autumn of

1881, not long after after the meeting with Muybridge. At the beginning of winter he left for Naples with the gun and small single plates, while waiting for the completion of the cine camera-gun prototype, for which he tried to use existing parts or elements. Practising with a one-shot gun, he photographed, among others, a boat at sea, single birds and insects in flight.

Marey then increased the pace. On 3 February 1882 he wrote to his mother:

> My technician is working at the same pace as I am … I have a photographic gun which is anything but deadly and which takes images of birds in flight or a running animal in less than 1/500th of a second. I do not know if you can imagine such a speed, but it is an amazing thing.

On 9 March he announced in a letter to the Académie des Sciences the success of his first experiments, while on 22 April 1882 *La Nature* published a detailed article, with illustrations.[238]

> I have been able to construct, in the shape of a hunting rifle, a machine that photographs twelve times a second the object under aim; each images requires, in terms of exposure time, only 1/720th of a second. The barrel of this rifle is a tube that contains a photographic lens. Behind, solidly fixed to the rifle-stock, is a large cylindrical breech where one will find the clockwork mechanism … When one pulls the trigger of the rifle, the mechanism goes into motion … A central axis, which makes twelve revolutions a second, controls all the parts of the machine.[239]

Two rotating discs, one with a single aperture, the other with twelve, functioned as shutter and intermittent transport for the sensitive plate. A crank and a latch ensured the regularity of the movements and the stops. The focus was accomplished by either elongating or shortening the barrel of the rifle, in other words moving the lens forwards and backwards, controlling it on a piece of ground-glass. A circular clip 'analogous to those already available commercially' held twenty-five plates that could be loaded in succession without being exposed, simply by leaning the clip over the breech and making the next plate slide into its predetermined space.

For the first experiments Marey used normal glass plates cut with a diamond into circles or octagons, with a diameter of approximately eleven centimetres. They soon proved too fragile and heavy and he switched to the new Balagny film, cut and glued on vulcanised india-rubber discs; according to Marey they had a mass that was half that of the plates and made the mechanism function more securely.[240] In fact this also allowed him to shoot at twice the original speed, with exposure at 1/1440th of a second.

Naturally he did not expect that anyone would require proof or controls for the technical data he gave.

Before applying this instrument to the study of flight, I submitted it to a few experimental tests, and the results that I obtained were satisfactory.[241]

He describes in detail the filming of a black arrow on a white background, the rotating velocity of which (at the extremities) was five metres per second, having obtained on the rotating plate twelve stable images of the same arrow. He then shot a pendulum and 'for greater security in the measuring of lengths' also used the graphic method, recording with the pneumatic system the trace of the movements of the rotating plate together with a chronograph or a tuning fork. Subsequently Marey would comment on the limitations of shooting with the photographic gun, which was able to give the position of the bird and the positions that followed but not movements in space nor the velocity of movement in space.[242] In the *La Nature* article he had in fact stated that the photographs did not add a great deal of new information to what was already known about the mechanism of flight. But he did point out that 'to give a reasonable opinion on the matter' it would be necessary to wait until a great many images of various birds in flight had been collected, with reference to the different types of flight.[243] That partial impression was based on the initial results (the article was written only a few days after the beginning of shoot-

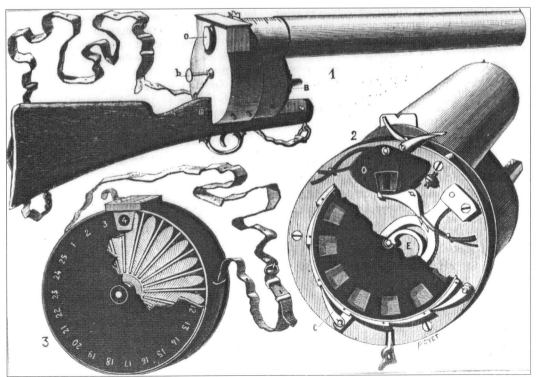

Marey's photographic gun, showing the interior and plate holder.

ing), which consisted of black silhouettes on the white background of the sky.

In the same article, Marey wrote that not only had he photographed birds, but likewise horses, donkeys, dogs, men on their own two feet or riding on bicycles.

> However I did not follow up these experiments: these fall within the programme that Mr Muybridge is undertaking with such great success.

In truth – at this time – Marey was only interested in studying 'by photographic means the mechanism of flight in various species of animals.' Subsequently with the invention of new chronophotographic machines, he would return to the study of the earthbound movement of humans and animals, despite Muybridge.

The fact is that for him the gun was just one episode, one of many instruments which, throughout his scientific career, he had to create to move ahead with his research. In the world of photography however, the idea of a photographic gun (as already the revolver) was a real find, a curiosity that would develop further and even have a few imitations, the creative level of which was not very high, but which makes us appreciate even more Marey's invention. This is demonstrated by the 'photographic gun' of Sands Hunter of 1885, which was exhibited at the London Science Museum, but which instead of being a refinement of Marey's gun, looks like an antiquated and primitive attempt, as it allowed only for one photograph at a time to be taken with eighteen small round plates of about three-and-a-half centimetres in diameter placed in a small brass cylinder next to the camera-shutter and which, after the exposure, passed on to another small cylinder.[244]

The idea of a photographic gun has remained alive up to this very day, albeit with increasing rarity. In the 1960s in the display of an exclusive Parisian shop specialising in clothing and equipment for exotic travels, one could still buy a modern repeating gun that only worked as a camera.

Marey did not concern himself with how he appeared to others when armed with his photographic rifle. His devoted assistant Lucien Bull (who lived to be ninety-four and whom we had the opportunity to interview) has confirmed what he wrote in a commemorative article.[245]

> Professor Marey had been nicknamed by the Neapolitan 'natives' 'the madman of Posillipo', since to them it was incomprehensible that a man, even though the owner of a villa and therefore respectable, showed himself to be satisfied by his catch after pointing a rifle at a bird, without a shot ever being heard.

The filming undertaken by Marey in 1882 took place in Naples, not only because he happened to be staying there at the time, but also to make the most of the strong sunlight, thus obtaining results that were photographically more advanced.

The exposure time was extremely fast, the sensitivity of the emulsion then available still very limited. The first series of birds in flight gave very contrasty images in which the outline of the bird was seen against the clear sky with no detail.

To demonstrate the possibilities of his machine Marey photographed a horse drawing a coach, which he not only shot at 1/720th of a second, but with a telephoto lens at a distance of 150 metres. He then published an enlargement, using a new technique for reproducing photographs lithographically, to show that 'not having been photographed against the luminous back drop of the sky, it is not a simple silhouette, but reveals some detail.'

Marey was now looking for new technological hypotheses and to invent and perfect methods for recording and analysing rapid movement. Having experimented with the gun at a shutter speed of 1/1440th of a second, he discovered that the vibrations could compromise the sharpness of the images. He had reached the mechanical limits of the mechanism. Returning to Paris in the spring of 1882, by the beginning of summer he was presenting at the Académie des Sciences a new filming machine, based on very different principles.

The title of the presentation of 3 July 1882 was: 'Analysis of the mechanism of locomotion by means of a series of photographic images collected on the same plate and representing the successive phases of movement.' The machine with which he undertook this filming was the first of many and various models which all came to be referred to as chronophotographic equipment.

In the clippings album that Muybridge kept with great care we even find the extract for the report on that sitting of the Académie in Paris. Perhaps Marey sent it to him, perhaps he obtained it himself. The text opens with these words: 'The admirable method first begun by Mr Muybridge ...' After this compliment and acknowledgement, the French physiologist passed directly to laying out the limits of this same method to the ends of scientific research. Then, in two short pages, he described his new technical proposal. This gave a methodological indication which in later years would at first seem to lead him on a complicated and at times contradictory path, but which actually constitutes the line of development of modern cinematography and especially scientific cinematography.

> The prints and plates that I have the honour of presenting to the Académie were obtained from the physiological station at Parc de Princes, where I work with the assistance of Mr G. Demeny.

Marey wanted it to be known that he now had at his disposal an adequate experimental laboratory. A dozen years later, still full of enthusiasm, he would write that in his Station Physiologique he had access to 'opportunities which do not exist anywhere else.'[246]

One should also give the perspective of Lucien Bull, his assistant from 1895 until his death, and thereafter a passionate exponent of his work. Bull said that at Parc des Princes the heating did not work very well so it was only possible to work during warm months. In fact Marey had a laboratory and mechanical workshop set up in his house at Passy where the assistants and technicians of the Station

Physiologique could go to set up equipment, prepare the instruments and work on the results. One has to keep in mind the practical conditions under which this was undertaken: the rooms were illuminated by gas and if a few amperes of electricity were required, they had to resort to potassium bichromate batteries which were awkward to use. The mechanics used a foot lathe for small bits, while for bigger jobs they had to go to a workshop that had steam powered equipment.[247]

The period between 1882 and 1883 was full of studies, ideas, experiments in all directions. Marey on the one hand was satisfied by the technological results and the success of the photographic gun, but on the other he did not think that the small square images of just a few centimetres were really good enough, especially as the resolution was poor and hard to enlarge, making it harder to extract the data he needed. At the Académie, Janssen proposed that the glass disc or sensitive film should be wound by a fast continuously rotating motor, to get past the mechanical problem of intermittence. The 'shutter' action would take place indirectly, illuminating with brief flashes the subject being photographed.[248] Marey considered the full extent of this proposal and had to disregard it: the images would come out blurred owing to the correlated movements of the disc and the subject, even in the brief period needed for each individual flash. In the same way he considered and rejected (sometimes after testing them with specially constructed equipment) projects based on multiple lenses variously placed in relation to a single static plate. Essentially it was a variation of Muybridge's method which the latter went on to use in Philadelphia. In any event, in Paris some were already pursuing this approach, such as Albert Londe, head of the photographic service of the Hospital at Salpêtrière, in the same way that Thomas Eakins in Philadelphia paid for his own studies to imitate Marey's methodology instead of Muybridge's.

Marey's new idea was based on the uniqueness of the camera (while Muybridge continued with a series of independent cameras) and on the singleness of the lens (while Londe and Muybridge at one point proposed or used even a considerable number of lenses). For Marey these two techniques might be used in a few cases but had the fundamental flaw of 'seeing, if one can put it that way, the object being photographed from different angles.'[249]

His new machine was again one born of scientific necessity and methodological rigour.

Marey needed images that could be compared with each other, for the whole succession of the phases of the dynamic action under consideration, with the possibility of identifying exactly the spatio-temporal coordinates of every image in relation to the others.

Therefore the desire was to achieve a single point of view, a single fixed plate on which the images would be recorded side by side (since the subject would be in progressive motion), with the separation between each image regulated by a shutter that would open and close the lens for as many phases of movement as one

Marey's first fixed plate chronophotographic apparatus, 1882.

wanted to capture. The shutter was made up of a rotating disc with an adjustable window 'so as to vary the length of the exposure according to the brightness of the light or the speed of the rotation of the disc. With a narrow window and a slow rotation, one has images very far apart from each other. A quick rotation gives images closer together, but with an exposure time which may be insufficient if the window was not widened.'

Naturally, for this technique to work, the plate would have to be exposed several times, equal to the number of the phases of the movement being analysed, without the plate losing its sensitivity. To obtain this result Marey appears to have wanted to push the plates to the limits of what was then possible.

It is necessary that there be absolute darkness in front of the machine and that the person or animal that passes in front of it emerge in white on a black background.[250]

This new methodology was perfect for the study of a whole series of physiological mechanisms. At the Station Physiologique, Marey had enough space to create a circular running track for animals and humans moving in front of a large black background, built three-dimensionally with special materials so as to avoid any reflected light. Only the subject was to be illuminated by the sun.

Perpendicular to the housing for the black background was a rail track bearing a small wagon, on which the recording equipment was mounted.

The shutter disc was 130 centimetres in diameter (which, as we have seen in the way it functioned, prefigured a modern shutter with variable speed and aperture). The plate could reach very large sizes so that subjects could be shot from a variety of distances and in a number of positions as required. The objective limit was determined by the size of the fixed plate and by the fact that if there were too many images for a movement that was brief in space and short in duration, the images would end up by partially overlapping. This could have even suited Marey's purpose, but beyond a certain point it would be confusing and render any analysis difficult.[251]

The circular track at the Station Physiologique.

By using a number of technical expedients, Marey was able to maximise the usefulness of the data and capture many important images; for example, by dressing in white only those parts required, the rest of the subject remained 'invisible' because dressed in black (in front of the black backing)

… except for thin strips of shiny metal which, applied along the leg, thigh and arm, marked fairly exactly the direction of the bone structures of these limbs.[252]

Small white circles indicated the head and joints.

Having thus reduced to its essentials the space occupied on the plate for each photograph, one could multiply by a factor of ten the number of images to be recorded clearly on the same plate: if the shutter disc with a slit recorded five images by making five turns in a second, putting in a disc with ten slits and making it turn at the same speed produced fifty images in a second. Naturally, the spatial and temporal details were also recorded on the plate: metric scales on the bottom to measure the movement of the subject in each shot and a large clock hand which made a complete revolution in one second. It was with this technique that Marey made those splendid chronophotographic plates which graphically synthesise the dynamics of human movement and which, apart from providing him with all the elements he needed for his physiological research, constituted valuable iconographic documents which were to be influential on the development of the figurative arts.[253]

The fixed plate chronophotographic machine may seem, from the point of view of the development of the modern cine camera, a step backwards when compared to the results obtained with the photographic gun. Marey himself in some of his writings and conferences towards the end of his life described the evolution of his chronophotographic machines not in chronological order, placing the fixed plate machine before the gun. The latter is in fact a real cine camera in the modern sense, its sole limitation being the small number of images recordable on a single disc.

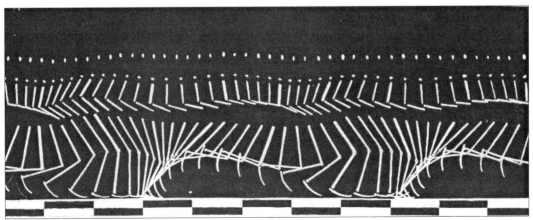

Fixed plate record of a man in motion with lines and points in white creating a geometric chronophotograph.

In terms of usefulness to his work as a physiologist, however, it is clear that the fixed plate machine was in fact a step forward. With it he could obtain a larger number of images, which were bigger, better defined, with faster intervals and exposures, and more easily adaptable to each occasion.

The focus (problematic with the gun since the bird in flight constantly varied its distance, requiring a quickness of response in the shooting not always compatible with the best quality) could now be measured and controlled, with the black background and the variable distance of the chronophotograph mounted on a wagon running on rails. Finally, the spatio-temporal parameters of every single shot were easily recordable and usable for scientific interpretations of the images, whereas with the gun the spatial movements of the subject being filmed (a bird in flight) were not measurable.

Marey went on to use his fixed plate machine in Paris to photograph the flight of birds, still one of his main areas of research. However he could only use white birds, or ones with white markings. The photographs were only possible when the bird flew in front of the black backing (which was fairly large however: fifteen metres across by four in height, three in depth, to reduce light reflection), but these limitations did not stop him obtaining excellent results. For instance, when he was able to photograph a pigeon at 1/900th of a second flying parallel to the backing, he obtained images 'able to bear enlargements from ten to fifteen centimentres.'[254]

The reliability and flexibility of his experimental plant allowed him to undertake research and experiments in various directions: studying not only the dynamics of different and successive phases in the flight of various birds, but also making a comparative analysis of a single phase, observed over and over again so as to identify the constants, the details and characteristics which might escape a single recording.

In this case Marey applied the stroboscopic technique, but not simply as an optical effect (as was the case with Plateau and Stampfer's machines), but as a research document, recording on a single plate a series of close-ups and comparable images of the same bird captured in exactly the same phase of its flight. This was achieved by perfectly matching the periodic cycle of a wing beating with the rotational cycle of the shutter disc. Of course, to research these results he made use of data previously obtained with his graphic method. In his writings he went on to state that chronophotographic research was, for the most, not so much about making new discoveries, but rather in confirming in detail what he had already observed with his earlier graphic method.

24. Chronophotography, new research instrument

With the development and the extension of the chronophotographic experiments at the Station Physiologique, Marey began to consider the autonomous and methodological importance of using serial photography as a research tool. Thus, in 1884, while preparing a new edition of his 1878 treatise *La méthode graphique dans les sciences expérimentales*, he wrote a special supplement of more than fifty pages entitled: 'Le Développement de la méthode graphique pour la photographie.' This supplement would eventually be sold separately. In the preface, dated 22 May 1884, Marey wrote that he had

> ... tried in using photography to find the solution to some problems which were not being dealt with by the procedures for the mechanical recording of movements. The success of these attempts has been so complete that I consider it necessary for these new procedures to be known. Chronophotography ... bridges an important gap in the graphic method. Not only physiologists, but more generally, all researchers will find in chronophotography the solution to a great many of their problems.

The text is a systematic statement on the application of serial photography to the study of complex movements. In the introductory historical review, he cites as among the first experimenters Dr Onimus and the photographer Martin, who in 1865 photographed on the same plate the opposing extremities of the hearts of live animals. He then describes the experience and results of Janssen and Muybridge. From then on to the end Marey presents, interprets and comments on his own experiences, starting with the photographic gun to arrive at the most sophisticated technique for the cinematic analysis of the movements of animals and humans. Sometimes the movements required detailed extracts and reconstructions of the various data obtainable from the comparison of the photographed images. Marey was scrupulous in giving the terms and technical details of the various solutions he experimented with, such as for the 'determination of the synchronicity between the different points of many trajectories recorded simultaneously' (as in the cause of the movements of arms and legs), when he suggested that one of the windows on the shutter disc should be twice as wide as the others so that, at known intervals, one could obtain more intense images so as to act as points of reference for analysis.

From the 1884 supplement it is also clear the extent to which Marey had become fascinated by the language of images and how this had, and would continue, to push him to keep using the chronophotographic method, even outside the area of physiological research. This can be seen in the short chapter on the determination of trajectories of inanimate bodies in differing movements. In conclusion comes the candid confession of how the austere and respected scientist, wearing gloves and a mask, dressed himself entirely in black to record with the chronophotograph a series of linked rings, created by rotating at speed a lighted ball at the end of a rope. The stated aim, perhaps little more than a pretext, was to test the sensitivity of the plate, though he then admits to having, for reasons of pure enjoyment, written his own name with a small lighted ball, creating his signature on the plate.

In 1884 in France as well as the rest of Europe there was a cholera epidemic. At that time the *vibrio cholerae* had not yet been discovered. Marey decided partly to abandon his physiological research into movement, believing that his investigative method, based on the recording of dynamic phenomena, might be usefully applied to an epidemiological situation that was still uncontrolled and the dynamic of which could therefore be studied with the data of the actual evolution and development of the morbid condition using the standard spatio-temporal coordinates of his graphic method.

The Académie de Médecine asked him to present a *Rapport sur les résultants de l'enquête sur l'épidemie de choléra on France en 1884.*[255] The analysis of the pathological phenomena was based on a socio-statistical investigation, using the methods of cartographic notation, so as to arrive at the conclusion that water was the principle factor in the transmission of the illness. These techniques used by Marey would be developed and re-used by other academics in cases of typhoid, poliomyelitis and in much research on pollution.[256]

Despite this well-motivated shift from his main line of research, Marey never really abandoned his research on movement, as shown by the continuing papers to the Académie des Sciences. There is a decrease in 1884–85, but in 1887 eleven reports were presented, nearly all of them on human movement and bird flight with invaluable use of chronophotographic research.

In some experiments, Marey once again gave evidence of his technological and engineering abilities: the need to obtain data of a certain quality and quantity to understand certain physiological phenomena by visual means, led him to resolve mechanical and optical problems – in other words to take apart time and space, to make visible and interpretable that which escaped the human eye. When the need to take many images in a short time with a single plate created confusion and superimpositions, he built a machine with two plates side by side with a lens each, but with a single shutter. In this way on one plate there would be uneven numbered images (1, 3, 5, 7 etc) and on the other the even numbered ones (2, 4, 6, 8 etc). When he needed to, therefore, as in the case of a seagull in flight, he was able to obtain phases at very short intervals which were clear, not overlapping, isolated but comparable.

Even more impressive was how he resolved an even more complex dilemma: how to analyse the flight of a bird moving in the direction of the camera, which is to say without that perpendicular spatial movement required to record successive images in different places on the fixed plate.

Marey invented a technique that it still used today for filming at ultra high speeds: using a rotating mirror to capture the images and transmit them slightly displaced one after another. This mirror, incorporated in a camera, was moved by a clockwork mechanism. Its movement ensured that the individual successive images were placed one after another, instead of overlapping as would otherwise have been the case with the bird flying towards the lens. Many years after the invention and perfecting of cinema on moving film, a principle similar to this would be used to increase the number of frames which can be filmed in a fraction of a second. Even in this case it was necessary to overcome some technical hurdles, just as noted by Marey with his first model for the photographic gun: the mechanics of the intermittent pulling of the film, the problems of inertia and resistance of materials do not allow for certain speed limits to be overcome, meaning that other solutions had to be found. Developing Marey's original idea, a rotating prism was placed between the lens and the film which went back to being fixed (for example a strip placed inside a drum), just like the fixed plate in Marey's machine. Revolving at a very high speed, the prism reflects and registers on the film strip many images which can be used to analyse a very brief phenomena which occurs in a fraction of a second.

Still in 1887 Marey considered, in relation to the flight of birds, the issue of three-dimensional space in those movements. Seeing that two-dimensional images were insufficient and that stereoscopic images could not provide scientifically measurable data, he decided to proceed with a series of shots of the same phenomena on the intersecting spatial phases. He first established the theoretical model which would require:

Marey, pigeon in flight, 1887.

... three black backings and three chronophotographic machines, to obtain simultaneously three series of images aligned on three planes perpendicular to each other.[257]

Then, since he could not accomplish the whole project in one go, he proceeded by successive experiments rather than simultaneous ones. To do this he had to make a practical frame fourteen metres high on which to place the camera facing downwards, using a black backing on the ground of great size and (to reduce reflection) other vertical screens. In the end, under these difficult conditions, he did succeed in recording a bird in flight from above while also photographing it from the front and side. From a photographic point of view, the shots from above were the most critical; in fact, owing to the speed of the filming and the limits of the black backing, he had to make do with barely perceptible figures that could barely be timed so as to compare them and integrate them with the other two phases of movement. From the perspective of physiological analysis, Marey used synoptic plates to study and indicate the global characteristics of beating wings. By now though he was too aware of the importance and novelty of the scientific language of images to forgo the plastic reconstruction of the analytical images which he collected with the chronophotographic filming: 'To make the successive attitudes of flight more intelligible, I modelled the images in relief.'[258] However, what might appear to be a form of satisfaction and gratification from the results of original research, became for him yet another scientific puzzle.

Cast in bronze in Naples, using the old technique of lost wax casting, the images of the seagull in the various phases of a single beat of its wing opened up the problem of the fidelity of its representation of the fourth dimension, that is to say the spatio-temporal one. The speed of shooting with the chronophotographs was such that for each single position of the bird (relative to a time of 0.005th of a second) there was not a movement in space as long as the entire length of its body. Therefore the images which Marey with such innovativeness and technical ability was able to keep from overlapping, now had to be spatially intersected to represent the dynamics of the movement of the bird chronospatially. He thus created, beyond the single figures, a plastic composition of great conceptual originality, its fusion in bronze anticipating by decades the analogous dynamic sculptures of Italian Futurists.[259]

Marey probably did not consider the artistic value of his plastic representations of a bird in flight, but at the same time he cannot have been indifferent to the beauty of those scientific models. In his book of 1894 he referred to a proposal to create 'photo-sculptures' to make a plastic image starting from a circular series of contemporary photographs and even published the image of a small statutette created from a series of chronophotographs.[260] We have seen how his basic interest in scientific research pushed the French physiologist to invent his own investigative technique, consisting of visualising the phases of movement. Having reached this objective (which was both research and documentation), the series of images obtained were nearly always studied singly or comparatively. There seemed no need to reproduce the movement, reconstituting it through a synthesis of the analytical images. If such a series of analytical images could create the illusion of real movement when viewed with the Phenakistiscope or Zoetrope, then it meant that truly those phases were the elements of actual movement.

For Marey, even the aspect of the 'reconstruction of movement' was of research interest: he discovered that the Phenakistiscope offered the perfect illusion of continuous movement, from the moment in which at least eleven images were placed on a disc on which was impressed the rotation speed of a turn per second. Now, since the seagull completes five beats of its wings in a single second, he was obliged for the purposes of analysing a single phase, to record the equivalent of fifty images a second. By placing around the disc of Plateau's machine just the images that show a single beat of a wing and watching the movement in a mirror with the disc rotating a turn per second, one saw the movement at a speed five times slower than in real life.

> It is the slowing down of movements that makes the use of the Phenakistiscope valuable, allowing the eye to follow easily all the phases of an action that would be missed by direct observation.[261]

But that was not all. Using the plastic models of the phases of the flight of a pigeon and a seagull, Marey invented the three-dimensional Zoetrope, putting inside the machine the models of the bird figure instead of the paper strips with drawings or photographs.

Various people could watch therefore, looking through one of the numerous slots, at the pigeon or seagull in flight. Anticipating holograms, Marey described his new experiment thus:

> The great advantage of figures in relief is that it allows one to see the bird under all possible angles ... depending on which part of the bird one is focusing, one sees the bird escape, pass or come close: from these three points of view, one can study at will the movement of wings and slow down the speed as one likes, reducing more or less the rotation of the zootrope.[262]

Today, functioning examples of Marey's Zoetrope are exhibited at the Science Museum in London, the Národní technické museum in Prague and the Musée Marey in Beaune, proving to our eyes, made sharper by our familiarity with moving images, the truthfulness of the presentation that the French scientist had created over a century ago.

This simple machine, essentially scientific but still fascinating for those watching the uninterrupted flight of seagulls, stimulated the imagination of artists such as Max Ernst, who made it the subject of a graphic transcription where one of the figures takes off and flies away.[263]

Zoetrope with seagull models in successive positions of flight.

25. Twenty images per second

By this point, Marey had no doubts about the importance, originality and irreplaceable nature of research undertaken by way of the new language of images.

> What was missing up until now was that the movement of human beings be as well known as that of the celestial bodies, or of those inert masses that move inside our industrial machines. What was missing above all was the perfect knowledge of the positions that each part of the body assumes in specified moments, since our eye cannot follow these movements, which are too rapid. Chronophotography has filled this gap.[264]

It is still the physiologist speaking here, the sole motivation behind the research being the study of movement. However, by now Marey had become a specialist, a pioneer of this new way of seeing, communicating and understanding these things not based on words but images instead. After years of intense research and of advanced results, he considered – still for reasons of scientific exactness – the issue of the distortion of perspective and the parallax effect relative to the use of short focal lenses compared with those with long focal lengths. He had to face considerable difficulties to make comparative studies of the beat of the wings of a seagull and a pigeon: the latter has a beating rhythm (approximately nine cycles per second) almost two times greater than the other, so Marey was forced to film the successive phases with an interval of just 1/100th of a second between images.

Marey was conceptually ready now for the steps towards the final stage of technical development of cinematography as we know it today, which is to say a camera with moving film. In 1887 in France, Eastman began selling a new sensitive film placed on a paper strip that could be rolled on to a bobbin, which would be destined eventually to replace glass plates. This was to avoid the problem of their weight and the fact that they were hard to handle, but also because the new film allowed the camera to be loaded just once for a whole series of photographs. The manufacturing company looked not only at the flowering market of professional photographers but to the growing and promising field of amateur photographers. They had no idea of how far this little roll of photographic paper would reach, despite their industrial efforts. Not even their research laboratories were thinking of the cinema. Eastman in 1888 launched the prototype for the Kodak camera which would become famous with the slogan: 'You press the button, we do the rest.'

Marey asked the photographer Balagny, an artisan manufacturer of sensitive materials and already his supplier, to make him some strips of his new type of emulsioned paper. Having gained experience from the photographic gun of the various types of chronophotography (with fixed plate, multiple lenses, mobile plates), Marey was about to construct a new series of filming machines: 'filmstrip chronophotography.' Between 1887 and 1889 he built a number of models which proved how his medical training had in no way reduced his talent as a constructor of machines. On 29 October 1888 he presented to the Académie des Sciences his first results in a paper entitled: 'Décomposition des phases d'un movement au moyen d'images photographiques successives recueilles sur une bande de papier sensible qui se déroule.'[265]

I have the honour to present ... a series of images obtained at a rate of twenty images per second. The apparatus I have constructed for this purpose has running through it a strip of sensitive paper that can reach 1.60 metres per second. Given that this speed is greater than my current needs, I have reduced it to 0.80 metres.

Speaking of such an experience he would say a few years later: 'I took advantage of this idea from commercial photography ...' as if the only problem left unresolved was that of the sensitivity of the film.[266] At that time Balagny was still supplying him with strips that were one metre in length and nine centimetres wide.[267] With regards to the technical descriptions of the first film cameras, one cannot but be astonished by the series of brilliant inventions that we owe to Marey – they each constitute genuine qualitative leaps compared with the technology of the day and even his previous work. The first model, in which the apparatus was housed entirely in a camera obscura from which the lens emerged, used an ingenious system to move the strip intermittently. The strip, driven at a constant speed, was stopped periodically by an electromagnectically operated clamp, just as the shutter opening passed the focal plane. The second model was already portable since the entire mechanism for rolling and unrolling the paper strip was housed in the machine which was no greater than a camera for plates measuring 18 x 24 centimetres. Marey also invented 'protective tails', that is to say two paper strips of a different colour which were glued to the front and tail of the emulsioned strip, permitting the loading and unloading of the rolls in normal light condition and ensuring that there was no confusion between those that had already been exposed and those still to be used.

With renewed enthusiasm he thought of a whole series of new research areas opened up by the potentially unlimited possibilities offered by the filmstrip chronophotograph. It would no longer be necessary to photograph white subjects on a black background; there would be no more problems with images being superimposed on the same plate. Marey was completing his work on animal flight (the treatise *Le vol des oiseaux* was published in 1890) but now he thought that it would be interesting to start, or return to, the experiment with insects, reptiles, amphibians and mammals of various sorts. He considered new problems in the analysis of quadruped locomotion: studying the running of a dog compared with other animals, starting with horses, so allowing him to deepen his understanding of the differences and the analogous elements, establishing relationships between anatomical characteristics and physiological functions. He became drawn to entirely new areas, such as the possibility of studying the movement of fish and microscopic organisms.

26. Edison discovers Marey

In Paris in 1889 another universal exhibition was held, an expression of the impetus of the expanding industrial society on the basis of recent scientific developments and applications. The newly-constructed Eiffel Tower, monument to the vanguard of new iron technologies was illuminated by hundreds of light bulbs, symbolising the practical uses being made of the latest discoveries in electricity. Edison had booked a large pavilion to illustrate his many new inventions, from the Phonograph to a variety of electrical applications, for the purpose of selling products, patents and licences. Having arrived in Europe for the Paris exhibition, he was bestowed with various honours and receptions. While visiting the Italian pavilion, Edison saw exhibited an allegorical statue by Bordiga with the title 'The triumph of electricity': a winged woman, a telegraph, a cogwheel, a telephone and a voltaic battery. The woman was stepping on the gas lamp and brandished instead of the torch of the Statue of Liberty, an electric light bulb, all made of Carrara marble. Edison bought it for the entrance to his new laboratories in West Orange, New Jersey.[268]

Marey met the American inventor on several occasions and on one of these showed him his new film Chronophotographe. One recalls the episode when Muybridge in 1888 was in West Orange for two presentations of his Zoöpraxiscope discs and suggested to Edison the combining of his projects with the Phonograph. It is said that Edison refused, or anyway let the matter drop, at least as far as Muybridge was concerned. In actual fact Edison asked one of his main colla- borators William Kennedy-Laurie Dickson to work on a prototype 'optical phono- graph.' This was based on a rotating cylinder covered by sensitive material on which a number of small images could be recorded rapidly which, once fixed, could have been viewed by one person at a time through a lens. In October 1888 the Edison Company even presented a patent caveat for this idea. The project did not proceed, however, owing to unsatisfactory results, and the notion was abandoned. However, Edison and Dickson were not going to pass up the possibilities offered by the rolls of sensitive paper now being made by the Carbutt Company and by Eastman. In 1889 the latter launched a new product, substituting paper (which was delicate and fragile) with a thin transparent nitro-cellulose film which greatly simplified not just the use of rolls of photographic material but also the developing and printing processes.

'Films' were thus born, but at this moment the term only referred to photographic film.

Edison must have been impressed by Marey's chronophotographic machine and by the images captured with it, as well as by Marey himself – this figure of the pure scientist, so engrossed in problems of physiological research that he would invent dozens of machines, ones of a complex and sophisticated nature, simply to study how humans run or birds fly. The great artisan inventor, however, bestowed with the practical spirit of an industrialist, saw a completely different type of opportunity. He thought (also given the worldwide successes of the Phonograph) of trying to do something analogous for images. Not for scientific purposes, but to sell strips of moving images with unusual or amusing subjects, available to view on request through his machines, in the same way that people paid to listen to his phonograph recordings. Returning to America, he began brand new plans for this project. After seeing what Marey had achieved with the possibilities offered by the new rolls of film, in November 1889 he deposited another caveat which used the word 'film', still only used to mean the way that the sensitive material was used. In that project lay the idea for one of the most important technical principles for the development of cinematographic projection: the perforation of the film to guarantee the regularity of the movement. While Edison was in Europe, Dickson (responsible for a number of the inventions and developments made at the Edison company at this time) continued to work and make plans. He had Eastman send him their new film, and making the most of the prestige of the Edison name, ordered many more, to be made to measure: he ordered film strips with a width 3/4 of an inch and at least fifty-four feet in length, and if possible double that.

Edison, in a press release on the occasion of the commercial launch of the Kinetoscope in 1894, made reference to the research of Muybridge and Marey as the inspiration for his machine.[269] Marey for his part wrote in 1892 that Edison had without doubt been inspired to create his Kinetoscope by the strips of images taken with the Chronophotographe, which he had shown to him on an 'electro-photographic' Zoetrope at the 1889 exhibition.[270]

Strange as it might seem, dealing as we are with an inventor tied to science and technique, there are no other concrete items linking Edison's activities to the birth of scientific cinema. As to the merits and the type of interests Edison had in the complex affairs surrounding the birth of entertainment cinema, much has already been written.[271]

With the benefit of hindsight, one could simplistically claim – as some historians have done – that in the following years Marey failed to see the advantages of the Edison-Dickson film perforation. Some even go so far as to say that had Marey adopted it he would have invented cinematic projection. On the other hand, with the same method, one might point out that Edison did not really see the value of Marey's technique, which from the beginning of his experiments made film move intermittently. Instead, in Edison's Kinetoscope the film moved continuously (though his camera used intermittent movement), and to get a stable image it was necessary to have brief light flashes through the images. Most importantly, the period of viewing needed to be very short, making projection onto a big screen impractical; viewing was limited to individuals through a magnifying lens.

In 1890, long before Edison and Dickson had made their Kinetoscope prototype, Marey developed a newly perfected Chronophotographe (and in this case also patented it, which was unusual for his scientific activity). The film was now on a transparent support of cellulose nitrate, the intermittent movement achieved with a mechanical system, so abandoning the electromagnet. It also included a series of enhancements to avoid tears, breakages and irregularities in the movement of the film, which had to move roughly and at a fairly high speed, but which also had to be able to stop for an instant many times per second.

> The originality of the system consists in arresting the movement of only the film during the pause, and letting the transport mechanisms keep turning.[272]

Thanks to the cutting edge characteristics of the Chronophotographe, Marey was able to enter into a new phase of experimentation. Subjects did not have to be placed against a black background and so were not limited to the Station Physiologique. The new camera was portable and could photograph subjects of any type on any background. He had already made some experiments in Naples in the winter of 1889–1890 with marine photography in an aquarium.

Filming the aquarium at Naples, 1890.

In 1891 he experimented using the Chronophotographe through a microscope, photographing some infusoria. The main limitation was that although Balagny could supply highly sensitive rolls of film, they were very short, starting at a little over a metre to a little over four metres in length (while Eastman in the USA was providing Edison with much longer rolls).[273] Despite this, Marey immediately decided to undertake a technical challenge that would test the limits of his machine and which would eventually provide him with new data for his research on movement. He was thus able successfully to realise some shots taken at a speed of fifty frames per second. To put this in context, one should remember that the film was nine centimetres wide, was not perforated and was essentially made up of a short length. It was thus necessary to reach the high transport speed immediately, and even with the obvious difficulties inherent with such a large surface, ensure the regularity of the fifty pauses per second (of a single duration of less than a hundredth of a second). Marey himself calculated that the velocity of the transportation of the film, without the time taken up with the fifty pauses for exposure, reached 1.80 metres per second.[274] If we consider this in light of modern day 35mm perforated film, for filming at twenty-four frames per second this would give a transport speed of approximately 0.9 metres per second, while for 16mm this drops to 0.4 metres. To obtain such extraordinary results, and at the same time record on the short piece of film a sufficient number of images (about fifty), Marey was obliged to reduce the minimum height of each frame. Thus on a base of nine centimetres one had an image that was only 1.8 centimetres in height, with vertically transported film.

Between 1891 and 1893 a number of modifications and refinements were made to the Chronophotographe camera, and in June 1893 Marey patented the machine again. One of these models (from 1891) could be used either with filmstrips or fixed plates. The shutter speed could be varied from 1/200th to 1/2500th of a second; by altering the cams of the arrest mechanism of the film and the shutter windows, one could vary the format of the images from 9 x 9 centimetres to 9 x 1.8 centimetres, in the latter case making it possible to obtain sixty images a second. At the same time Marey was working on a Chronophotographe projector. One of his prototypes had as its light source the sun. In this case, though, the practical results were not satisfactory. This was not the fault of using the sun, but because the positive prints taken from the negatives filmed with the Chronophotographe, when projected resulted in jittery images. This was due to the small difference in the spacing between one image and another, leading to the images not overlaying each other exactly on the screen. This was not a problem for Marey since he analysed the images one at a time. When he wanted to reconstruct the dynamic of the movement visually, for demonstrations or for additional research in slow motion, he placed each image on a Phenakistiscope or on the strip of a Zoetrope, so that the defect was irrelevant. To get past this with his projector, Marey resorted to the laborious process of cutting out and trimming the photographs one by one – with the most precise equidistance possible – and mounting them on a tape of gummed canvas. He did achieve some viable results, but the machine overall was clunky, noisy and not very reliable. The result was that, having given the details of his new machine at the Académie des Sciences on 2 May 1892 and announcing a demonstration for the next scheduled gathering, he then cancelled it and let the matter drop for a few years.[275]

With regards to this technological stalemate, the only one that we really know about in Marey's long, varied and productive career as a constructor of machines, it is difficult, but not impossible, to find an answer to it. If we examine the technical structure of the intermittent mechanism, we can see that it would not have been easy to insert the mechanical binding element for perforation and therefore for the cog wheels as well. It would have been necessary to have to start with a completely new functional structure. It is perhaps true that the technological genius that he demonstrated on so many occasions would have seen him eventually resolve the problem. In our opinion, however, he lacked a strong motivation to go in that direction. Not so much, as others have written, because he did not want to adopt a solution found by someone else, but rather that projection itself was not of great interest to him. The fact that he did deal with it may have been due to various factors: his meeting with Edison, who was only interested as a future industrialist in the entertainment industry; his long collaboration with Georges Demeny, his assistant since 1881, who was receptive to the temptations of commercialising equipment developed for scientific purposes (we will return to this argument when we look at Demeny's own work); finally – why not? – the search for the public adulation which a chronophotographic projector could have brought with the possibilities of presenting his results in a hall with a large screen.

In practical terms, Marey dropped the idea in 1892. In his book *Le mouvement*, published in autumn 1893, the very last page was dedicated to chronophotographic projection. After outlining the way it worked technically, he underlined his strictly scientific conception for its uses: 'to capture the nature of a movement well it is opportune to reproduce it a certain number of times.' He proposed the use of a strip of film made into a loop so that a continuous series of images could be studied. He announced that he had built a machine to do this, which could function electrically or with solar power, and be projected on a screen.

> The instrument gives extremely bright images, but it is noisy and the projected images do not have the absolute stability that must be obtained. Having reached this point in our research, having learned that our assistant had obtained in another way an immediate solution to the problem, it seemed convenient to postpone any new attempts.[276]

27. A cat always falls on its feet

During this period, Marey continued his physiological research with the Chronophotographe. In 1893, among the various presentations made at the Académie, we find a study of the swimming movements of the Thornback Ray (filmed in an aquarium in Naples in 1891), but also work on hydrodynamics. In 1894 he achieved a notable feat: he filmed a cat (later repeating the experiment with a rabbit) falling on its feet after being dropped upside down from above. The paper 'Des mouvements que certains animaux exécutent pour retomber sur leurs pieds quand ils sont précipités d'un lieu élevé', resulted in debates and discussions.

> One day there presented itself a controversial case of animal mechanics. A popular proverb says that a cat always falls on its feet; mechanics however taught us the opposite of this; that in the absence of an external pressure point an animal is incapable of righting itself during a fall. Now, experience has proved the proverb to be right ... By the time that the animal has fallen 0.25 metres it has already righted itself. By examining the succession of images we can see how this happens. Chronophotography has therefore played an important role in correcting a mistaken formulation of rational mechanics.[277]

It is interesting to note that for the visual presentation of his experiments, Marey – unsatisfied with his own prototype projector – used, as in the past, a Zoetrope which also allowed him to show the event over and over again but with variable speeds,

The falling cat, 1891.

slowing it down to the limits of the persistence of the optical effect of the machine.[278] A number of academics commented on the demonstration since its findings appeared to contradict a mathematical principle contained in a theory known as *le théorème des aires*.

Some even made fun of it, ridiculing their colleagues for participating in frivolous activities. In truth Marey's short film constitutes the first recording on moving film of a rapid, dynamic phenomenon which could not be analysed by the naked eye, but only with the use of recording equipment. It is one of the main principles of scientific cinema, one of the historical reasons for its birth, and one of the main ways in which it distinguishes itself from entertainment cinema.

Marey was a firm believer in the importance and irreplaceable nature of chrono-photographic analysis as an instrument of scientific research. In the preface to *Le mouvement*, he wrote that each chapter of the book was actually a programme of work which interested scientists could undertake within their own specialist fields. He was not just addressing physiologists but also those studying geometry, hydraulics, naturalists, navigation specialists, those in the military and even artists. He said that the book was aimed at all of them 'because it deals with their main concern, the desire to understand, among the phenomena of life, that which escapes even the most careful observation.' The inclusion of the military among the parties interested in chronophotography raises the issue of some of Marey's financing, the provenance of which (the Ministry of War) might have indicated a not entirely scientific orientation in some of the research.

In the correspondence between Marey and Demeny, especially in recently discovered letters, there are a number of interesting references to some research of this kind. In the physiological area this refers to some aspects of the *marche de l'homme*, when soldiers carried a load, such as a rucksack, others in the field of ballistics.

From the parts that have thus far emerged, it appears clear that it was Marey who, with the importance of his scientific standing, exploited a relationship with the military to have more materials at his disposal, and even worked with some of them to make certain tests, such as those on bullets, which allowed him push his equipment to its limits.

Chronophotograph of a soldier marching with pack. c 1891.

Almost as a way of demonstrating the unusual applications of the Chronophotographe as a research tool, Marey frequently undertook tests outside his specific area of study. For example, he dealt with hydrodynamics and invented a technique for visualising large wave movements using small silvered wax spheres with the same density as salt water which, when illuminated, provided beautiful images of the fluid movements of the water, as well as the actions and reactions to obstructions or to floating or submerged objects. One can still recall the lovely chronophotographic images on a fixed plate of the trajectory of a white ball, the movements of a stick thrown in the air, the vertical fall of a ball or the vibrations of a flexible rod determined by the point from which it was held. These tests and experiments were mainly undertaken during the winters spent in Naples between 1883 and 1886, about half a century before the equally fine stroboscopic images produced by Edgerton and others. In a small way these works served as a means to test and refine the equipment and to check its reliability. Mostly however they expressed Marey's interest in studying dynamic phenomena by means of the method he had invented.

Subsequently he experimented with stereoscopic images, achieved by a Chronophotographe with two lenses. In *Le mouvement* he published some fine images of solid volumes produced by rotating a straight line or circle around an axis. These images come across as extraordinary precursors to the geometric creations which one can obtain on a monitor with the help of an electronic computer. Marey however used this stereoscopic technique for physiological research, such as the trajectory of a man's pubic region while running (1885).

28. Marey and aerial navigation

Aviation, aerodynamics, man's conquest of flight, is a fascinating area of research that Marey linked strictly to his specific interest as a physiologist. In 1869 he had published a work on the mechanical reproduction of insect flight. In the same year, using the graphic recording method, he let birds fly while suspended from a circular frame, enclosing them in a kind of harness and providing them with 'exploratory drums' which allowed him to record the curve of the wings in a backwards-forwards direction, also up-and-down. Marey also built a cylinder with a black backing for insects which were pinned at the abdomen with small silver surgical pliers fixed on a very light screw, which rotated freely. To record the trajectory of the wings he glued a sequin onto a wing, then exposed the wooden box containing the machine to the sun to record the reflection of the luminous point. In *La machine animale* he wrote:

> We have no hesitation in confessing that what has sustained us during the complex analysis of the phases of the flight of birds has been the certain hope of getting to the point of being able to imitate in increasingly less imperfect fashion this type of admirable aerial locomotion, which yesterday was still thought of as a utopia but which today is being addressed in a truly scientific fashion.[279]

This was certainly true for Marey as well as for other pioneers. However, speaking of Utopia, at the beginning of the twentieth century the problem of human flight was still seen in these terms: controlled aerial locomotion would have as its first consequence the abolition of customs borders, but would above all bring an end to all wars. Fortifications would be useless. Wars would lead to such atrocities that just to think of them people would be terrified and make governments find reasonable solutions to the problems they had between them.[280]

As president of the Société de Navigation Aérienne, Marey was part of the organising committee for the International Aeronautics Congress which was held as part of the Paris Universal Exposition in 1889. During this event he was able to have discussions with many other pioneers and researchers of flight. Some of his students at the Station Physiologique dedicated themselves exclusively to designing and experimenting with flying machines with beating wings, for gliders and steam-powered craft.

From his book on bird flight (1890) we know that Marey built machines that imitated the beat of a bird's wing and more than one functioning model of a mechanical bird, animated by circular or straight translation, with recording up to 1/100th of a second.

Discussing studies of air resistance when compared with bodies in motion, he predicted the use of wind tunnels (*souffleries aérodinamique*). He would later go through with this project, even receiving financial contribution from the Smithsonian Institution for his research into aerodynamics. Marey remains one of the founders of the visualisation methods for air and smoke streams which are still in use today.

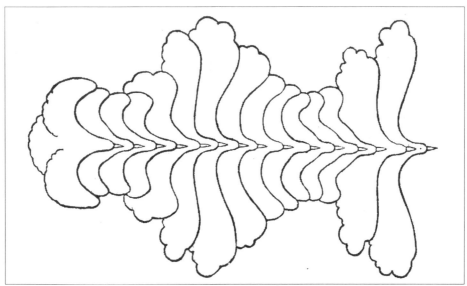

Marey's analysis of the flight of a seagull, from *Le vol des oiseaux* (1890).

In 1891 he presented to the Académie a work entitled *Emploi de la cronophoto-graphie pour l'étude des appareils destinés à la locomotion aérienne*. Otto Lilienthal, one of the pioneers of glider planes, wrote in 1895, clearly referring to the works of the French physiologist:

> The phenomena of natural flight have been analysed, anatomically and mechanically, by optical means through instantaneous photography and graphic reproduction.[281]

In a conference in 1899, while discussing three dimensional filming of the beats of a bird wing, Marey said that: 'This is how I was able to understand the mechanism of flight which consists of a real spiral beat of the wing.'[272]

It is therefore no surprise to read Wilbur Wright's words: 'If I have been able to fly, it is because I read *Le vol des oiseaux*, Marey's famous book.'[273] Wright praised Marey further in 1912 when in Berlin to inaugurate the first aeronautic salon.

29. The Institut Marey

In the last years of the nineteenth century Marey, ignoring both the arguments over the birth of cinema and the patent wars ignited by the first cinema shows, continued to work with his usual calm, scientific method.

He was close to seventy years old and continued to perfect his Chronophotographe. Between 1896 and 1899 he refined new models which were both 'analysers' (i.e. filming equipment) and 'projectors.' He continued to use his old terminology,

The Institut Marey.

so that even by 1890 in *Le vol des oiseaux* he makes reference to 'analyseur photochronographique à bande sans fin.' By now film rolls had reached thirty metres in length and in his last model it was possible to use various types of film, 'perforated or not', including that which would become standard 35mm film. In its own way it was an acknowledgement of the reality created by the industrial technology of the growing film entertainment industry. After announcing it in 1897, two years later he built an electrical photographic gun, 'a portable machine which one can aim at the subject.'

The mechanism was powered by an electric motor, while the magazine held a twenty metre roll of 35mm film. Compared with the large, heavy and complicated hand-cranked cameras which cameramen the world over would continue to use for a few decades, Marey's prototype comes across as a science fictional prophecy of modern portable cameras.

In 1899 he also perfected his Chronophotographe-microscope equipment, introducing a technical development of great importance. The lighting of the area being photographed was automatic and only occurred while the shutter was open, to reduce the problems of overheating and thus the survival of the biological subject. Just a few years earlier, Marey had written: 'Microscopic chrono-photography could, in the hands of someone more expert than we, produce important results.'[285]

Marey's prestige and fame as a scientist had for many years stretched beyond his own country. At the International Congress of Physiology held in Cambridge in

Marey gun-camera, 1899.

1898 it was decided that the methods of physiological research should be unified and made compatible, and Marey was made the president of this work group. In the years that immediately followed, the decision was taken to create an international association for the control of instruments, and in recognition of the importance of his research, the organisation was named the Institut Marey in his honour, and was based at the Station Physiologique at the Parc des Princes.[285]

30. Marey and Lumière

In 1900 Marey was made president of the organising committee of section 12 of the Musée Centennial at the Universal Exhibition in Paris. The event acquired a special solemnity coming as it did at the end of a century characterised by extraordinary development and considerable progress in the fields of science and technology. For such a celebrated scientist, already showered with honours, this appointment might seem rather unbecoming or even inadequate, if one does not take into account a particularly delicate and complex situation. The section of the Exhibition which Marey was supervising also included in its 'Photography' section all the various types of equipment for cinematic filming and projection.

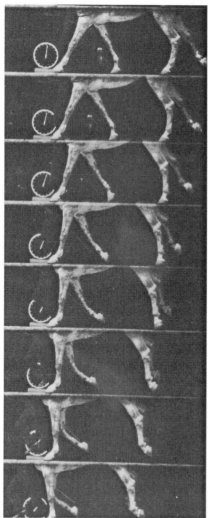

Marey chronophotographic film showing the locomotion of a horse, 1895.

In those years this new form of entertainment, after arousing the curiosity, interest and enthusiasm in the royal courts and in aristocratic and bourgeois society, had already reached, thanks to itinerant projectionists, huge popular audiences, first in fairs and market tents, before establishing itself in actual cinema halls. In the decade that sat astride the nineteenth and twentieth centuries there were hundreds of patents taken out for cinematographic machines, resulting in an actual patent war in the USA, with huge legal, economic and even criminal ramifications. In 1897 the New York representative of the Lumière company was forced to board a French steamer in secret having reached it at sea in a launch to escape from trumped up charges. Up until that time American protectionism had decided to exclude European productions (before invading the rest of the world with its own product). Meanwhile the most cutthroat competition broke out on the old continent, aiming to impose differing types of equipment and their films.

The importance of the task given to Marey now may seem a little clearer: to set up a centenary exhibition on the progress of inventions and developments in the area of photography and cinema. With all the various fights, arguments, technical and economic low blows between adversaries and rivals going on unabated, it was a requirement of the job that the man appointed be of high prestige, outside of and above the rabble.

Marey got straight to work, albeit not without a little hesitation, and his report 'Exposition d'instruments relatifs à l'histoire de la chronophonographie' was a scientific document which made tremendous efforts to be objective and avoid the easy trap of nationalism (acknowledgement was made towards Edison's work), and not descend into a spat between Frenchmen over who deserved recognition for this invention (even though Marey, beyond commercial or industrial aspects, would have been a frontrunner).

In the catalogue for section two of the Musée Centennial, Marey published an interesting essay: 'Applications scientifiques de la chronophotographie.' Rather than the work of famous seventy-year-old scientist, it reads like the views of a young researcher that has discovered a promising route of inquiry and experimentation, talking of it with all the missionary zeal and the enthusiasm of a propagandist:

> Animated projection, which has caught the public's interest so greatly, offers but a few advantages from a scientific point of view: in actual fact it does not provide anything that cannot be seen with great precision with the human eye.

It is as if he wanted to then add: however, with chronophotography... He goes on to review analytically its wide-ranging applications for the study of movement, geometry, mechanics, physics and physiology.

> The difficulties that Galileo and Atwood had to overcome to determine the laws on falling bodies will in future, in all analogous cases, be avoided by those that make use of chronophotography.[286]

At the Exhibition the Lumière company presented a gigantic cinematograph show: a screen over twenty metres wide and fifteen metres high. The projected images could be watched on either side of the gigantic screen, kept wet so as to be translucent, and in the immense machine gallery where the shows took place up to 25,000 people could watch. The Lumières had built a special machine for the event (using large-format film) to increase the image to such a size, though in the event this projector was not completed in time. However, the giant images were successfully projected with a standard 35mm machine. The exhibition in any event was overflowing with cinematographic attractions: from the unfortunate Cinéorama (an enveloping 360 degree projection system using ten synchronised machines; it failed to open), to a number of ephemeral attempts to match the two marvels of science: the Phonograph and the cinematograph.

A question arises at this point: what was the relationship between Marey and the Lumières? This question is not only relevant with regard to the Universal Exhibition of 1900 and the arguments that would follow from it, but also to the basic issue of their respective contributions to the invention of cinema.

The Lumières, as is known, made their first exhibitions (first in private, then in public, and then for payment) in 1895; in the same year Marey was not only president of the Académie des Sciences but also president of the Société Française de Photographie. In June of that year at Lyons (the Lumières' home town) there was a meeting of the Union Nationale des Sociétés Photographiques de France. During a trip organised for the occasion, Auguste Lumière shot some film of the participants disembarking from a riverboat and of Janssen in conversation with a local councillor.

These short films were shown the next day at the final meeting of the congress. On the same occasion, Janssen, who was presiding over the event, gave the speech in which he paid tribute to the Lumières and gave them the honour and the credit for having made a considerable step forwards in the amazing illusion of animated photography. With skill, Janssen referred to his photographic revolver and paid tribute to the eminent president of the Académie and the Société Française de Photographie who had successfully transformed his original machine, adding, however, a subtle distinction to differentiate the analytic photography of movement (i.e. the scientific use of Marey's Chronophotographe) and animated photographs (i.e. the naturalistic reproduction of scenes of movement by the Lumières).

Marey was not present at this meeting in Lyons and we do not know if he attended the presentation screenings held in Paris by the Lumières before and after it. This might make one think that the old scientist had had a negative reaction to the success of the two young industrialists in resolving a problem on which he had stalled. We have already seen, however, that scientific detachment of Marey's with regard to the problems surrounding projection (see the last phrase of his book *Le mouvement*, autumn 1893, which refers to the successes that his collaborator Demeny would have in this arena). This is also demonstrated by the apparently contradictory fact that Marey, even after the appearance of the Lumière's equipment, continued to perfect his projection Chronophotographe without any impetus in a competitive, commercial or entertainment sense. His wish was to make use of an additional scientific instrument to view dynamic phenomena which would of course offer a synthesis of movement, but with the additional possibilities for study and research offered by the movements being slowed down or speeded up during the projection. In addition Marey always kept in mind the typically scientific and pedagogic importance of a projector that could print images in a loop, enabling the observation of those characteristics of movement that might be missed with a single viewing.

Marey had absolutely no interest in filming real or made up scenes to exhibit them for a fee, and had no intention of commercially exploiting equipment developed for scientific ends. He took out only a few patents and even these may

Auguste and Louis Lumière.

only have been undertaken to guard against the possible commercial exploitation, with a few adjustments, of his discoveries by strangers or even his collaborators. By far the majority of Marey's inventions, rather than being patented, were instead presented to the world via papers delivered at the Académie des Sciences containing all the details relating to their construction, thus making them automatically and freely available to all. Among Marey's papers only one case has been found in which he referred to the possibility of selling a Chronophotographe. It was in 1892 and Marey thought that by doing so he could, at least in part, get back some of the money spent on constructing the prototype. It has been suggested that the only model to be sold ended up in the hands of the Lumière brothers, either directly or through their father Antoine, who had founded the company.

It has been written in many places that the young Lumières had frequented Marey's laboratories and so were aware of the technological characteristics of his chronophotographic equipment and of the results obtained in both filming and projecting phases.[287]

On the other hand it is known that the Lumière company became a supplier of film and plates to the Station Physiologique, and it is said that they did this at a special price in consideration of their special relationship with the scientist.

At a conference in 1899 Marey summed up the developments of the Chrono-photographe and spoke of the work of the Lyons industrialists, after mentioning the well-deserved earlier success of Edison's Kinetoscope:

> The Lumières found, in 1895, the sought-after solution. Although using one of Edison's principles, the perforation of film, they nonetheless discovered a new procedure for taking and projecting film images ... This admirable invention reached perfection almost from the very beginning. It achieved ... under the name *cinématographe*, a considerable success and this name, which is nothing but the name of this particular machine, will remain for a long time associated in people's memories with all syntheses of movement.[288]

The following year, in the already mentioned paper for the exhibition of instruments and on the history of the Chronophotographe, he repeated the same concept, without mentioning the 'borrowing' from Edison, emphasising rather that:

> ... the Lumière cinematograph permits the projection on a screen of animated scenes that can be viewed by large audiences providing the perfect illusion of movement.

The Lumières, for their part, acknowledged Marey's important place among

> those scientists that thought of using photography for the purposes of fixing transitory scenes to be able to subsequently study and think about them in their own time ... To him we owe a great number of very ingenious pieces of equipment ...[289]

They were among those that underwrote the monument erected to Marey in Paris in 1914. However – even before the disagreements began – they strongly defended their own place, their right to consider themselves the inventors of cinema. Forgetting the initial scepticism over the possible future of the cinema after the surge of interest for this 'scientific curiosity' (see the famous phrase attributed to them in connection with Méliès' which many historians of the cinema have quoted), from 1897 they began to say, and have others say, that:

> Since there is a tendency too often to forget it, we permit ourselves to insist on this point and repeat, whatever the historical and documentary value of the predecessors, that cinematography dates, from a practical standpoint, from the invention and distribution of their machine.[290]

The first Lumière patent (February 1895) only referred to a chronophotographic machine, using and developing, even in its terminology, the earlier results by Marey. In addition, the technique for the perforation of film had been commercialised in the Edison Kinetoscope, which had already been exhibited in Paris in 1894. The name Cinématographe, which they inserted in to their second patent request, had already been used for the machine patented by Léon-Guillaume Bouly in 1892.

On the other hand, one cannot overlook the fact that the Lumières were, above all, industrialists. Their stimulus, their motivation to succeed in presenting their machine (using the best devices and technical solutions already used by others and then adding something new like the eccentric mechanism and the claw for the pull-down of the film), was essentially a question of prestige and the establishment of their company. Only a few years after the huge success of the cinematic entertainment, when the Lumière company, solidly placed especially in the field of photography, gave up on an impossible hegemony and to a place of importance in the film industry, did they try, especially in the case of the younger brother Louis, to pass themselves off as scientists. In fact Louis Lumière in 1899 succeeded in getting elected as a member of the Académie des Sciences. However, in 1900, on the occasion of the Universal Exposition and the centennial museum, the Lumières were not only present with their gigantic cinematograph, but also applied pressure to be included in the jury to select the equipment to be exhibited.

Since Marey was the most senior member, those pressures were mainly directed at him. After vacillations and doubts, Marey wrote to the minister in charge to ask that Louis Lumière be put on the jury, even going so far as to offer his own place in view of his many other commitments 'which I have rather unwisely accepted.' To back up his proposal, he claimed that the Lumières were 'not only industrialists and businessmen of the first order, but also distinguished scientists. Inventors of the cinematograph ...'[291]

This letter, which was for the minister's eyes only, had the desired effect of inserting Lumière on the jury, but also confirmed Marey as president, almost as guarantee that the entry of an individual with related economic interests, should be under the leadership of a scientist not involved in business affairs.

Until his death (1904), relations between Marey and the Lumières seem to have remained good, even if characterised by two profoundly different points of view.

The disagreements and disputes, by turn angry, contorted, quibbling, sometimes even malicious and vulgar, only began several years after his death and so he was in no sense involved in them. The Lumières, being much younger, outlived him by almost half a century, and subsequently were careful – when the polemics exploded – to stay in the shadows, letting others act on their behalf with personal attacks, regarding one who had undoubtedly acted as a kind of spiritual father to their activities as inventors.

We have already said that the 'affaire Lumière-Marey' was typical of French internal debates. Starting from the assumption that the cinema was a French invention, this led to problems when the time came to establish which of the many Frenchmen who had distinguished themselves and contributed to its birth could be labelled as the actual 'inventor', thereby creating the ritual celebrations, commemorations, plaques in preparation for later anniversaries. Having cleared the field of various minor players, there remained two main contenders, each represented by ranks of pugnacious supporters. A pretext was found for the polemics to explode finally at the beginning of the 1920s when a committee of old Paris proposed putting up a commemorative plaque to celebrate the thirtieth anniversary of the first public film shown by the Lumière brothers. Marey's supporters were incensed, especially scientists at the Académie de Médecine, while for the Académie des Sciences the controversy remained internal now that Louis Lumière was a member of it.

Marey (left) and Georges Demeny (centre) at the Station Physiologique.

Today, reading the detailed reports of the disputes that went on for years and which led to innumerable articles, conferences, brochures, pamphlets, radio programmes as well as placards, committees and even books, has an odd effect: it tends to emphasise its sectarian and partisan spirit, as well as its malicious and spiteful nature.[292] Marey would certainly neither have tolerated nor accepted such a state of affairs. The issue of the plaque had reached almost comic levels: one plaque was to go up at Boulevard des Capucines for the Lumières and another at the Station Physiologique for Marey; in vain were attempts made for a single plaque that honoured the Lumières and also valued Marey's methods. In 1925 Lumières supporters won out, but hostilities were soon taken up again.[293]

A Marey committee was even created outside Paris, in the USA. Any pretext was good enough to start the debate up again: the celebrations for Marey's centenary at the Académie de Médecine, the fortieth anniversary of the Lumière Cinématographe, the plaque at the house where the Lumières had stayed etc. At the Paris Universal Exposition of 1932, Marey was presented as the inventor of the Chronophotographe, the Lumières as inventors of the Cinématographe. However, because at the entrance to the Palace of Cinema there were busts of Louis Lumière, Gaumont and Pathé, the Marey committee in protest placed one of the chronophotographic machines there from the Museum of the Conservatoire National des Arts et Métiers. Lumière was proposed in vain for a Nobel prize for physics, while Marey's supporters met up and one of them at his own expense published *La voix de Marey, histoire de l'invention du cinématographe*, to teach the public

to venerate the name of he who created this marvellous instrument, not for entertainment, but for the instruction of man and the progress of science.[294]

In the text, many brief references to Marey's scientific works alternate with such rhetorical statements as:

… Inside his laboratory, or looking on the sunshine to take the flight of birds, he seemed to be perpetually to be affected by the need to be useful to all … (p. 37); … the name of Janssen is to be removed from the list of the precursors of cinema… (p. 48); … faced with the weaknesses of Janssen and the mistakes of Muybridge, professor Marey would now march alone with timeless perseverance, towards the discovery of the instrument for which he was searching … (p. 57).

Even today, in his home town of Beaune, there is still an Amis de Marey association.

These disagreements made the supporters on both sides lose their perspective. Marey's allies made slightly exaggerated claims for some of his results (for example on the workings on the chronoprojector) which Marey himself probably would not have subscribed to. On the other hand, proponents of the Lumières were not too subtle either: they altered or ignored that which was not grist to their mill, minimising or depreciating Marey's work. One of them, in full flight, stated that:

> Much earlier than Marey, troglodytes of primitive times without doubt had tried to reproduce movement.[295]

A group of old students of Marey (scientists, university professors including some from overseas, directors of the Institut Marey) published a protest pamphlet that concludes thus:

> Marey's work shows clearly the connecting thread leading to the cinematographe, an invention perfectly and definitively defined, by 1897, in its fundamental aspects. The Lumières clearly did nothing but add technical improvements to this initial invention ... Marey is and will remain for informed and impartial people the creator of animated photography, of analytical and synthesised chronophotography and transparent film, in a word, of the cinematographe.[296]

In the two camps there were also those that switched sides. The film pioneer Grimoin-Sanson (inventor, among other things, of the Cinéorama which we referred to earlier in the section on the Exposition of 1900) went from supporting Lumière to becoming president of a Marey committee, and declared:

> Was there another inventor of cinema if not Marey? ... Lumière was nothing but a brilliant populariser, one of the first to have the idea that the cinematograph could become an entertainment.[297]

In the other direction, the ex-secretary of the Marey committee passed to the side of the Lumières and as a consequence saw the distribution of a facsimile of the letter (23 March 1900) already cited that Marey wrote to the Minister of Commerce asking that Lumière be added to the judges for the Exposition. Left undisturbed for many years, this letter could only have come from the Marey archives or from those of the ministry. Unless Marey himself had made a copy for the Lumières, in which case they would be the origin of the circulation of the letter.

A reference to the letter can be found in a book published in 1932, in a partisan and tendentious essay by G.M. Coissac in which he once again reiterated his view of the Lumières as sole inventors of cinema, and naturally he cites Marey's phrase.[298] In the same book, an essay by Dr Noguès (of the Institut Marey) takes the opposite view ('the first infant's cry of the cinema, its birth complete, is found in Marey's works'), but is preceded by an editor's note which seeks to distance itself and comments on the need for differing opinions to be heard. A copy of Marey's letter, as already mentioned, was circulated anonymously in 1938, the leak attributed to the deserter from the Marey committee. There were whisperings, saying the Lumières sent a cheque to Marey to thank him for the letter.[299] To our knowledge the Lumières never took a clear position on such delicate issues and it is clear that it was in their interests not to do so.[300]

So, in France, to defend beyond all measure the figures of the Lumières, a situation was created which ended up by damaging Marey and the importance of his work as creator of scientific cinematography.

Henri Langlois, founder of the Cinémathèque Française and a genial, albeit disorganised figure, of the modern cultural history of cinema, in an attempt to overcome this impasse in 1955 at the Musée d'Art Moderne de la Ville de Paris organised a large exhibition:

> À l'occasion du 125 anniversaire de E.J. Marey: 300 années de Cinématographie (1655–1955) – À l'occasion du 60 anniversaire du Cinéma: 60 ans d'Art cinématographique (1895–1955).

In his introduction to the catalogue, without taking anything away from Louis Lumière, he wrote:

> Marey, in the genealogy of cinematography, is the tree trunk that unites the roots and from which sprout all the branches that represent its development.

In 1963, Langlois organised another exhibition at his Musée du Cinéma, an 'Hommage a E.J. Marey.' In the imaginative introductory text he compared the scientist to Leonardo da Vinci, saying that he 'created the machines that made it possible for the cinema to appear'; he considered him an artist for the beauty of his chronophotographs which prefigured, thirty years in advance, the art of the first decade of the twentieth century. The show included works by Marcel Duchamp, Max Ernst and Gino Severini, whom he had invited to participate. The text of the catalogue (edited by E.-N. Bouton, Marey's nephew) claimed that:

> Marey's invention of cinema is incontestable, as otherwise one would have to claim that the members of the Académie des Sciences, from 1882 to 1890, were the collective victims of an illusion.

Even the fine exhibition dedicated to Marey between 1977 and 1978 at the Pompidou Centre in Paris, subtitled 'The Photography of Movement', suffered from this inferiority complex, clashing with the tacit self-censorship of those wishing to value properly the reputation and work of the scientist without casting aspersions on the myth of the Lumières. The important catalogue published for the occasion particularly avoids taking a position, limiting itself to providing a large and often valuable documentation.[301]

The Marey-Lumière *querelle*, created more than anything by intermediaries and for not always acceptable interests, seems to us to be now dated, and in any event not very scientific. Marey, a stranger to these diatribes, brimful of scientific honours and acknowledgements as a scientist, died in Paris in 1904; he had requested a civil funeral and that his body be cremated. As a result of the necessities of his scientific research and his technological talent, Marey undeniably built and made work a number of film cameras, he discovered and, with brief film sequences, gave scientific value to the new language of moving images, inspiring the special techniques of scientific cinema. If his results in the field of the analysis of dynamic phenomena were huge, in the field of the synthesis of movement reproduced by chronophotography alone Marey's contribution was exceptional, identifying the educational and cognitive value of the observations of phenomena at speeds different from those in real life. He was a scientist and he required the methods and equipment of cinema to develop his research interests. It was no fault that he was not interested in exploiting his equipment for the purposes of entertainment. In any event, there were others, before and after, that saw the possibility and acted on it. For Marey the importance was cinema at the service of science. It is undeniable that he gave birth to and developed this kind of cinema, and that today we have access to a new non-verbal language of enquiry, study and communication that for over a century has continued to enrich human culture.

31. Anschütz' Electrotachyscope

In looking at the history of the real birth of cinema, among the small crowd of pioneers and inventors who more or less contributed (with theories, anticipations or in practice) we will limit ourselves to referring to those who operated in the scientific sphere or who at least worked with a scientific spirit.

The first of these is the German Ottomar Anschütz (1846–1907), born in Lissa (Leszno, in the Poznan region), then part of Prussia and now part of Poland. Anschütz's father was a pioneer professional photographer. His son followed the paternal route but with some additional ambitions. When at the end of the 1870s Muybridge's first photographs reached Europe, the young Anschütz was so impressed by them that he decided to undertake similar experiments, with equipment of his own design, to emulate and possibly supersede the results already obtained. Anschütz specialised in instantaneous photography, which was not available to all amateur photographers. Using dry plates, only recently introduced on the market, he got himself noticed in photographic circles and received press coverage for his brilliant images of military manoeuvres by the Kaiser's army, but especially for his many photographs of birds in flight. During the 1883–1884 period he enjoyed a success with photographs of storks taking off and then landing on their nests. These images captured the various physiological poses of the birds with sharpness and richness of detail. The pioneer of human flight Otto Lilienthal (the first man to fly with a glider) kept the studies in mind for his first experiments, which were also based on the work of Marey.

As with Muybridge, it is clear that the limits of scientific interest for this kind of image lay in the impossibility of reconstructing the precise order of succession of the various phases of flight, in the absence of spatio-temporal terms of reference. A few years later than Muybridge and Marey, but with a typically German sense of precision, Anschütz made plans for many series of serial photographs, rigorously separated in time, the results of which, albeit obliquely, would make him a participant in the birth of scientific cinema. Financing from the Prussian ministry of culture allowed him to construct a photographic apparatus made up of a complex of twenty-four cameras electrically wired to each other. A whole series of photographs could be undertaken in 72/100th of a second, but the chronophotographic mechanism allowed for all the variations of intervals up to ten seconds (still for the complete series of twenty-four images). The signal for the beginning of the operation could be given by the passage of the object of the photographs or manually with a clockwork mechanism or a metronome.

This is evidently exactly the same method as used by Muybridge. Even the dates confirm it. Anschütz' first series were taken in autumn 1885, not only many years after Muybridge took his photographs at Palo Alto, but also after he had already taken thousands of photographs at the University of Pennsylvania.[302] Why is it worth referring to Anschütz at all then? Mainly for the technical quality of his photographs, which were praised by Marey.[303] But not only for this reason. Anschütz is perhaps the first case of the appropriation of the nascent scientific cinema by the military. On his own he had taken some serial photographs of sporting movements and animals. However, in 1886 his first customer was the ministry of war, which asked him to transport his equipment to the Equestrian Military Institute at Hanover to take one hundred series of photographs of horses in regular and irregular motion for the purposes of study and training. Also for military purposes, he photographed a bullet shot out of a barrel.[304]

There are few details left of how Anschütz attained his serial photography, so few in fact that even Marey, while speaking positively of the results, bemoaned the fact that the technical details had not been made available, as was the norm in scientific circles. This was not due to simple curiosity, since Marey used very different methods and, as we have seen, much more advanced ones at that. Rather, it was for the principle that anyone, if they so wished, should be able to repeat the experiment.

It appears that the twenty-four cameras were gathered into a single box or a type of cart.[305] The negatives were very small – the figure of a horse was about 20–25mm. The quality must have been excellent, however, as they could be enlarged up to thirty times in size. In addition, Anschütz had set himself the problem (one practically ignored by Muybridge) of the parallax: the shift, in other words, in perspective between the twenty-four cameras. This, as we know, was one of the reasons why Marey did not use this type of shooting. To try to get around this, at least to a significant degree, Anschütz used high luminosity Voigtländer lenses with a long focal length to place up to thirty metres between the cameras and the subject being photographed.

Anschütz' Electrotachyscope, 1889.

In his own time, which is to say independently of his own military commitments, Anschütz took many impressive photographs of various animals and humans in motion, usually in sports-related activities. He published these himself and sold them with such success that he decided to turn them into Zoetrope strips. He even built his own model, called the Schnellseher, in which the cylinder could rotate on both its vertical and horizontal axis. He also built a gigantic Zoetrope (the strip with the series of enlargements was two metres long), allowing a number of people to watch the figures in motion at the same time.

In March 1887 he first presented to the Ministry of Culture in Berlin a new machine, which would later be called the Electro-Tachyscope, dozens of models of which would subsequently be manufactured by the Siemens and Halske Company.[306]

It was a machine that, in its various versions, could either be used by an individual like a kind of viewer, or even with a token (thus anticipating the technique of Edison's Kinetoscope), or for projection on a screen.

There were still twenty-four images, with 10 x 10 cm slides rotating on a large disc. Passing in front of frosted glass (which constituted a small screen), each photograph was illuminated by a powerful spark made by a Geissler tube lasting approximately 1/30th of a second, giving the viewer the illusion of movement.

With reference to Muybridge's Zoöpraxiscope, it is interesting to note that, right from the start, Anschütz made use of photographic enlargements and not coloured drawings derived from photographs. Another link between them is that both were present with their machines at the Colombian Exhibition in Chicago of 1893, where it appears that Anschütz had a great success with a small scene showing an elephant 'dance.'[307]

However, a version of the Electro-Tachyscope had already been presented at the Universal Exposition of Paris in 1889. In fact, Marey had wanted to show it to Edison when he visited Paris.

Hendricks' detailed and thorough historical research on the origins of the cinematograph in the USA has confirmed that, from 1887, Anschütz machines had been described in technical journals, and in 1889 (the year of the Paris Exposition) offered for sale by an American company. It is no surprise, therefore, that Edison, having returned from his European trip, used for his Kinetoscope some of the technical innovations of Anschütz' machines, in addition to those inspired by Marey's Chronophotographe. Hendricks speculates that in Edison's laboratories at West Orange, where W.K.L. Dickson worked, there was by the end of 1889 one of Anschütz' Tachyscopes or a reconstruction of the same type of machine. One should remember however that the American had shown with his book *The Edison Motion Picture Myth*, among its many other demystifications, the impossibility of the story of how Edison, on his return from Europe, showed images with sound using a Kinetoscope prototype with a projected image of Dickson taking his hat off and making a greeting while an electrically synchronised Phonograph reproduced words of welcome.[308] Hendricks states that the only even vaguely possible way that something similar could have occurred, albeit a few months later, would have required the use of Anschütz' Tachyscope (or a similar type of machine).

However, the greater or lesser importance that the machine of the German photographer may have had in the development of the Edison laboratories' industrial and commercial activities has little relevance to our subject. As we have seen, Anschütz had only a limited interest in science, except for his military contracts. What is more, Anschütz and his supporters had been disturbed by Muybridge's presentation in Berlin in 1891. There were debates in the press and Anschütz wrote bitterly of how the same artists that had dismissed his serial images in 1886 were now all ordering copies of Muybridge's plates.[309] Being a good craftsman and businessman, Anschütz followed the growing wave of interest for animated photography and at the end of November 1894 in Berlin he gave a series of brief public screenings for payment on a screen that was 6 x 8 metres, using two Tachyscopes which were used alternately so as to extend the brief duration of each rotating disc.[310]

32. At the hospital of Salpêtrière

Another of the principals in the birth of scientific cinema was the Frenchman Albert Londe, in some senses a true disciple of Marey, although he worked and experimented by himself. In fact Londe worked in the photographic laboratory of the hospital of Salpêtrière at the same time that Dr Charcot, specialist in nervous illnesses, worked there. In 1883 Londe built a machine with nine lenses placed in the shape of a crown with electromagnetic shutters activated by the impulses of a contact metronome. The nine small images (3 x 3 centimetres) were recorded on a single plate measuring 13 x 18 centimetres. In his role as the hospital's scientific photographer he made use of the equipment to record serial images of the phases of hysteria and other nervous ailments. By 1892 Londe had perfected this technique with a machine with twelve lenses placed in rows of three, recording the images on

Albert Londe operating twelve-lens camera at Salpêtrière, with Marey seated on the right, 1892.

a single 24 x 30 centimetre plate. He was thus able to obtain usable 7 x 7 centimetre stills for a series of projectors with one or two lanterns, to study clinical cases or for purposes of teaching. The twelve images could be taken in an overall minimum time of 1/10th of a second.[311] In the meantime, passionately interested in the problem of analysing movements, Londe had also made various series showing such subjects as acrobats, women dancers and men at work.

The bulk of his results remained fundamentally tied to series photography for medical purposes, but his interests in the field were wider.

An expert technical photographer, he published various specialist works on developing, instantaneous photography, photography applied to medicine, and a more general work, *La photographie moderne*, which went through more than one edition. Londe became a supporter and populariser of the ideas and theoretical principles already established by Marey: in particular the fact that, for scientific purposes, projection was useful as a method of confirmation, while what was important for research was chronophotographic analysis. He was insistent, however, on the importance of slow motion and speeded up images so as to study phenomena that would otherwise be invisible. He also published photographic books and articles on anatomy and the artistic physiology of movement as well as an *Album de photochronographies à l'usage des artistes* (Paris, 1903).

In 1896 he wrote an article on the popular success of the cinematograph, which was obtained with effective marketing undertaken by capitalists interested in a successful financial operation. In detail, he pointed out how its results had already been achieved in scientific laboratories, and which large commercial interests were and would be behind the processes of synthesis of animated photography, the cost of which, he stated, could not be borne either by private researchers or by the state laboratories, 'not being able to pledge themselves to such an expensive road which would yield very little real progress.' Only 'American style' capitalistic enterprises such as Edison's or those of industrialists like the Lumières would be able to undertake it. The latter had the merit of having started early, but already there was a sense of the competition between the many companies which were set up to do business with the cinematograph.[312]

As we can see, Albert Londe was a good prophet even if he was motivated to a degree by resentment, or, more properly, frustration with regards to the two industrialist brothers from Lyons. It appears in fact that Londe took part in some meetings in June 1895 at the Société Française de Photographie, which we have already mentioned and during which the Lumières projected their films. According to Sadoul, at the same meeting Londe was supposed to present a prototype projector, probably for scientific use, limited to twelve photographs at a time, but after the great success of the presentation of the Cinematographe, Londe decided not to present his machine.[313] In the closing arguments of the meeting, Jules Janssen – who was presiding – also marked Londe's work as among the most significant, although he was referring to his serial photography anatomic studies, and praised their high scientific value: 'serious studies, which can only be fully appreciated by physiologists and doctors.'

33. 'Je vous aime'

The third figure entering the field in this chapter is another Frenchman, another close collaborator of Marey, and one who was rather more than a mere second lead. He was an emblematic and contradictory figure who summed up well the difficult relationship between the birth of scientific cinema and entertainment cinema, lived in a critical and self-critical key.

Georges Demeny (1850–1917) was born in Douai, in the coal-mining region of Northern France, and moved to Paris in the mid 1870s.[314] He began and then interrupted his university studies to launch himself enthusiastically in a pioneering activity: the establishment of a modern school of physical education teaching, a field which at that time was non-existent. He created a circle of rational gymnastics, and it was due to these professional interests of a scientific-technical nature that he was drawn to Marey. Taking part in his classes he soon got himself noticed and by 1881 Demeny was offered the position of technical assistant to the great scientist. The Station Physiologique at Parc des Princes was about to be set up and Marey needed an enthusiastic assistant who would be interested in experimentation.

Demeny quickly became Marey's principal assistant in setting up the experimental plant in the new laboratory. In the second half of the 1880s he would present, on his own and as Marey's collaborator, numerous physiological works on human locomotion to the Académie des Sciences. In 1890 and 1891 he would publish in the journal *La Nature* a series of articles, on the same theme, illustrating them with chronophotographs obtained 'using the method and equipment of Professor Marey.' From the heavy long-term correspondence between the scientist (whom one will recall passed many months of the year in Naples) and his assistant, it is clear that Demeny set up and undertook at the Station Physiologique series of experiments that they had discussed and agreed upon, even in Marey's absence. Marey, for his part, continued directly with other projects and experiments, creating and building prototypes for new machines and equipment.

Within both of their research areas, Marey and Demeny were interested in using the Chronophotographe to record the human face while speaking and shouting. In his book *Le mouvement*, Marey recalled the series of ugly expressions and strangely contorted aspects of the face of a guard at the Station Physiologique filmed while he was clearing his throat; however, in watching him speak, Marey added, the man had nothing out of the ordinary in his expression.[315] It was one of the many surprising and curious effects of analysing, image by image, a movement that normally we see in fusion.

Professor Marichelle, of the deaf mute institute, having read Marey's article on the importance of chronophotography in physiology, including the study of the expression of human faces, saw the possibility of using this method with deaf mutes. He discussed this with the scientist, who passed him on to his assistant. Subsequently Demeny developed a line of enquiry, using the Chronophotographe to record the visual expressions of a person speaking certain words, in an attempt to help deaf mute students learn how to speak on the basis of observing and imitating lip movements. Once again we find scientific requirements, and in this case didactic ones too, at the basis of a series of technical developments that will eventually bring about entertainment cinema. Demeny in fact *had* to film close-ups. There were, it is true, some sporadic precedents by Muybridge, with his photographs showing the details of hands. But here we see the true antecedent of the classic cinematic close-up of a human face, to put into relief all its expressive and mimetic detail. At the end of the 1880s however there were still many hurdles ahead. To get a good reproduction of the mouth in motion, Demeny needed to shoot at least eighteen frames a second. One must remember how insensitive emulsions were then and the difficulties there were in lighting the reddish-yellow tones of the skin evenly. After many setbacks some satisfactory shots were achieved. The face, which in close-up said the words 'je vous aime', was strongly lit with a mirror focused on the light of the sun. Even though Demeny, in describing the episode, uses the third person, he was the subject who stood in front of the Marey's Chronophotographe and pronounced the romantic phrase.

> The position of the subject constituted a real martyrdom and one could not ask him, given the circumstances, to exhibit an alternative expression; in reality the result was a grimace.[316]

The resultant eighteen images showed an altered face, which was partly due to the rays of the sun obliging Demeny to keep his eyes almost shut.

When showing these to deaf mutes, however, the desired result was not forthcoming: that is to say, recognition of the phrase simply by watching the various images. What was valued for all other physiological research, where the objective was a frame-by-frame analysis of movement, in this case did not work. It was

Georges Demeny says 'Je Vous Aime', 1891.

essential to reproduce the synthesis of movement itself, perhaps slowing it down, but preserving its dynamic fluidity.

Demeny continued to work on the problem and achieved some good results at the beginning of 1891. In that year he put the finishing touches to a machine he would call the Phonoscope. It was based on the classic model of Plateau's Phenakistiscope, taking some technical and structural elements from Anschütz' Tachyscope and from Muybridge's Zoöpraxiscope. It was made up of two discs rotating on the same axis, but at very different speeds. On one disc were the images, while the other, fitted with one or more slits, functioned as a shutter. Paper discs were made for direct viewing, and glass discs for direct viewing or projection. The following year Demeny patented (3 March 1892) a projection Phonoscope and exhibited it at International Exposition of Photography in Paris. In July 1891, however, Marey had given a presentation to the Académie des Sciences on the Phonoscope, illustrating it, not without some hesitation, with the possible results for the education of deaf mutes.

At this point the situation was thus: to photograph his images, Demeny used Marey's film Chronophotographe, clearly with his consent. To prepare the discs for the Phonoscope required a massive amount of patience, as Demeny would later describe himself. It involved putting the negatives on the disc, ensuring that every single photograph was perfectly placed, and then contact printing on large emulsioned glass discs (with a diameter of fifty centimetres) the positive images: all this to reproduce a cyclical movement of not more than two or three seconds. In attempting to simplify these laborious and delicate operations, but not to have to use Marey's machine to make the negatives, Demeny constructed a 'reversible' Phonoscope, for shooting and projecting. On a 25–centimetre disc he could take, through rotation, a series of negative images. Contact printing a positive disc, one could view it in the same machine.

In this period, while still working as an assistant with Marey at the Station Physiologique, Demeny found himself strongly attracted by new opportunities. He was convinced that his Phonoscope could be a big commercial success, and not just as an instrument to help deaf mutes learn how to speak. That had been the scientific part of the research, the pretext and the occasion to refine the instrument. For demonstration purposes, after 'je vous aime' he filmed and recorded (still with himself as the subject) the phrase 'vive la France.' Demeny believed that the Phonoscope, mass produced and therefore made available at a low price, could become present in many households as a way to keep an eternal record of the dearly departed. He thought along the lines of a 'living portrait', a technological and positivistic version of the ancestral traditions of the cult of the dead. These moving portraits, accompanied and synchronised with the voice recorded on a Phonograph, would replace family photograph albums which were then becoming popular, the first tangible proof of the socio-cultural revolution being brought about by the invention of photography. All classes, even the most modest, should and could permit themselves this luxury, once reserved only for a few noblemen and some rich members of the middle classes, to have portraits made of themselves and their beloved at the most solemn moments of their lives: birth, weddings, military service, great trips that might occur, new homes, until old age and death.

> These people seem happy to be able, for an instant, to look again at the semblance of a loved one now gone! In the future immobile photographs, fixed in their frame, will be replaced by an animated portrait to which one may, with the turn of a handle, give life. It will conserve the expression on a face as the voice is conserved on the phonograph. It will be possible to unite this with the phonoscope to complete the illusion ... This application will greatly enrich the activities of amateur professional photographers. There is a great interest in enriching with real and varied expressions those portraits, which too often mummify, and so leave behind us some documentation of our existence, which can be brought back to life, like real and actual apparitions!

So wrote Demeny in the journal *La Nature* of 16 April 1892.

Some months earlier (December 1891), after he had presented the Phonoscope to the Conservatoire National des Arts et Métiers during a conference on the photography of movement, he had got busy putting together funds and finding business partners to create the Société Française du Phonoscope.[317] Its aim was to produce and sell his machine industrially, for both domestic single viewers and for projection. To set up the company, Demeny created his own laboratory in an industrial suburb of Paris, where he made numerous experiments, built prototypes, but most of all gave practical demonstrations of the results that could be obtained with the Phonoscope, especially to financiers (French and foreign) interested in his initiative. By doing this however he was putting himself in position that went against his obligations to the Collège de France, which did not allow such external activities. Demeny wanted to set himself up in business, but he could not ignore the fact that he had done all his early scientific research for Marey's laboratory. He made a number of attempts to be independent of Marey's Chronophotographe. In 1892 he even tried making (following on from, or perhaps ignoring, the failure of the Edison-Dickson experiments) a cylindrical optical phonograph.

Despites its limitations, and some desultory defects in its functionality, Marey's machine remained the better one and Demeny needed it to make the negatives for his Phonoscope. This created a very delicate situation for him. As far as can be gathered from what is known, Marey tried to give his collaborator the maximum amount of freedom: he allowed him to use his equipment at the Station Physiologique, he presented the Phonoscope at the Académie to great acclaim, and complimented him for the results he presented at the 1892 photographic exposition. He probably pretended not to know about the business activities being undertaken by his technician and which would otherwise have meant the end of his work at the Station Physiologique. Perhaps Marey did not want to lose a valuable collaborator. In 1892 they collaborated on a series of plates which would be published the following year under the title *Études de Physiologie artistique, faites au moyen de la chronophotographie*. In July of the same year, Marey believed that Demeny had managed to solve the problem of chronophotographic projection, and he wrote him, 'If you have succeeded, it is not worth my looking as well.'[318]

However, at the start of 1893 Demeny was asked by his associates at the Société Française du Phonoscope (officially created in December 1892) to negotiate with Marey for the use of his film Chronophotographe to produce images for use with Phonoscope discs commercially. If they had simply asked to buy some of his machines he would probably have agreed, since he had already done this for one of his technicians to offset some of the expenses incurred in creating his proto-types. Demeny's company, however, offered to make Marey a partner in the deal. Demeny's approach was probably based on the naïve hope that if he were able to get his mentor involved in the deal, he would then be able to stay on at the laboratory and get Marey's help in solving the still quite considerable problems that stood in the way of making the Phonoscope commercially viable.

Predictably, Marey walked away from the deal and in fact got so suspicious about some of the recent interest in his machines that, contrary to his usual practice of making all his discoveries freely available to the public, he took out patents on his most recent refinements to the film Chronophotographe. This took place in June 1893, before the breakdown of the negotiations with Société du Phonoscope. Demeny and the company therefore decided to look overseas for the series images they need. Clearly from that point onwards the personal relationship between Marey and Demeny was destined to deteriorate. In that year, though, Marey was still prepared to praise the efforts of his assistant in the field of chronophotographic projection in his book *Le mouvement*. A few months later, though (February 1894), he had to ask Demeny to allow someone else to take on his position of assistant, on account of his commercial commitments. Marey however did write and say that he would still be able to obtain a substantial municipal grant (equivalent to double the salary Demeny received at the Collège de France) so that, if he wished, he could continue his research.

Marey once again showed that he was not motivated by any animosity or malice, even in the face of situations that could clearly be seen as being provocative: such as the fact that Demeny in October 1893 patented a chronophotographic machine that was in practice the same as Marey's but with a modification (to the eccentric bobbin for taking up the film) which helped in keeping the filmed images equidistant. Demeny himself admitted that he had to find something to patent as his own machine, since he had not had any success with any of the other avenues he had explored, and he did not want to have to continue to use Marey's machine since most of its features were in the public domain.

34. Between cinema and gymnastics

Demeny was already in the grip of the vortex of commercial-industrial-financial machinery that he himself had set in motion. He refused Marey's requests and suggestions, practically breaking off all contact, considering himself fired. Having said that, he never criticised Marey while he was still alive. Afterwards, even when discussing his replacement as chief assistant at the Collège de France, he did this in a self-deprecatory way since, as he said, in attempting to achieve success in the business world, which he then found uncongenial, he had lost his right to a pension. Demeny never sought to give greater weight to his role in the invention of Marey's various chronophotographic models. Marey remained his great mentor, even if Demeny did use parts of their considerable correspondence for his own benefit.

The many letters that Marey wrote to Demeny, recently re-discovered, allow us to be more precise in establishing their respective roles.[319] A very clear picture emerges, in which Marey treats his collaborator and employee with great fairness and friendship. He got him his job at the Collège de France even though he did not have all the qualifications required; he inspired him on several occasions to follow the lines of research or experimentation he indicated; he did not just consider him as someone to fulfil his orders but showed great interest in his ideas, to which he would often offer his authoritative support. With regards to the machines, especially the various Chronophotographe models, it appears to be confirmed that Marey modified and built following his own lead, sometimes using Neapolitan workers or technicians or sometimes using Otto Lund of the Station Physiologique. He discussed problems and solutions with Demeny by letter, sometimes even making sketches in them.

As in the traditional relationship between academic and technician, especially when the teacher was one of Marey's calibre, Demeny had his own space and autonomy, but not within the sphere of the work space of a principal who, even if he made mistakes, took all the responsibility for his choices. Demeny did not, then, give Marey significant input into the creation or perfecting of the Chronophotographe machines. Rather, he was a valued undertaker of research and experiments, working side by side and under the leadership of the master.

What he undertook in his own sphere and of his own initiative, outside of the Parc des Princes laboratory, is clear enough: the success of the Phonoscope (in the papers and with specialised audiences) made Demeny believe that the outlook for 'living portraits' or the possibility of projecting animated scenes, made it worth leaving a secure job as a research assistant and technical collaborator of a famous scientist at an established national institution to try his luck as an entrepreneur. There were things in his favour: *L'Illustration*, the popular magazine, had published

Georges Demeny.

on its front cover the photographs of him saying 'je vous aime.' The newspaper *Le Radical* on 7 June 1892 wrote on the subject of the Phonoscope:

> One of these days industry will get hold of this brilliant invention, and on that day current photography will be overtaken by one hundred lengths – the animated portrait is certainly the photography of tomorrow.

During this period Demeny photographed a number of variety artists and comics (acrobats, magicians, sneezing men, maids dropping crockery etc), but the resulting plates were distributed through magazines and were used as promotional tools in his attempts to secure funding to launch the Phonoscope on the mass market.[320] It was at this time that through Demeny's private laboratory at Levallois-Perret passed not only possible financial backers but also a number of people from the same field who were developing similar machines, such as the Lumière brothers and Léon Gaumont. In fact it was the latter who, eventually, went into business with Demeny to exploit his patents. In October 1894 the Lumière brothers had decided against joining Demeny as partners in the Société du Phonoscope. They themselves were industrialists and were in a position to promote the commercial launch of an initiative with wide margins of risk without fear of going under from the effort and able to resist the inevitable competition from their competitors.

This was not the case for Demeny. The story of his successes and failures, his brilliant technical discoveries and the financial messes in which he was embroiled has already been detailed in traditional histories of entertainment cinema. It is said that Edison was impressed and influenced by the close-ups used by Demeny in his first Phonoscope pictures. Swiftly following the success of the Lumière Cinématographe, Gaumont launched the Bioscope (based on equipment patented by Demeny) in important Parisian venues such as the Châtelet and Olympia theatres, and the zoological gardens.

In this field, however, Demeny remained a failure. Attracted by the chimera of the success of the living portrait on disc, he spent great effort into perfecting Marey's Chronophotographe in an original way (he being the main contributor for the cinematographic technique of the eccentric cam). He continued to see it predominantly as a machine for filming, since he was mainly concerned with using the Phonoscope as an instrument for viewing or projection. Initially he did not realise that his modified Chronophotographe could work as a projector in a satisfactory manner, while the Phonoscope (like Edison's Kinetoscope) had the defect – as pointed out by Marey – of being based on the continuous movement of images (not intermittent), and which therefore suffered from poor illumination. Too late did he recognise from the Lumières the possibilities of a new type of exhibition based on animated images, even though he had had opportunities to note in his scientific work (in particular his experience with deaf mutes) that, while series of analytical images of a movement were appreciated by the few, the synthesising reconstruction of a movement was embraced with interest and surprise by all.

In November 1897, looking at the worldwide distribution of the cinema, he wrote:

> Since filmmakers have only commercial goals, they think it easier to set scenes up in front of the cameras, rather than to seek them out in nature. Apart from the inevitable discredit brought on this new art by compositions of the kind, one cannot deny that these scene are grotesque and that the movements appear false

and hasty…The simplest natural events, like two children playing unobserved or housewives that chat on their doorsteps, would be of far greater interest …[321]

Whereas Georges Méliès opened the door to fantasy and the fantastic for this new kind of entertainment, Georges Demeny anticipated the position of absolute realism which seems to us to have been conditioned by the many years in which he collaborated with scientists like Marey.

His failure as a businessman meant that over twenty years later he was forced, with some bitterness, to return to his first interest: physical education. In this field, however, he went on to have many successes. Applying his studies of movement and the observations he made through chronophotographic analysis, he wrote numerous manuals on physical education for young men and women, for the military, as well as studies of physiology applied to the exercise of certain professions, such as violinists. In these fields he was thus able to gauge the real importance of analytic chronophotographic documentation, which allowed him to establish experimental data, even in cases where athletes, for example, refused to recognise themselves in photographs which documented discrepancies between traditional theoretical ideas about sport gymnastics and the reality of people's behaviour.

At a conference that he held in 1909 on the 'Origins of the Cinematograph' at the Ligue Française de l'Enseignement, Demeny summed up his attitude as a pioneer disappointed by cinema, an embittered scientific technician, a man tested by destiny who none the less had managed not to be overcome and in fact in the end had been able to find a satisfying place for himself:

> The cinematographe draws its origins from the machines that we used, Marey and I, at the Station Physiologique to study the movements of man and animals, machines known to everyone. It represents a sad period in my life, an unhappy incursion into commerce and industry, two untrustworthy fields, where those who deal in science should not venture, until the day society gives inventors a fair recompense or acknowledgement, equivalent to the usefulness that it derives from their work.[322]

35. The Industrial Revolution and the study of movement

In the preceding chapters we have seen *how* cinema was essentially created to serve as an instrument for scientific research and documentation. Before looking at its subsequent developments, we must examine *why* this occurred in its particular socio-historical context.

Too much has already been published on the causality of so many scientific and technological discoveries and on the happy coincidences that allowed observations that would then gave rise to progresses in human understanding. Without wishing, as a reaction, to fall into a mechanistic determinism, the birth of scientific cinema certainly offers a useful opportunity to evaluate and reconstruct the diverse influences through which a specific historical framework allowed for the flowering and development of a new language, which would later be described as having opened up the era of the 'civilisation of the image.'

The beginning of the nineteenth century is generally considered, from the point of view of social developments, by the establishment of the Industrial Revolution: a revolution in the full sense of the word, even if this phenomenon did not have a direct bearing on the great event that instead defined the end of the preceding century: the French revolution.[323] The nineteenth century is often defined as the age of the steam engine, but towards the end of it, one must increasingly define it as the century of electricity.

Between these two broad definitions, both of which can be seen to be accurate, comes the massive technological and scientific progress that occurred in the space of twenty years, despite wars and social upheavals. Now with historical hindsight, it is clear that the birth and impetuous development of modern industry, which took place in that century, did not grow from the manufacturing and artisanal activities that preceded it.[324]

The origins of the Industrial Revolution derive from the earliest experiments of the first modern scientists that emerged from the 'century of light' and which collected themselves in academies and scientific societies. Techniques could no longer be based on skill, developed down the centuries, in corporations and artisanal shops; it was about to turn into technology, that is to say, industrial science. For the traditional artisan and even for the most able manufacturer one might use the ancient Italian proverb 'practice is worth more than grammar.' The new technician of the nineteenth century (whether a scientist or inventor, industrialist or machinist) had to know his grammar, which is to say mathematical analysis and calculation, laws of physics and chemistry, fields which were just about to differentiate themselves (it is not by coincidence that it was in this century that we also see the birth of such new professions as the engineer). A direct link was forged between the new science and new technique, in effect the definitive elevation of the scientific method and the end of the deliberately misleading way of seeing the laboratory or rooms for scientific study as a kind of magician's den.

If the nineteenth century technology from which great industry was born is a direct descendant of science and its brilliant discoveries and applications, the dialectical nature of things meant that successive developments in scientific research would be ever more conditioned by the availability of adequate technology. It would be required for laboratory experiments, for the equipment itself (which essentially means the machinery) that had become part of scientific laboratories. This would be made even more necessary by the new objectives of scientific research which now pointed to avenues of research which had hitherto been unthinkable or at least impossible: for our purposes, this means the analysis and study of movement. The limitations of our sensory perceptions had been for thousands of years an impossible hurdle. Galileo had to fight simply over the credibility of those visual enlargements offered by lenses. However, now that the steam horse seemed to be able to multiply the work capacity of man endlessly, now that voltaic batteries offered the promise of a new kind of energy for the future, the scientist was left in no doubt as to the possibility, in fact the necessity, of extending the restricted limits of our senses. Thus began a systematic investigation which not only explored the celestial bodies with the newly available telescopes, but also analysed the infinitely small by using microscopes, up to then a practically invisible world and ground for dispute over the issue of spontaneous generation. The vacuum pump and the first instruments based on static electricity gave great impetus to the new science of chemistry, which itself helped foster new industrial developments. In the case of the study of movement, however, it presented characteristics and differences which made it all the more difficult to find a solution to its main issue: finding the right methods and techniques for undertaking the research.

As we have seen in the chapter on the prehistory of scientific cinema, the initial link in the chain of research and investigations that focused on movement in the first decades of the nineteenth century, was made up of a series of observations, initially casual or fragmentary, and then systematic, relating to our particular (and defective) sensorial perception of rapid dynamic phenomena. In the titles and texts of the scientific communications of Roget, Faraday, Plateau, the expression 'optical illusions' recurs and it is from this term of reference that the new research on the physical, rather than physiological, characteristics of ocular vision takes off. It should be recalled that Plateau, the inventor of the first scientific apparatus for breaking down and re-composing the phases of movement, took his degree with a dissertation on visual perception. A typical example of the traditional scientist, he did not hesitate, though in positive danger of losing his own sight, to make experimental studies of the behaviour and the limits of the retina's sensitivity with regard to solar light. He was able to establish important points of stability regarding the phenomenon of the persistence of images on the retina, accurately measuring the duration of this physiological process in relation to the duration of the image-stimulus presented to the eye for a very short period of time.

It cannot be by chance that at the same time, and independently from each other (at least at the beginning), scientists of different countries, differently educated and with different angles of activity, conducted the same research and arrived at the same type of results with similar experimental equipment (Faraday's wheel, Plateau's Phenakistiscope, Stampfer's Stroboscope).

The factual elements at the base of their research are not new; but in the first decades of the nineteenth century there was also the burgeoning industrialisation based on applications of steam and the beginning of railways: elements that profoundly transformed social and economic life in conjunction with the exploitation of the movement of machines.

This movement of wheels and gears, pistons and connecting rods, became the characterising element of the *culture* of the period, meaning by culture not the restricted, overarching and traditionally humanistic acceptance of the term, but the broader and all-encompassing form of expression of human thought that creates the life of a society through its inventions, researches, applications, together with the other canonical forms of philosophy, history, and fine arts.

It is curious to note the considerable discordance between the scientific aims that research in the field of the study of movement poses right from its beginnings, and the results that can be realised in practice. Beyond experiments on the limits and defects of the visual perception of moving images, we see that researchers like Faraday (who was absorbed in his fundamental work on electricity and therefore dealt only marginally with these problems) stopped at the phenomenological confirmation of particular visual effects relative to the forms and figures in movement. Others, specifically motivated in investigating the subject more deeply (such as Plateau and Stampfer), identified rather the principles of stroboscopic theory, which would allow the slowing (in observation) of a movement that was too rapid to be studied and even the stopping to a single phase of a periodic movement. They succeeded too, within the limitations of simple geometric figures, but remained distant from any possibility of practical scientific-industrial application. The fact is that by the mid-1820s – as is known – photography had not yet been invented and therefore those optical techniques based on drawings or geometric forms developed by scientists attempting to modify the relationship between the real time of execution of a simple movement and its visual perception, did not exist.

It was possible, however, indeed it was the aspect that gave resonance and fame to the research of Plateau and Stampfer, to achieve the artificial synthesis of a movement created by a series of static images, which arbitrarily or schematically fixed individual phases of an object or person in movement.

Going to lengths of absurdity, though not excessively so, it could be said that in the march towards the analysis of dynamic phenomena that increasingly involved the interest of the researchers, man had first to pass through a theoretical stage that consisted of inventing and reconstructing movements to show himself that the possibility of analysis existed, given that a movement can be created by starting from phases of still images.

In reality, as we have already seen, Plateau had very clear ideas on the importance of the method he had created and a few decades later the physiologist Marey acknowledged this in his introduction to *La méthode graphique*, referring to the 'fine experiments carried out by Plateau on the *stroboscope*.'

When an object animated by very rapid periodic movements offers our eyes only confused images, this object can be given an appearance of immobility, by making it visible only during the same instants of its periodic movement. In other situations, its apparent movement can be made much slower. If there is vibration in a tuning fork that one wishes to make one hundred or one thousand times slower, the experiment is set up in such a way that the shaft of the tuning fork is visible only for a few instants, each separated from the other by intervals, each of which being equal to a vibration plus one hundredth or one thousandth of a vibration. This fine method was considerably developed and found numerous applications in Germany. It not only serves to correct the imperfection of our eyes, in which the persistence of the images produces confusion, but it can remedy the defects of certain apparatus, the inertia of the needle of the galvanometer, for example, or the needles in pressure indicators.[325]

Marey sensed and underlined the importance of Plateau's method, not only for its specific applications, making it possible to exceed the limits and defects of our senses, but also because the Stroboscope lent itself as an instrument for investigation and documentation that was superior even to that of other methods of recording and measurement, even though these might be based on more modern principles and techniques.

Despite the anticipatory enthusiasm of Marey, the scientific and technological uses of the stroboscopic method up to the halfway point of the nineteenth century remained limited, while the various types of optical toys enjoyed great popular success. These derived directly from those principles and aimed, rather than at the analysis of movement, at its apparent reproduction.

As far as these optical toys are concerned, however, it is of interest to note how these served a recriprocal scientific function. In fact, it is undeniable that Muybridge took inspiration from Plateau's Phenakistiscope, through all the technical developments and improvements that succeeded each other, in order to increase sales when he realised his projection Zoöpraxiscope. As far as Marey is concerned, it is well known that he had theorised and practised the use of the stroboscopic equipment, both in the disk and the drum (Zoetrope) forms, not so much to reconstruct the movements he was studying, but rather to analyse them dynamically in slow motion. D.B. Thomas of the Science Museum in London goes even further in maintaining the importance of optical toys in the historical phase of preparation for the birth of cinema, because he states that 'many of the pioneers obtained information on the design of shutters and the rate of taking and projection images from examining the action of optical toys.'[326]

The evolution of research and the great experimental results obtained by Marey offer further triggers and references in the relationship between technological or industrial research and development. When, towards the end of the 1860s, he finally abandoned medicine and clinical research to devote himself to his preferred studies of animal and human physiology, the process of the invention of photography (1826 is the commonly accepted date, if one places Niépce's work first) had already undergone some technical development that made it largely practicable, but it was still far from being considered as a possible research method in the analysis of movement, given the long exposure times required. The very idea of instant photography had yet to be born.

We have seen how a scientist like Janssen, an enthusiastic supporter of the scientific use of photography, expressed trust in the future progress of the same science that it would improve the basic technical conditions that would make this means of studying movement possible.

It is within the logic of the modern development of technologies that the requirements of research stimulate the identification and perfecting of new methods, whose applications then take autonomous pathways that will lead to important results in other sectors, which may well not be scientific at all. This, *inter alia*, is the very obvious case of cinema, born, as it was, as a research tool.

Before this happened, Marey had clearly focused on the fact that the two basic obstacles to be overcome in order to progress in the study of the physiological processes of movement, were the limits and imprecision of our senses and the inadequacy of the words to describe, document and explain those phenomena. The graphic method and the pneumatic techniques seemed to him to be the best way to confront the difficult analyses of the dynamics of the horse, the first attempts at studying the movement of man, even to attempt to understand the laws of the flight of birds. Marey's book *La méthode graphique* was a brilliant treatise which showed, through an abundance of experimental results, that the route he chose was not only right, but was then the most modern and adequate means to overcome our sensory defects and the difficulties of representing the data and the discoveries made. Marey had considered electricity as a possible research method, but he had discarded it. Photography seemed to him a concrete revelation, a new way forward, after seeing the results obtained by Muybridge. We know all that happened afterwards: how he mastered that technique, developing the new method of chronophotography, laying down the basis of the new language of images. But what had happened earlier, so that photography became competitive, indeed innovative and qualitatively superior for the research and scientific language that Marey pursued? Paraphrasing from Potonniée, a historian of both the origins of cinema and photography, we can synthesise in three phases the progress of the first forty years of photographic technique: the Daguerreotypes required exposures lasting minutes; with slides of wet collodion it was possible to go below a second, down to 1/10th of a second; with the dry slides the unexplored horizons of the 'instantaneous' opened up at 1/100th of a second.[327]

Obviously these phases have to be considered as mere terms of reference and comparison, because it is evident that in particular conditions and with good lenses it was possible to achieve much faster times, as shown by the work of Muybridge with various types of negative plate.

However, in addition to these summary indications, there is a need to highlight how the great technological progress made by passing from wet plates to dry ones, was not the result of industrial research by the burgeoning production and commercial companies that were springing up in various countries, but was rather the work of one scientist, Dr Richard Leach Maddox. The story of how the first dry plate was created by the Englishman Maddox is amusing. In 1871 (ten years before the marketing on a large scale of the new type of dry and faster emulsions) he wrote a letter to the *British Journal of Photography* to announce and describe his gelatine emulsion, which could be spread and left to dry on the slides without losing sensitivity. He added, however, that his profession as a physician did not leave him enough time to perfect the procedure and he therefore invited anyone interested to continue with the experiments.

Maddox subsequently made it known that he had made the effort of finding a new type of emulsion, not because wet collodion did not suit him, or to seek an easier availability of plates or greater sensitivity, but simply because in the small, warm room with glass walls where he photographed histological preparations under the microscope, he found the smell of the ether he had to use to prepare collodion slides particularly unpleasant.[328]

Of course, what Maddox wished for happened: others continued the experimental work he had begun, with ever better results in the quality and the effects of the emulsion, and in the increase in sensitivity. Manufacturers launched the new product commercially. The dry plates, light-sensitive to the point of allowing the famous instant photograph, constituted a real qualitative leap forward: from this was born the large-scale industrialisation of photography, so that it finally left the restricted circles of pioneering professionals and wealthy amateurs. Now machines with multi-plate loaders could be produced, portable apparatuses could be conceived of, there was no longer any need to take a whole chemical laboratory around with you in order to take a photograph. Thus the beginning of all this process of development took place in a scientific laboratory where a medical doctor used photographs as an instrument for research and documentation.

The manufacturer of dry slides, George Eastman, with the universal brand, Kodak, that he introduced in 1888, was involved in the other great technological event that would provide the final leap to popularising photography, and which in particular – as far as we are concerned – would be the definitive product from which cinema, in the modern sense of the word, would be born. This was the use of a flexible and transparent support for photographic emulsion; what in practice transpired as the invention of film.

The authoritative historian Beaumont Newhall, after describing the revolutionary Kodak apparatus, recounts the episode as follows:

George Eastman had done more than invent a camera; he invented a system and worked out machinery for producing standardized material in quantities sufficient to back up the system. In 1889 he further improved his system by substituting a clear plastic (nitrocellulose) for the paper base, thus eliminating the delicate stripping operation. Amateurs could easily process their own exposures.[329]

All this was true, above all for the underlining of the system that would definitively lead photographic techniques out of arts and crafts and into one of the greatest of modern industries, multi-national in character and, in a commercial sense, dominant over a large part of the world. There are, however, reservations to be expressed about the historical accuracy concerning the invention of celluloid, leading as this did to the radical innovation of film. Newhall does not state, in fact, that Eastman had invented the transparent plastic support, but only that he had perfected his system with the introduction of this technique. He forgot to add that this support had been patented as much as two years earlier by a priest and that other small entrepreneurs had started out on the same route within their limited means, before Eastman.

The inventor of the photographic film was the Episcopal pastor Hannibal Goodwin (1822–1900), not a scientist but an educator. Goodwin, apart from his activities as a priest, dedicated a large part of his time to what we would call today the cultural activities of the parish and the city of Newark, NJ. A frequent user of the magic lantern, he was enthusiastic about photography, for which 'he foresaw the possibilities as an instrument of education.' He 'devoted his inventive talent to the improvement of that art' and was the inventor of 'photographic film … that has proved so potent an agent for the instruction and entertainment of mankind.' These quotations are taken from a commemorative tablet dedicated to Goodwin by the Essex Photo Camera Club in 1914.[330] Only thirteen years after his death did the US bench definitively recognise his rights as inventor. For a long time, Goodwin attempted in vain to affirm his priority. The patent offices asked for costly experimental proof to give executive validity to his patent of 1887, while in 1889 Eastman had concluded the paperwork for his patent in a few months. It appeared, however, that the procedure patented by Kodak did not work very well in reality, so that it seems that the ever greater quantities of film produced in Eastman's factories were created in accordance with Goodwin's method. This would explain the repeated, though vain, attempts by Kodak to acquire the invention rights from the priest. When, finally in 1898, Goodwin obtained recognition of his patent rights, he set up a company to compete with Eastman's, which, in the meantime, had become an industrial colossus. The Goodwin Company sued Kodak and – as we have said – only many years after the death of the reverend inventor, did human justice sentence the multinational to pay its competitors the astronomical damages of $5,000,000. Some historians of this great episode in the patents war, which characterised the first decade of the development of the industry of cinema as entertainment, state maliciously that in reality Kodak lost nothing at all. After the death of Goodwin (who, moreover, was a minority shareholder in his own company), the Goodwin Company changed several times and at the end of the case was called the Ansco Film Company, a firm whose ownership was unclear. It is said that behind the scenes, it was Kodak that had to keep the 'competitor' formally alive so as not to come up against the anti-trust law.[331]

The final touch to this whole business, significant for its conflict between a free company founded on private initiative and the emerging reality of monopolistic economic power, is provided by the omissions or self-censures of the historian of photography, Beaumont Newhall. These become clear once it is realised that he had been for many years the director of George Eastman House, the Museum of Photography created by Kodak at Rochester, NY, where the great factories of the same company were to be found. In fact, in Newhall's book, not only is Goodwin ignored, but likewise the photographers and small industrialists Balagny (French) and Carbutt (English transplanted to Philadelphia) who had made the mistake of preceding Eastman in creating film. Even now, in the tourist information of the city in the State of New York where Eastman was born, he is presented as the inventor of the film that enabled Edison to invent entertainment cinema.

Here, then, is the progress of photography, by now firmly entangled with the specific technical conditions that would permit the birth of cinema as entertainment; that is, outside the laboratories and experimental terrain where it had been invented and utilised for scientific purposes.

36. Scientific research and technological problems

The historical framework in which these technological innovations developed shows us that their authors were scientists or (in Goodwin's case) people who moved in the cultural circle of research. The new industry was born of the intensive exploitation of these inventions and the creation of a market that became ever more lucrative, because it was based on a need brought about in ever wider layers of a society that now pegged its progress to science. A small, but significant, example is in the fact that in 1880 the Société Française de Photographie launched a public competition to find a support for the emulsions of photographic plates to replace glass. If we compare the dates of the earliest work of Marey in chronophotography, we can see that it was at the end of 1881 that he attempted his experiment with the photographic gun and came up against the mechanical and physical difficulties of making even such a small plate of glass move with a very fast, rotating movement while having to overcome the inertia of twelve stops and re-starts per second. The obstacle could be overcome by adopting the first, still experimental, photographic paper (prepared by Balagny), which Marey then glued to disks of hard rubber (ebonite) that were much lighter than glass and were not breakable.

Examples of the close interconnections between scientific research and

technological problems, both in the sense of negative conditioning and favourable predisposition, were innumerable throughout the course of the nineteenth century and, in the restricted field of the birth of cinema as a research
instrument, quite determinative. We have seen how the astronomer, Janssen,
was obliged to use Daguerreotype plates instead of those with wet collodion,
in order to have his photographic revolver work in 1874, thus taking a step
backwards with respect to the best existing technology; dry plates, in fact, though
already invented by Maddox, would only become available commercially several
years later.

The long series of experiments carried out by Marey, and the results he obtained,
shows us that where he was able to intervene personally (or with the help of his
research structures, such as the Station Physiologique and its laboratories) on the
development of the technology, extraordinary progress was achieved, both in the
innovative concepts of the various types of chronophotography and with their
relative applications to different research fields. For the sensitive emulsions,
however (on plates, paper, strips, and finally films), Marey depended – as did Edison
– on the producers of these materials. These small artisan companies, while
technologically advanced, were limited in practical terms because of their lack of
adequate equipment: for example, Balagny in Paris or Carbutt in Philadelphia, could
supply strips or films of good sensitivity before anyone else, but of ridiculous length
(one metre, or a metre and a half). On the other hand, the industrial companies of
a certain size and even more those in a phase of great development like the Lumière
company or Eastman-Kodak, paid little attention to the scientific requirements of a
Marey or even those of an inventor-industrialist like Edison. The Balagny films
would be produced commercially some years later, also by Lumière, but Marey
found that the more artisanal products of Balagny were of higher sensitivity. Not
having strips and films available that were of sufficient length, Marey was obliged
first of all to record many images on fixed plates, carrying out what, for certain
aspects, might seem to be a step backwards compared to the earlier photographic
gun; then he was obliged in a number of ways to reduce the height of each individual frame to the minimum so that he could record the greater number of images
on the very short strips of film.

Edison had advantages over Marey, soon being able to have films for his
experiments that were ten or fifteen times longer than those available to the French
physiologist. Eastman, in fact, was equipped to produce rolls of film that were
twenty metres long for its Kodak cameras with glass supports. It had no problems,
therefore, with supplying Edison with rolls of film of a width different to normal
photographic supplies; not imagining for a moment that the width of film required
by Edison (35 millimetres) would become the universal standard of the
entertainment cinema and one of the major components of the future global
triumph of the producer company.[332]

It was quite clear, wrote Muybridge in 1901, that

> The improvements in the modern instruments are due to the invention of celluloid, as a substitute for glass for receiving and exhibiting the photographic images.[333]

However, the industry that specialised in this type of production lagged behind experimental and scientific requirements.

> The film was short, hard to find on sale, of very uneven sensitivity, difficult to treat; it hid surprises; either the emulsion became detached from its support or electric discharges affected the sensitive layer and appeared during development.

So we are told by Demeny, recalling the period of his work with Marey; in other words, before 1894.[334]

Dickson, the Edison experimenter, complained more or less of the same things. But at least Eastman provided them with film in long strips. It was only because of this that the Kinetoscope could appear before Lumière's Cinématographe. The Lumières, in fact, well informed about Marey's work, to whom they supplied film, as well as that of Edison (the small Kinetoscope films could be seen in Paris by September 1894), sought desperately to achieve their own production process for long strips of sensitive film, but they could not manage it. On the other hand, since they were one of the largest producers of photographic plates in France at least, they certainly could not ask their competitor Eastman (already attempting to invade the European market with its products) to sell them film. And even if they had done so, apart from showing their cards in advance, they would have received evasive answers, as occurred apparently to the Skladanowsky brothers of Berlin who, having asked the Rochester firm for a supply of some strips of film for their experiments, received the response that Eastman would accept an order only if it was in excess of one thousand marks, a figure so high as to force the Skladanowskys to give up and thus delay the trials of their Bioskop.[335]

According to Sadoul, the Lumières, in the summer of 1894,

> for their first experiments, used strips of perforated paper sensitised with silver bromide. Subsequently they bought in the United States, from the New York Celluloid Co., some crates of celluloid in sheets. They spread the emulsion on this support of excellent quality and Moisson [head mechanic of the plant] perforated the film they obtained with an apparatus he had invented based on a sewing machine.[336]

On 5 November 1895, some weeks before the historic public debut of the Cinématographe, Louis Lumière wrote: 'It is very difficult to spread the emulsion on the American films and, unfortunately, up to now we have not managed to do so.'[337]

However, they urgently needed to be able to produce a certain quantity of rolls of film, beyond the more or less long sections prepared as best they could to form the negative and positive copy of their first chronophotographic films, which dated back to the beginning and then the summer of 1895. Towards the end of the year, not having succeeded on their own, they decided to involve Victor Planchon, a small manufacturer of sensitive photographic material. They convinced him to close down his laboratory in the North and to move and join them in Lyons. Planchon recalled the period as follows:

> The first films were spread and allowed to dry on six-metre sheets of glass. The length of these sheets had to be increased to seventeen metres, then to fifty and finally to sixty metres.[338]

Things were not going much better in America, despite the advantage Eastman had as far as experience acquired and the quality of its technical equipment were concerned. Charles Francis Jenkins, one of the many inventors of cinematographic-type equipment (a projector deriving from the Kinetoscope) wrote in 1895:

> The strips of celluloid currently being used are not fully satisfactory. They are not flexible enough, they dry out, they twist, and they break.[339]

From all these concerns, some conclusions can be drawn. Edison was involved in a somewhat curious way in the so-called invention of cinema. He was already famous, a rich man, a celebrity, who dealt with many things at the same time, and in fact the work on the optical Phonograph project, which then became the Kinetoscope, had been delegated mostly to his assistant Dickson. Except, of course, for requiring all the various caveats and patents to be in his own name. Whether it was Muybridge or not who gave him his first inspiration, it was nevertheless obvious that, as far as Edison was concerned, the idea of cinema was born as an affiliation of the Phono-graph and even – in alternating phases – as an association with the Phonograph. Edison had no perception of the problems of the new language of images and its expression, nor even less, the scientific requirement for analysis and research into movement. When Edison spoke or wrote of the future of the cinema in mystical terms which bore little relation to the reality of the experiments in his laboratories, he did so exclusively in terms of entertainment, indeed reproducing those already in existence. His favourite expression was: we are about to achieve an invention that will allow you to see and hear, in your home, a whole opera at the Metropolitan. Apart from such assertions being quite unsustainable on a practical basis, what comes across strongly is his lack of interest in the fundamental technical problems involved.

Gordon Hendricks, in *The Edison Motion Picture Myth*, impressively brought to light some errors in the descriptions Edison attached to his requirements for caveats and patents, errors which concerned the very bases of photographic

Thomas Edison.

technique; for example, confusing negative and positive. But even on the more general level of optics, shutter problems, speed of takes, etc. there are traces of a veering between the subsequent experimental phases, an effect of intuitive research that took empirically here and there from the work of European and American scientists and technicians, but gave no consideration to the theoretical and methodological bases of the problems. After the success, primarily prestigious, of the Kinetoscope (and we now know that this was due more to Dickson's work than to Edison's) before the appearance of the Lumière Cinématographe, it became evident that it was technicians outside the Edison company who would develop American projection equipment. More than one episode in the patent wars showed the way in which Edison appropriated the work of others. As, for example, when he 'convinced' Thomas Armat to assign to him the glory of the invention of the Vitascope (a projection apparatus) with the following argument: exploit the established name of Edison as a guarantee of success, but above all use *his* perforated *patented* film, otherwise he would be sued in court.[340]

Edison, however, assumed contradictory attitudes. On the one hand, he neglected the advancement of technical and experimental research concerning the prototypes of the Kinetoscope, on the other, he allowed himself to make public declarations that were boastful and unfounded; when he patented the Kinetoscope, he made the mistake of doing so only for the United States (wrote the imaginative Terry Ramsaye, 'to save a hundred and fifty dollars'), as if he did not believe in the enterprise's possibility of development and success, save for committing himself to making war on imitators and competitors.

A fairly convincing explanation of these contradictions can be found by seeing the questions of the Kinetoscope in the overall context of the Edison enterprises. The genius inventor and self-made man had by now been swallowed up by the figure of the great industrialist, who had important patents such as those concerning electric light and the Phonograph. He had interests in many countries and, at this particular time, there was another project that was perhaps closer to his heart, considering the time and financial resources that he dedicated to it: the perfecting of a patentable industrial method for the electro-magnetic separation of minerals. This was applied technology, albeit avant-garde, risky for the investment it required, but very promising in its possible results. The undertaking did not work out well for him, indeed it could almost be considered a failure; this explains even more how the research in the direction of the 'invention of the cinema' was mostly marginal for Edison and more than anything a question of prestige, as a derivative of the Phonograph. He certainly did not dedicate the thought, theoretical studies, or experimental investigations that he would have found necessary if he had had a strong scientific motivation, or even that of a simple inventor-industrialist who placed all his bets on that enterprise. Perhaps a mitigating factor was his specific ignorance of the problems of optics and photography.[341] Claims made *a posteriori*, and the legal doggedness that led Edison and his collaborators to deny and tamper with acknowledged reality, formed part of the requirements for prestige and success that were not only personal or related to the company, but sprang from the myth that he had created around himself. In this particular case, it identified also with the nationalist requirement, *America first*.

In Europe, the situation was different. We have seen how the majority of the pioneers were scientists driven by their research interests. Even when these were photographers who studied (or only postulated) the ways of making the photographic image dynamic for the reproduction of reality (and to explore possible recreational purposes), the motivation was always technological research within this framework. This itself was somewhat a mythologised part of the social, rational and scientific progress that characterised the century. There was certainly no awareness or intention of making use of this technical progress solely for profit.

In this sense, the famous episode in which the French parliament – on the proposal of the scientist Arago – purchased the invention of photography in 1839 (in exchange for a life annuity) and placed it in the public domain, 'making a gift of it' to humanity, was emblematic. A few decades later, we see the Englishman Muybridge, fully immersed in American society and under the wing of the capitalist Stanford, carefully patenting his original method of automatic electro-photography (which no-one in practice ever exploited commercially) and placing a copyright on each photograph. Later, this same Muybridge, older and back in the England of his birth, underwent, by contrast, the conditioning of a different social environment: proof of this was his reserved and detached attitude at the invitation to come forward and make himself part of the disputes over the birth of cinema.

On the discovery and invention of the language of images in movement, Marey made his scientific attitudes clear. On the one hand, he theorised its novelty and originality, on the other he showed its application not only to his field of study, but to the most diverse sectors of scientific research and social progress, from flight to the dynamics of fluids.

As far as the Lumières were concerned, it was true that as young industrialists seeking their fame and fortune they focused on the cinematograph with the aim of increasing the prestige of the company. However, one must emphasise the characterisation of 'scientific curiosity' that they attributed to the invention, and the incontrovertible and significant fact that – after only a few years – the Lumière brothers withdrew on their own initiative from the nascent cinematographic entertainment industry. And regarding the production of sensitive materials, the cinematographic film remained largely secondary to photographic plates and films for the Lumière company.[342]

Considering the importance of scientific research for the development of modern industry in the nineteenth century, we must also note that science itself, in order to move on, has always had need of avant-garde technology, provided by industrial bases.[343] However, the nascent industry had not yet developed, nor was there a pressing need for the advanced technological research sector to do so, because it had ample opportunities for exploitation of those scientific novelties already available. It progressed, therefore, and developed its own initiatives, only in accordance with the laws of the market-place.

The consequence of this was that developments in scientific research (and some important practical applications of the theoretical results) were slowed down or at least conditioned and made possible only by the availability of the most advanced technologies. In this way, that fundamental characteristic of our modern society was born, an indissoluble interdependence between scientific culture and quality of life.

37. Scientific cinema and entertainment cinema

What happened to scientific cinema after the birth of entertainment cinema?

We are still far from the expression of a cinematographic art. The very short and jumpy little films were presented and viewed in the same way as going to see a lady shot from a cannon or a horror ride. Not by chance did Charles Pathé, one of the first *parvenus* (as he defined himself), who made his fortune out of the nascent commerce of travelling cinema, start out by going around to fairs and saint's day festivals with an Edison Phonograph bought on installments, having people pay to listen to short recordings (often made at home) of songs, operatic arias, monologues. He then moved on to the Kinetoscope (pirated examples, manufactured in England), which had the disadvantage of being usable by only one spectator at a time, while for the Phonographs (even before the adoption of trumpet horns) there already existed headphones linked to the apparatus by flexible tubes that allowed twelve people to listen at the same time.

When entertainment cinema arrived, its development ground was that of peddlers, wooden stalls at markets and suburban festivals. Nothing serious, then: a funfair curiosity. It was not for this that scientists and technicians, academy members, all driven by research interests, had worked so hard. Furthermore, in May 1897, in Paris, on the occasion of a traditional charity sale not far from the Champs-Elysées, a disaster took place. In the cinematograph set up for the occasion among the tents and wooden huts of the Bazar de la Charité a sudden fire broke out, and among the flames, fed by the inflammable materials, with the confusion caused by the darkness of the room and the press of the terrified spectators, around 140 people died, mostly women. The disaster had been caused by the carelessness of an operator when lighting the ether saturator lamp of the projector: in public opinion, the cinematograph had become something that was terribly dangerous. Questions were asked in parliament and solemn funerals were held at Nôtre-Dame for the victims.[344]

It was a hard blow and the prestige of cinematographic entertainment suffered the consequences. From the cultural point of view, once the first wave of curiosity for photographic images that moved on a screen had passed, the content of the first films (each lasting only a few minutes) was hardly very exciting.[345]

With regard to the cinematograph, conflicting opinions were expressed. Maxim Gorky, having attended the showing of the same films in his town (Niznij Novgorod, June 1896) wrote a long article in the local newspaper. In inspired style, he spoke of the 'Kingdom of Shadows', grey and silent, and of the exceptional impression created by the projected images and described the films he had seen.[346] However, he commented sharply that a notorious place had been selected for the showing of this latest progress of science, a place where – said Gorky – only vices were encouraged, where the victims of society and layabouts were to be found.

> I do not yet see the scientific importance of Lumière's invention but, no doubt, it is there, and it could probably be applied to the general ends of science, that is, of bettering man's life and the developing of his mind ... I am convinced that these images [reference is being made to women workers coming out of the Lumière factory] will soon be replaced by others of a genre more suited to the general tone of the 'Concert Parisien.' For example, they will show a picture titled: 'As She Undresses', or 'Madam at Her Bath' ...[347]

It seems that, at the beginning, there was a sort of inability to communicate between scientific cinema and entertainment cinema. Each was on its own riverbank, so to speak, without the two ever meeting. Marey had a good relationship with the Lumière brothers, but seems not to have been present at the Lyons meetings of the Société Française de Photographie, nor at any other screenings of the Cinématographe. He did not even obtain one of the Lumière pieces of equipment, continuing to develop new prototypes himself, even when he surrendered to using perforated film, at least as an option. Demeny, through letting himself be seduced by profit-making enterprises, was practically outlawed by the scientific world, exploited for a while by the real industrialists and businessmen (in his case, Gaumont) and then put rudely to one side. Nonetheless, between scientific cinema and entertainment cinema a series of connections and interactions were inevitably created, and the main results of this should be considered from the development of techniques. The particular case of the Institut Marey was in fact, unique and virtually unrepeatable: a centre of physiological research that was to become, through the passion and creative spirit of its founder, a focal point of cinematographic, technological research applied to the most diverse experiments and practically to almost all sectors of scientific research.

Despite the practical limits of Marey's Chronophotographe (especially the shortness of the films), the anthropologist Félix Regnault used this apparatus in summer 1895 (the Lumière Cinématographe had not yet been exhibited) for scientific documentation purposes, by filming Senegalese natives at the Paris Colonial Exhibition. In the following two years, he made further chronophotographic films of the locomotive behaviour of African natives (in particular, ways of climbing trees). In 1900, probably as a result of the projection of his films, though perhaps on his own initiative, the Ethnological International Congress (meeting in Paris), approved a document that said:

> All museums of anthropology should add adequate film archives to their collections. The simple presence of a potter's wheel, a few weapons or a primitive loom are not enough for full understanding of their functional use; this can only be transferred to posterity with precise cinematographic recordings.[348]

Regnault's pioneering work was to produce copious fruit, in view of the great development that ethnographic cinema has enjoyed since (if not always in the strictly scientific sense). To be precise, it can be observed that he had been assisted in glimpsing the importance of the cinematographic instrument for anthropological documentation through his previous research in the field of behaviour and locomotion, which had brought him to Marey and his chronophotographic method.[349]

An example of the use of chronophotography for early scientific research purposes (given the limits of the technology available) was that by J. Orchansky, who at the Institut Marey in the last years of the nineteenth century filmed (in Marey's words) 'the saccadian trajectory followed by the eyes during reading and was [therefore] able to discern in this movement that which referred to the optic muscles and that which could be attributed to the movements of the head.'[350]

Another type of pioneering application of cinema to scientific purpose was offered by the French astronomer Camille Flammarion. Known also as a great scientific populariser, he had emphasised in *La Nature* the importance of Janssen's photographic revolver from the moment of its first construction. In December 1897, he projected a film lasting almost three minutes for the French Astronomical Society that showed two rotations of the earth as seen from the moon against a starry background. Obviously, these were shots of a small model. Flammarion called his technique *cosmocinematography* and announced that he proposed carrying out other astronomical demonstrations on the Sun, Mars and Jupiter.[351]

In 1898 in Paris, a strange personality drew attention to himself by expounding his ideas on the need to create 'cinematographic deposits'; that is, in practice, cinémathèques (although the word had not yet been coined), because cinema was *A new source for history*. This was how a booklet printed at his own expense was entitled. He sent it to the newspapers, to personalities all over Europe, to monarchs, ministers, generals, doctors and scientists. Some months later, still at his own expense, he published a further booklet, *La photographie animée*, where he included in the appendix extracts from newspapers that had commented favourably on his first initiative. His name was Boleslaw Matuszewski, a Polish photographer (though with a Russian passport since his native city was then part of the Tsarist empire), who lived between Paris, Warsaw and St Petersburg. Little is known of him, and from his writings, though rich in ideas and proposals, some far-fetched, others brilliant, little biographical information can be gathered. He said that, as an official photographer, he had taken numerous cinematographic records of the meetings in 1897 between the Tsar Nicholas II and other heads of state (including the President of the French Republic), as well as other events, military or private, concerning the Imperial family. He stated that in the same period he had filmed surgical operations such as amputations, complicated births, and the nervous movements of people with mental diseases at hospitals in St Petersburg and Warsaw. However, he added that his first medical films were flawed on account of imperfections in the apparatus and that he had not screened them. While in Paris in April and May 1898 (he indicated the exact dates to state his priority), once the problem of fixing the image was resolved, he would start filming numerous 'interesting cases' in the hospitals of Saint-Antoine and La Pitié.

From his writing it seems clear that he was a lucid enthusiast of cinematograph as an instrument for culture, documentation, and teaching. He was clearly not interested in entertainment cinema; the name of Lumière is never quoted on his pages, he used the current terms *cinematograph* and *cinematographic*, but where showing greatest commitment (starting from the title), he preferred *animated photography*. He announced the project of a European cinema journal (which should have come out at the end of 1898, but in fact was never published) which was to have been called *La chronophotographie et ses applications*. It is not by chance, therefore, that he quoted Marey several times, and that Marey too, in a lecture he gave the following year, spoke of Matuszewski as follows:

I have received from a Russian living in Paris a curious little work in which with bold perspective he reviews those fields which to him seem open to chronophotography in the form of projection. He is saddened by seeing it used only as an entertainment and quite rightly asks that it become a useful tool for all kinds of scientific teaching. But he goes beyond this. He sees this invention that so excites him become a way of transmitting information on industrial processes, as a way of communicating good agricultural methods and in general as a teaching aid for all forms of apprenticeship ... Mr Matuszewski also wants chrono-photography to record and study the various phenomena of nervous diseases, to avoid the repetition of vivisection, filming experiments once and for always, presenting aspiring surgeons with model operations undertaken by masters. He hopes that chronophotography will come to be considered one of the most reliable sources of history and asks that in all circumstances which one might predict will be of historical importance, there be an official chronophotographer, just as we call for a stenographer wherever important words are spoken. He proposes the creation of documentary *cinematograms*, analogous to libraries and archives. Finally this new invention seems to him to be able to provide documents for teaching, to the fine arts and even for the police! All of this will one day happen, but certainly not quite as soon as supposes the ingenious author of *Photographie animée*.[352]

With his usual scientific detachment and perhaps a crumb of complacent irony, Marey spoke to the public at the Conservatoire des Arts et Métiers about this supporter of cinema in its most widespread social applications. If many of the rather wild but often acute proposals of the Polish photographer were eventually fully or partly carried out, this was not achieved either by him or as a direct influence of his writings.[353] Nothing more is known about Matuszewski, not even where or when he died. As a pioneer he was not very lucky.

38. Doctors with a cine camera

A lot more luck, however, was had by another pioneer, though it would perhaps be better to refer to him as a user of scientific cinema. Doctor Eugène-Louis Doyen (1859–1916) was a famous surgeon, much talked about at the time because he was a non-conformist who operated in private clinics, had rich clients and was well known in Parisian society for his duels. A personality of this kind was not going to be looked upon kindly by the leaders of the medical profession and the use he decided to make of the cinematograph looked like provocation. Some of his operations had already given rise to scandal because of their courageousness and innovative approach: filming operations to screen them outside the small amphitheatres of the operating theatre was just too much.

Exponents of the medical classes went so far as to seek to have his screenings stopped. However, whether he was a 'first' or not, what is certain is that Doyen obtained – whether he sought it or through his detractors' polemics – the maximum renown for his initiative.[354] In July 1898, having encountered difficulties in his own country, he made a presentation at the 66th meeting of the British Medical Society in Edinburgh, projecting three films, including one of a craniotomy and one of an abdominal hysterectomy, as a demonstration of his statement on the usefulness of the cinema in teaching surgery and operation techniques.[355] Such was the interest shown that many doctors asked Doyen to show the films again the next day. After this success, he announced a similar statement to the Académie de Médecine in Paris, with new films. As he would himself recount in an article, he obtained authorisation to have a screening room set up at his own expense on the Académie premises, but – at the request of many colleagues – the Presidency did not keep its word.[356] More or less the same thing happened at the French Congress of Surgery (despite his being a founding member), and he was obliged to show his films outside the congress hall; nevertheless, it was a great success.

From the outset, for the realisation of his project Doyen had turned to Clément-

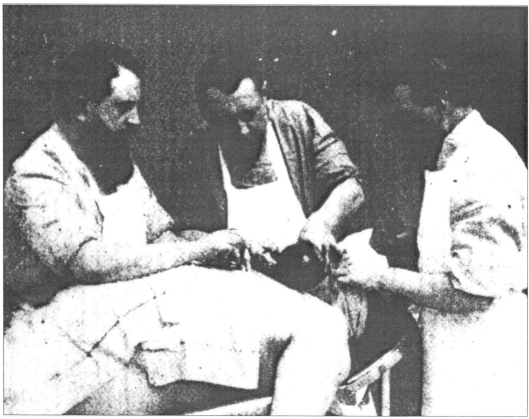

Image from a film of Dr Doyen (centre) operating.

Maurice, the technical director of the first public screenings by the Lumière brothers in Paris in the winter of 1895–96 and friend of Antoine Lumière, the father of Louis and Auguste.[357]

The surgeon's request was, in fact, not simple to meet. First of all, it was necessary to modify the cine camera and projector to make use of film bobbins that were much longer than those provided: films then only lasted a few minutes, there was no editing, except as a technical practice in eliminating cut-outs or inserting titles – the films were shot and the roll of film was projected effectively in real time. In the case of a surgical operation, there certainly could not be an interruption to allow the replacement of film. This difficulty was resolved by modification to the equipment, but there was another that was less easy to overcome: the low sensitivity of the negatives of the period made it possible to film with certainty only in full sunshine and, in fact, Clément-Maurice had first proposed shooting the operation in the open air, using a cadaver. Doyen refused and, since it was impossible to light the operating theatre adequately with artificial lighting, another brighter one had to be found, given that the best lenses then available had a maximum aperture of f:5 – f:6 and the operator would still have to obtain sharp negatives with a reasonable depth of field.

In this case too, therefore, it was for scientific reasons that technological progress in the field of cinematographic filming was achieved. Contrary to what was stated by his detractors, Dr Doyen was not seeking publicity that was alien to professional ethics, even if as a physician he seemed unorthodox. He proposed intervening with cinema in the modernisation of teaching and in the practice of surgery, replacing what he called 'surgery of the dead', (i.e. operating in amphitheatres) with true operations. In his statement in Edinburgh, Doyen indicated among the advantages of cinematographic projections 'the remarkable enlargement of *film frames* and the fact that their rapid succession prevented any re-touching', as well as the ease of reproducing a negative in multiple copies, so that the various operating techniques could become known the world over and people could judge the skill and personal qualities of every surgeon. From the didactic point of view, Doyen thought that the professor should present the operation, first with slides of drawings and of photographic images taken from film, illustrating the various phases of the operation, and then passing on to the projection of the film itself. Doyen brought to light a particularly important aspect of the 'animated photography of operations', namely the possibility for the surgeon of seeing himself and, consequently, of being able to improve, where possible, his own dexterity.[358]

> When I saw one of my operations take place on the screen for the first time I saw how little I knew myself … The cinematograph has made it possible for me to perfect my operating technique significantly.[359]
>
> Doyen said to me that he had learned from his cinematographic machine how better to control himself. Watching films of his operations, he was surprised by the number of unnecessary movements he made which made the operations appreciably longer. Thus, recording the same operation several times, he placed himself under strict scrutiny that allowed him to eliminate superfluous movements and significantly reduce the duration of operations.[360]

It is necessary to bear in mind the limitations of filming technique in the first years of the cinematograph. The cine camera had a fixed lens and framed the whole scene in wide shot: in the case in point, it took in the patient, the surgeon as well as his assistants, thus allowing Doyen to observe any errors in the arrangement of the instrument tables, useless gestures, wasted time that could be eliminated, and so on.

Doyen went to great lengths to have his efforts known both at home and overseas, even arranging screenings in commercial cinemas. This inevitably raised howls of protest from other doctors and the ire of police authorities, which sought to block further such screenings. It is said that in Rome one of the first cinemas opened by the photographer Felicetti was forced to close again shortly afterwards as a result of screening one of these early surgical films.[361] Doyen in the meantime suggested that it would be useful to show these films not just to surgeons but to the entire paramedic staff, including the volunteers in emergency departments. In addition he openly considered the usefulness of showing the films 'to all classes of society' so that they could appreciate what a well-realised operation was.[362]

In 1902 Doyen filmed the separation of female Siamese twins, which raised further outcries. One doctor wrote to *La Tribune médicale* (9 April 1902) asking for the immediate setting up of an order of doctors 'for the safeguarding of the dignity of the profession', which had been offended by the commercialism of men such as Doyen. According to the writer, the surgeon had dared to show his Siamese twin film in a fairground under a banner bearing his name. Doyen was able to show that not only did he have nothing to do with this, but that the film had never been projected under such conditions and that rather a colleague of his had in bad faith altered the details of a show in which people paid to see a wax figure of the separated twin 'after the operation by Dr Doyen.'[363] Doyen experienced a number of similar situations, though one is left in little doubt that, since these were invariably shown in fairground sideshows, the films were of doubtful origin, used by travelling projectionists exploiting the sensationalist nature of the material to attract audiences.[364] In any event, as late as 1922 the Gaumont company, which had a special catalogue of surgical films including around fifty of Doyen's films, gave strict warnings about the showing of the films to non-medical audiences without prior approval, under threat of the films' removal. It is said now of the Doyen collection that while some are only of historical interest, others are true 'classics.' Among them one can even find demonstrations (on cadavers or skeletons) of electric instruments such as a circular saw.

In 1911 the catalogue of Doyen's films, or rather of the 'cinematographic conferences illustrated by films' was presented as a paper by the surgeon under the title *L'Enseignement de la technique opératoire par le projections animées*. This brief text comprises extracts from a conference paper given by Doyen in 1903 at the international congress of medicine in Madrid. It contains summaries of his previously expressed postulates on the best ways to use film in surgical teaching. In the presentation, Doyen is referred to as 'the only surgeon whose technique passed the test of cinema'; it also claims that the 'general crusade' by many surgeons against Doyen's films was due to their fear of appearing inferior, even claiming that some surgeons who had filmed their operations had had the negatives destroyed for fear of displaying their mistakes. This paper, which on the whole successfully reclaimed lost ground for Doyen (it even proffered his amazing new immunisations to cure various illnesses), must have had some success as there is evidence that it had been translated into Rumanian by 1914.[365]

At about the same time in Rumania, a specialist in nervous disorders at the

Pantelimon Hospital in Bucharest, Dr Gheorghe Marinescu (1863–1938), was using cinema not so much for teaching purposes but rather to enhance scientific research and documentation in clinical fields. A frequent visitor to Paris, he was able to use the very first cine cameras and by the middle of 1898 he was filming cases involving problems of locomotion and the mimicry and gestures caused by nervous conditions, publishing the results in *La semaine médicale*.[366] The following year he filmed a patient suffering from hysterical hemiplegia, first taking its pathological manifestations, then treatment by hypnosis and finally the behaviour after treatment was successfully concluded. He presented the case to the Académie des Sciences in Paris (December 1899) and then published an article on it.[367] Referring to the film, Marinescu concluded the article by stating: 'Which other scientific document could be more valuable in the study of hysterical hemiplegia than this?' In his published works he included dozens of film frames (either directly or with detailed diagrams traced from the film) for demonstration purposes, theorising on their potential use and naming them *cinematograms*, a term used by the previously cited Matuszewski.[368]

Marinescu's use of film as part of clinical research was not a special case limited to his stays in Paris, but continued for many years through a number of publications derived from his films. He took a camera back to Bucharest and assigned the filming to his assistant Dr C. Popescu, receiving technical assistance, through a friend, from Boleslaw Matuszewski in Paris. His enthusiasm for cinema as a research was contagious: on 25 October 1899 at the medical faculty of the University of Bucharest, Dr A.I. Bolintineanu discussed his doctoral thesis for which part of the research had been documented with films, with subsequent extrapolations taken from a series of drawings. This was almost certainly the first time that the cinema had been used as part of a university thesis.[369]

39. X-rays in movement

In international scientific circles, the year 1895 meant not only the first public screening by the Lumière brothers but more importantly the year that Wilhelm Roentgen discovered X-rays.[370] The ability to photograph the inside of the human body through opaque materials could hardly fail to interest those first scientists thinking of the cinema as an instrument for research, documentation and teaching. In 1897 the Scot John Macintyre produced the first experimental roentgencinematographs, protecting the camera with sheets made of lead, filming the X-rays directly (after passing through the subject), and exposing the film through a small aperture protected by black paper. Naturally this kind of direct filming only permitted taking very small fields, such as a frog's leg, having a reproduction relationship of 1:1. In the same year in France, Jean-Charles Roux and Victor Balthazard used a similar technique to study the peristaltic movements of the stomachs of small animals using a contrast method to make movements visible.

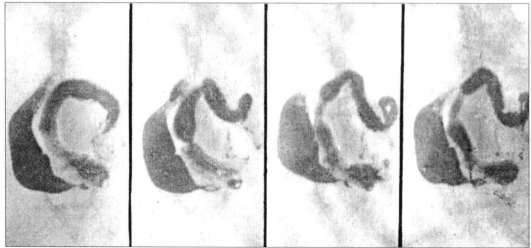

Carvallo X-ray film of a small animal's stomach.

At the Institut Marey at the turn of the century Dr Joachim-Léon Carvallo constructed a complex filming apparatus for direct roentgencinematography which used a special negative (with emulsion on both parts of the support to intensify the image, and a 60mm format), made especially by the Lumière company.

This particular camera was electrically automated to film at variable speeds between thirty frames per second and one frame every fifteen seconds. Between 1903 and 1906 Carvallo (who later became director of the Institut Marey) made a series of films on swallowing and digestion in small animals, down to speeds of five images per second.[371] The scale of the technical and scientific efforts demonstrated by this direct radiocinematography (which only allowed for fields of no greater than 6 x 6 centimetres) gives some indication of how, even after Marey's death, the institute that he founded maintained that engineering slant that had characterised his work. It also gives ample evidence of the extent to which it had become a centre for scientific cinematography.

Despite the low intensity of X-rays that could then be attained and the low sensitivity of cinematographic film available at that time, there were many attempts made to use the technique of direct roentgencinematography for physiological research or for diagnosis in humans, enlarging the filming area. For example, at the beginning of the century, the Dutch researcher P.H. Eijkman, to study swallowing in humans had to repeat the action fifty times (with exposures of 1/50th of a second) to obtain images that were sufficiently sharp. In Germany, before 1910 F.M. Groedel had constructed ingenious equipment which allowed, through a complicated and heavy precision mechanism, to record up to four images a second on a series of plates 24 x 30 centimetres in size (each of which was enclosed in a lead container).

The American L.G. Cole, by the end of the first decade of the century, had made direct roentgencinematographic films of gastric phenomena, although since the images were not sharp enough, he drew them all again one at a time and then re-photographed them again on 35mm film. Although it was not his intention, he can be considered as one of the pioneers of animated films.

To overcome some of the fundamental problems associated with direct filming of images produced with X-rays it was possible to pursue a different route: using normal film to record a fluorescent screen onto which X-rays projected the image being examined.[372] However, this alternative method, known as indirect filming, presented great difficulties generating images that were sufficiently luminous and detailed enough to be filmed, without giving the subject too high a dose of radiation. The first to gain satisfactory results in this manner were the French scientist Jean Comandon (of whom more later) and the radiologist André Lomon in 1911. They used a very powerful source of X-rays, but it was only activated for 1/32nd of a second, sixteen times per second (which was then the current speed used for shooting film), using a switch controlled by the movement of the camera (this technique had already been used by Carvallo for his direct filming system). The image that was formed on the special screen was shot with orthochromatic film (very sensitive to ultraviolet rays) through a specially constructed quartz lens with an exceptional aperture of f:1.5 which was made possible by the fact that, since the fluorescent screen was flat, it required no depth of field. The first films to be made showed the movements of the articulated bone structure of hands, elbows and knees of monkeys, of both live subjects and skeletons.[373]

40. In university laboratories

Those scientists who, during the first years of the development of cinema, showed interest in its possible applications as a methodology for investigation, as a type of documentation and as an instrument for demonstrations and teaching, can be for the most part divided into two main groups: those that became pioneers in the use of scientific cinema in their own fields, and those who became so passionate about this new language as to become, in essence, proper scientific cineastes.

Examples of the first group include the German Pfeffer and the Austrian Ledenfeld. The botanist Wilhelm Pfeffer, of the University of Leipzig, had by 1900 published some of the results he had obtained using cinematography to study geotropism and the growth of plants. If we leave to one side Janssen (1874) and a few of Marey's experiments, then Pfeffer can be seen as the first to use time-lapse photography to condense real time and so make visible and available for study extremely slow phenomena such as those that take place in the plant world. By shooting only a few frames per minute or sometimes only a dozen frames per day for a number of weeks, he was able to discover the rules and meanings of processes that up to that time had been incredibly hard to investigate in detail.[374] The marvellous possibilities offered by this technique had already been considered by the Austrian scientist Ernst Mach who, a few decades before Pfeffer's films, proposed the taking of a series of photographs of a man at regular intervals across several years, to cover the period from childhood to old age. He further proposed that these images be placed in Plateau's Phenakistiscope so that an observer could watch in a few seconds the changing phases of an individual's entire life span.[375]

At the opposite end of the scale of scientific possibilities offered by the dynamic language of images in 1903 we find Robert von Lendenfeld undertaking research into the flight of insects. His technique, as developed by Marey, involved taking a large number of photographs over a short space on a single plate using a rotating mirror. In this way one could obtain a number of ultra-fast images (with exposures of 1/42,000th of a second which gave a filming frequency of about 2,000 frames per second) so as to be able to analyse the otherwise invisible motion of the beating of the wings of a dragonfly.[376]

The Italian physiologist Osvaldo Polimanti (1859–1947), of the University of Perugia, in a sense represents an intermediate stage, albeit an exemplary one, between the two groups we referred to above. He was among the first to use cine-matographic means in his specific field: the physiology of the nervous system in relation to the movement of certain animals, in normal conditions as well as in experimental, atypical or pathological situations. In 1908 he published works based on observations and research undertaken by applying the methods of scientific cinema, but with Marey's work behind him he can hardly be given pride of place. However his interest in applying the methods of scientific cinema in general to research, documentation and teaching meant that by 1911 he had written essays on the topic, becoming a firm believer and proselytiser for this approach. F.P. Liesegang, the author and editor of *Wissenschaftliche Kinematographie* (1920), one of the most important works on scientific cinema, asked him to write the section devoted to the application of cinema to the various branches of science and teaching. Apart from the valuable documentation his work produced, there are also among his writings a number of sharp observations. In his work to 1911 he had pointed to the importance of using cinema in the research on human psychology. In 1920 he underlined a quality characteristic of cinematographic research documents: that of remaining open to further and even diverse interpretations. The recording of a phenomenon, one that it might not be possible to reproduce in the future, when undertaken with the techniques of scientific cinema in fact could, in the light of subsequent discoveries and experiences, be revisited and be the source of new interpretations, of new discoveries.

41. Profession: scientific cineaste

It was probably inevitable that the first professional scientific cineastes, so to speak, would come from France (even if they were not necessarily of French origin). They

Lucien Bull.

were from two distant poles: the Institut Marey on one side, and the growing entertainment film industry on the other.

The first protagonist of this type was Lucien Bull (1876–1972), whom we first referred to in his capacity as assistant to Marey in the last decade of his life. Irish by birth, he was sent to Paris by his French mother at the age of nineteen to perfect his knowledge of the language. During a short illness, his doctor mentioned Marey and promised to introduce him, since he was enthusiastic about photography. Although Bull was only meant to stay in Paris for six months, he discovered a passion for chronophotography and never left. For two years he worked as an unpaid volunteer, acting as a general factotum in Marey's personal laboratory at the Station Physiologique. He developed film and was the subject of some experiments. We can see him today as the man in white jumping over a hurdle in front of a black background at Parc des Princes. It is between 1895 and 1896. Bull had just turned twenty and apart from helping his master and learning from him, he also followed that which interested him the most in the field: the birth of the cinematograph.

173

Among the few not strictly scientific films made with Marey's chronophotographic equipment, there are a few made by Bull probably as practice exercises: scenes of traffic at the Gare St Lazare and the Place de la Concorde. Many years later Bull described the emotion he felt while projecting these brief films in secret on a small screen (owing to the weak light source), employing the same machine used for the filming.[377] He had to do this in secret since his patron Marey thought it a stupid waste of time to watch scenes of everyday life that could be seen with one's own eyes.

In 1902 Lucien Bull officially became an assistant at the newly constituted Institut Marey (of which, during his long life, he would later be deputy director and finally honorary director). This was a particularly important year for him as it marked the beginning of his own, highly original experimental activity. Marey gave him his start when he passed on a request from Professor Antoine Pizon for microscopic research using chronophotography. Marey, for his part, had made some micro-cinematographic films in Naples and the equipment had been described in *Le mouvement*. Pizon, however, had set a complex problem: to identify the evolution by germination of a botryllus colony (marine micro organisms that encrust submerged rocks), and given that this was an extremely lengthy process, to record it visibly by condensing real time. Bull constructed a new type of equipment made up of three separate elements (film camera, microscope, light source) and a device that allowed for the entire machine to be activated automatically to shoot a single frame every fifteen minutes, with a resulting acceleration (when projected) of approximately fifteen thousand. Pizon called them *biotachigraphic* shots, but for the history of scientific cinema they should be considered as the first important results of biological research obtained with time-lapse micro-cinematography. As soon as he had tested the equipment and shot the requested films, Bull began work on a research subject that was personally very important to him and into which flowed some of the scientific notions derived from his association with Marey and his technological interests. Going from the temporal condensation of a very slow event, he went to the opposite extreme, and became recognised as one of the fathers of high speed cinematography.

In 1902 he made experimental films at approximately 500 frames per second to capture the flight of insects and so decipher the physiological mechanism of the extremely rapid movement of their wings. This had been a topic dear to Marey some decades earlier. Bull seems to have inherited his ingenuity in inventing methodologies and techniques of research. His set-up was an original one. To obtain a very high number of images in a short space of time it was impossible to use a camera with an intermittent movement for the film: it would go beyond the limits of mechanical and physical resistance, for both camera and film. It was necessary therefore to move the film at a high speed in continuous motion, finding a new system to obtain the shutter action and therefore the capture of the single images.

Owing to the film's lack of sensitivity, a strong and concentrated light source would be required to obtain sharp and legible images with ultra-fast exposures. If the light source was constant (as for example with the sun), the heat directed at the subject being pictured could damage it or alter its behaviour. It was necessary therefore to have an intermittent light source. Drawing together these two concepts, Bull solved the problem in this manner: a strip of film was fixed to the inside of a drum which would then be rotated at the desired speed, only opening the shutter in the instant in which the event required actually occurred. The light source was provided by a fast series of luminous sparks produced with a Ruhmkorff coil. These sparks (or rather the micro-pauses of non-light between one spark and the next) functioned as a shutter.

The synchronisation between the sparks and the exposure of the film was obtained by linking the rotating switch to the axis of the film drum. Delicate problems remained to be solved as it was necessary to start the rotation mechanisms of the drum before the filming started, to get it to the correct speed, and then sustain it at the selected velocity and start the filming just as the pre-selected phenomena began. Bull found a brilliant solution to this problem. Having to film the flight of an insect for a fraction of a second, he adopted different strategies depending on the situation: a miniature pair of tweezers held the fly or dragonfly by a leg and then let it go through an electromagnetic command that also activated the camera; a glass tube trap with a flap that acted as a switch when a bee, for instance, took flight from the edge of the tube; a small swinging platform on which the insect, when it moved to take off, created an electric contact.

The film strip in the drum was made up of fifty-two frames from the first experiments at 500 frames per second. Bull obtained fifty-two images of what happened in a tenth of a second. Projecting this (at sixteen frames a second as was then common), that 1/10th of a second lasted a little over three seconds, with a slow motion factor of more than thirty. It is clear, though, that in these cases the true analysis of the film came through comparing one frame at a time.

In many of his experiments, to exploit the luminous power of the sparks to the full, Bull put the subject on the same optical axis, between the lens and the light source. Thus he obtained a silhouette, though this was not always readable in some important details. To get past this disadvantage he made his machine stereoscopic, doubling both the lenses and the strips of the film in the drum.

At the start of 1904, Bull reached filming speeds equivalent to a slow motion factor of seventy-five. On 21 March he gave a paper at the Académie des Sciences and later went to visit Marey who had been too ill to attend. As he himself later recounted:

… my last memory [of Marey] is of having gone to show him my first cinematograph of a subject that had been dear to him, the flight of the fly, taken at a speed of 1,200 images per second. This had, I think, really impressed him, since he congratulated me with enthusiasm, which was not a common occurrence and I shall always be proud of it. This meeting, unfortunately, took place only a few weeks before his death.[378]

In the following years Bull reached 5,000 frames per second, even if in the meantime others had followed his example and reached similarly brilliant results. Since then, thanks to him, one can at will modify the scale of temporal values, make real time relative, transforming it for scientific purposes in a filmic time that allows one to investigate the dynamics of a phenomena.[379] In those years, of course, Einstein was presenting his theory of relativity.

Lucien Bull's first high speed films have been conserved (following the closure of the Institut Marey) at the Institut de Cinématographie Scientifique in Paris, of which for many years he would in later life be the president. They constitute a precious record of the results obtained in Marey's shadow, in his teachings, his research and in the opening of new horizons in the language of images.

The military also recognised the value of high speed cinematography for the study of ballistics and analyses of the perforation of a bullet through various physical structures. Although Bull undertook some research of this kind, nonetheless he privileged work oriented more towards defensive concerns. During the First World War, starting with cardiological equipment, he developed a system of acoustic triangulation to identify the position of long-range enemy artillery, in collaboration with the British and French general staffs. For this he was awarded the Order of the British Empire. His longevity meant that he was able to deliver papers at the Académie des Sciences some fifty years after the beginning of his career as a researcher. Bull had a wide range of interests but was essentially a practical experimenter and a constructor of equipment. The bastion of his work remained his filming using sparks, with which he eventually obtained a frequency of 1,000,000 frames per second.[380] For Marey, chronophotography (even if he had sensed its novelty as a language) remained essentially an instrument for his studies in physiology, while for his pupil Bull it had become an object of research of itself.[381]

42. Disciples of Marey

The Institut Marey, especially in the first decade of the twentieth century, was a true breeding ground for young scientists and technicians. Coming from differing backgrounds and talented in various fields, they became researchers on scientific cinema, with particular emphasis on its special techniques. A case in point is that of Rumanian Ion Athanasiu who, after working as Deputy Director of the Institut Marey, went on to become professor of physiology and rector of the University of Bucharest.

In the first years of the century, while working on Marey's chronophotographic equipment, he undertook a series of research projects, from microbiology to botany. The ultimate goal, precisely on account of the variety of fields he tackled, was not so much to study the movement of the brow of a tiny mollusc or the growth of a volubilis, as much as to demonstrate new techniques such as high speed microcinematography (140 frames per second) or shooting in intervals via an original water-powered interval mechanism.[382]

Among these figures at the Institut Marey we also find Pierre Noguès who, after years of experimentation, created a high-speed 35mm camera with an intermittent pull-down. In 1909 he attained 180 frames per second, and a little while later 300 frames per second, which constituted the maximum physical limit for this type of filming. All higher speeds that were reached then and later were accomplished using different techniques (film without movement or in continuous movement, systems of optical compensation and/or vibrating mirror processes etc).[383] Shortly after Noguès' results at the Institut Marey, a private researcher (the engineer Labrély) finished a prototype for a standard high velocity camera, and it is interesting to note that in that period (the end of the first decade of the century) special techniques had begun to gain some interest outside of the scientific community. In fact the Debrie Company (manufacturers of film equipment) produced a commercial model of Labrély's machine, just as shortly afterwards the Germany company Ernemann would start selling micro-

Jean Comandon's microcinematographic equipment.

cinematographic set-ups which, on demand, could be provided either with a horizontal or vertical optical axis.

These two special fields of scientific cinema (high speed and micro cinematography) are those which would enjoy the most notable developments, albeit in a pioneering context, involving various people, institutions or companies in many countries. This can be explained by the fact that high speed photography, for example, interested the military for its application to the study of ballistics. In Germany the technique of cinematography with extremely high frequency, the film strip being in continuous rapid movement (which is to say the same principle as Bull's efforts), was developed with brilliant results by Captain Professor Carl Cranz. At the Berlin military academy, he built and used filming equipment for ballistics research, from 1909 overtaking the speeds reached by Bull. His images were extremely small, but good definition meant that they could still provide the necessary data.[384]

Regarding the application of the cinematograph to the microscope the situation was different: there were no military (or individual) interests pushing this research along, but many biologists had started to appreciate the great possibilities that microcinematography could offer them.

Once again the influence of the Institut Marey proved to be notable. In 1908, following the work of Bull and Pizon, the young Swiss researcher Julien von Ries of the University of Berne was able to capture the temporal synthesis of the segmentation of a sea urchin's fertilised egg (using time-lapse filming). In the same year a graduate in medicine, Jean Comandon (1877–1970), became interested in microcinematography.

He would go on to in subsequent decades to become a full-time scientific cineaste, contributing work that was as important in the field of pure research as it was in teaching and publishing. Although indirect, the influence of Marey was important in that Comandon became aware of the many possibilities of scientific cinema in the laboratory of Professor Charles Albert François-Franck, who replaced Marey as teacher at the College de France. From his predecessor, François-Franck had also inherited the method of applying chronophotography to research in the field of animal physiology.[385]

To study their movement for his doctoral thesis, Comandon wanted to film microscopic organisms like the trypanosome and the syphilis spirochete, much smaller than the infusoria filmed by Marey or the Botryl colonies filmed by Bull. He had innovative ideas regarding particular lenses and illumination techniques, but to obtain the results he sought he needed his own equipment. He turned to the enterprising cinema industrialist Charles Pathé who, probably for reasons of prestige (as we have seen, his background was in sideshow attractions at fairs), but equally with an eye to future earnings from educational films, gave him the technical facilities to set up a small laboratory at his offices at Vincennes. At that time the Pathé cine cameras were among the best available and through his professor Comandon was able to present a paper at the Académie des Sciences in 1909 based on a few films of trypanosomes and spirochetes of exceptional quality. Having launched himself with this first success, Comandon had then to face up to some difficulties. His experiments with powerful enlargements using an ultra microscope with a black backing resulted in unstable images on account of vibrations created by the camera motor, while the arc lights he was obliged to use proved fatal for the organisms on the slides. Comandon overcame these obstacles and obtained excellent shots of Brownian cell movements. As mentioned earlier, with the radiologist Lomon he was able to make the first indirect X-ray films. Pathé asked him to establish production of scientific films and Comandon requested the help of scientists from various fields to create a genuine film library to serve as the basis for the Pathé-Enseignement catalogue. It is worth adding, though, that Pathé took advantage of Comandon's films and presented them as 'sensations' in their travelling cinema programmes, which upset members of the academic world. Comandon continued regardless as a serious researcher and passionate scientific cineaste. Subsequently, he made some excellent research films (some of which can still be used for teaching today) and promoted a number of advances in the techniques of microcinematography with the construction by his collaborator De Fonbrune of auxiliary equipment such as micro manipulators and micro forges.[386]

43. From microbiology to icebreakers

The period between 1908 and 1910 was an extremely productive one for the development of microcinematography in biology. Again in Paris, in a restricted timeframe that makes it harder to give a precise account of who was the first, there were a number of other researchers aside from von Ries working on capturing on film the segments of a sea urchin's egg, including the biologists Lucienne Chevroton and F. Vlès. Accordingly to Polimanti, von Ries was the first, using his chronophotograph to publish some plates showing the successive phases in the embryonic development of the egg.[387]

Chevroton and Vlès, who did their research in the laboratory of Professor François-Franck at the Collège de France, found that the interval between images (Ries managed seven images a minute) had to be briefer to avoid discontinuity and to allow control during projection of the development of the phenomenon.[388]

Our interest in these detailed problems, while undoubtedly important as research, must not distract us from the fact that at the base of all this were questions pertaining to method and technique in this still new field of scientific investigation undertaken through the language of cinema, which made it possible to visualise, by enlarging, small organisms and to observe, by condensing the phenomenon into a few minutes, a process of development too slow to be followed in real time. Practically all of the various researchers that used scientific cinema worked with pieces of equipment that were prototypes (or nearly so), adapting them each time as became necessary, facing on a case by case basis the various problems that presented themselves. This succession of experiences contributed to the creation, brick by brick, of a corpus of special techniques.

A curiosity at how scientific cinema might permit all to witness images in motion of the most inaccessible and marvellous things from the world of laboratory research, particularly under the microscope, enticed other industrialists of the entertainment cinema to become involved. Thus Gaumont copied Pathé and offered Chevroton the opportunity to make films on microbiology, using them as sensational inserts in the newsreels that were part of his programmes.

A few years earlier in London, the enterprising producer Charles Urban (a Yankee who arrived in England as a representative of the earliest American companies and who later decided to go into business for himself) had had some small success with a few cinema shows on the marvels of science and nature. These were not scientific films in the strictest sense, rather short films such as THE BUSY BEES, NATURAL HISTORY, MARINE STUDIES and UNSEEN WORLD, made by F. Martin Duncan and presented under the title 'Nature on the Stage!' at the Alhambra theatre in London in 1903.[389]

Almost ten years later, an analogous event took place in Tsarist Russia, where the biologist U.M. Lebedev made an instructional film with the cine microscope and the producer A. Chanzonkov presented it to the public in 1912 under the title TUFEL'KA [Little slipper], since the infusoria featured in the film was of a similar shape. Lebedev had started using his microcinematographic machine for research and teaching purposes. In Russia at the end of the nineteenth century Admiral S.U. Makarov had used a camera to film the testing of the icebreaker 'Ermak'; on the basis of this, the constructor Krylov, analysing the movement of the bow frame by frame, had calculated the pressure that the ice was exerting on the ship. In 1905 the surgeon Medlinskij had some of his operations filmed, while in 1910 the pioneer of Russian aviation N.E. Zukovskij utilised the camera for experiment on the dynamics of fluids and filmed aircraft for his lessons on aerodynamics.[390]

In Italy, apart from the work of Polimanti, one should also mention a rather curious pioneer, Roberto Omegna. It is well known that from the early 1900s Italy had a flourishing entertainment cinema industry; in fact for over a decade it was the most important film making centre in the world. Omegna had been a technical collaborator and then director of Ambrosio Film, one of the first and most active film companies in Italy, established in Turin in 1904. Essentially he was a camera operator and a skilled technician. He gained praise for his cinematography and the special effects for the first film version of GLI ULTIMI GIORNI DI POMPEI [The last days of Pompei] (1908). But we must point out his predilection for scientific cinema, to which he would later dedicate the majority of his life as a maker of instructional films. In 1908 Omegna filmed a number of nervous pathological cases on behalf of the University of Turin. This is how he described it to a newspaper at the time:

> Professor Negro wanted a genius idea, to apply the cinema to the teaching of neuropathic illnesses to provide to students at small universities where 'living' clinical material is rare, a collection of cinematographic 'types' and 'cases.' The extremely successful experiment of Professor Negro will certainly create a stir in the scientific world since it puts into sharp relief and maintains the shape of 'movements' which mere photographs could not reproduce.[391]

Between 1908 and 1910 Omegna undertook a pioneering work with his scientific teaching film LA VITA DELLE FARFALLE [The life of butterflies], in which, among other things, he presented a complete series of time-lapse sequences condensing the entire process of the metamorphosis of an insect, with fine technical results. His technical ability in special filming would be confirmed in subsequent decades when – probably for the first time – at the end of the 1920s he showed on film the complete cycle of the development of a chicken embryo right up to the hatching of the egg and the emergence of the chick.[392]

44. Special techniques

Through the work of the first scientific cineastes we have seen the development, following Marey's original creative impetus, of the various special techniques that characterise the scientific use of cinematography.

For many years after the birth of entertainment cinema, technological research in the field of filming, special techniques in particular, remained almost exclusively in the hands of scientists in their laboratories.

The emergent industry that, initially at an artisanal level, produced cinematographic equipment for entertainment cinema, was dedicated to improving projectors, while the cameras remained essentially unchanged. From the point of view of filming techniques, only Georges Méliès, with his interest in the fantastic and his persona as a conjuror and illusionist readily exploited the possibilities of the new language of images in presenting his marvellous shows. The variation and reversibility of the speed of filming with respect to that of projection (forward and backward movement, filming one frame at a time, multiple exposures etc) allowed him to make his naïve, but frequently amazing stage effects; all this without the author realising what he was contributing to the birth of a grammar and syntax. Méliès' films are now historical artefacts in which he utilised tricks and techniques of prestidigitation and theatrical illusion. In other words, Méliès' special effects were used to alter reality, to create a more fantastical one, while the special techniques of scientific cineastes were used to reveal the secrets of reality itself. Méliès could be considered a finder-poet of the new language of images. Scientists and technicians (which includes the Lumières naturally, and others) following Marey directly or indirectly would instead be the founders of the logical basis for this visual language.

Bull, in his previously cited article on 'La technique cinématographique au temps des pionniers', pointed to an indirect contribution in the development of special techniques made by a standard-bearer of entertainment cinema. He referred to the method used by Emile Reynaud back in 1877 to present his animated drawings.

> Even though photography was not being used at that time the principle of his machine [the Praxinoscope], the 'optical compensation', picked up again and perfected, today constitutes one of bases for ultra-fast cinematography.

It is worth noting on this point that Reynaud used this technique of optical compensation just for presentation, while scientific cinema would adopt it for filming to increase the frequency of the images being recorded. One could add that Reynaud, before becoming an unlucky showman had been a technical lecturer and science teacher, hired by the Puy-en-Velay administration to hold courses on science with the aid of luminous projection.[393]

In the first years of its rapid development, broadly speaking the world of entertainment cinema did not make any significant contributions to the evolution of scientific cinema. The forefront of technical research was undertaken for purposes (military, industrial) other than for scientific ends, while for the film industry, it bears repeating, projectors remained more important than film cameras. Indicative of this is a work from 1926 by F.P. Liesegang entitled *Zahlen und Quellen zur Geschichte der Projektions-Kunst und Kinematographie,* in which through a logical inversion projection was given pride of place over cinematographic filming.

It is also interesting to note how, during the period which saw the origins of American science and technology, it contributed so little to the birth of scientific cinema, despite the presence of Edison and his overwhelming presence among the fathers of entertainment cinema. This might seem strange given the view of the United States as a nation that was still young, modern and completely taken by the mythology of technological progress. However, one must keep in mind the difficulties and mistrust encountered by Muybridge, admittedly a controversial figure, at the University of Pennsylvania. It is also true that in the United States, entertainment cinema started as a popular attraction and that the future motion picture moguls were for the most part improvised adventurers, recent immigrants without any money who made it out of New York to make their own private conquest of the West, which at the time was still open to the kind of colonisation which would see the establishment of Hollywood and its empire.[384]

Historical research on the scientific origins of cinema is still in the early stages. With more attention given to the topic from academics from around the world, it will be possible to acquire new information, rediscover unknown or previously thought lost documents and provide a more in-depth perspective on the birth of scientific cinema.

Conclusions

The so-called media age in which we currently live bombards us every day with audiovisual messages, in an often barbaric expression of this new language. Understanding how this language was born, identifying its scientific bases and cognitive possibilities, can help us not to become its slave, and learn how to master it and make use of it.

The lucid intuition of Marey ('the defectiveness of our senses' and 'the insufficiency of [traditional] language') is still valid as a positive spur for the development of this instrument for discovery and communication.

Scientific cinema, despite the establishment of the hegemony of entertainment cinema, has continued to make incalculable contributions to technological and scientific progress in the twentieth century, in a wide variety of fields, in the most disparate of applications. It is a story that is yet to be written: the very vastness of its applications and the breadth of its results makes such a project difficult, requiring a multi-disciplinary effort.

The special techniques of the pioneers may have marked the upper limit of their potential, and one might think that the majority of all possible discoveries have now been made. This does not mean however that scientific cinema is reaching the end of its cycle of development. Traditional techniques have been, and are continuously being integrated into fields of electronics, computers and holography. The methods of analysis, investigation, and documentation, utilising the language of moving images certainly can not exhaust themselves, and neither can the search for knowledge.

Some of the characteristic expressions of scientific cinema have become so integrated into everyday life that they are no longer even recognised as such. One need only think of action replays during sports coverage, to the visualising of the inside of the human body, 'live' images from the moon, as well as the synthesis and manipulation of images in movement via digital electronic means.

The language of images is not merely a phenomenological reproduction of reality – it has become a method of mass communication. The invention of its instruments is considered to be at least as important as that of the printing press. This new language is not a total replacement for the verbal and written varieties. It is another language, one with specific and particularly expressive possibilities. It is only at the beginning of its development, but it could become a universal language. Scientific cinema is its grammar.

Coda: The results of new research

The Italian edition of this book (1984) ended with the preceding chapter. This chapter has been especially written for the English edition which is being published over a decade after the Spanish language version. Further historical research has led to the discovery of other pioneers of scientific cinema and of new filmographic materials on its origins.

Prior to the publication of the 1984 edition, Dr Hans-Karl Galle, then director of the Institut für den Wissenschaftlichen Film (IWF) of Göttingen (Germany) had proposed to the author the making of a film which would bring together the proto-cinematographic materials of the pioneers mentioned in the book. The project had a long gestation due to many inherent problems: acquisition of materials, restoring them, transferring them to 35mm film to ensure their possible re-use in the future. In the end the project got underway in the form of an international co-production (German-Franco-Italian, with British collaboration) of a series of scientific teaching films entitled THE ORIGINS OF SCIENTIFIC CINEMA-TOGRAPHY.

From the single film which was first planned, three were eventually produced. The first, THE PIONEERS (1990, 52 mins, colour), illustrates the activities of Janssen, Muybridge and Marey. The second film, TECHNICAL DEVELOPMENTS AROUND THE TURN OF THE CENTURY (1992, 17 mins, colour) deals with other pioneers that undertook experiments and developed the various techniques of scientific cinematography. The third film, EARLY APPLICATIONS (1993, 30 mins, colour) presents a selection of the first applications of the cinema as an instrument of research, documentation and teaching in various scientific fields, culled from those original materials available.[395]

The three films in the series were made predominantly for teaching, as well as to promote wider understanding. They have a modular structure, which is to say they are based on chapters and sequences that can be enjoyed sequentially, separately or in the order one prefers. For example, in THE PIONEERS there are three chapters dedicated to Marey and two to Muybridge. With modern technological support for the reading and analysis of images in movement the chapters on Marey and Muybridge can even be viewed in the form of short films dedicated solely to one or the other. The modular form which structures the films was also adopted to facilitate the use of the materials within the ambit of thematic cultural programmes on television and for teaching at different levels, on an individual basis and in groups.

The making of the film instigated new research, the results of which will now be presented. Readers will be able to find in the second and third films the audiovisual sequences which relate to the results of this research.

Ernst Kohlrausch of Hanover (Germany) was an academic and, like Demeny, a teacher of gymnastics and, as we would term it today, a sports physiologist. In 1891 he published a description of his machine with which he had been able to capture serial images of sporting activities: diving, exercises on the parallel bars, etc. The originality of Kohlrausch's machine lay in twenty-four small photographic cameras mounted on a disc about one metre in diameter. With the rotation of the machine, the series of individual images was taken from a single point of view, bypassing parallax problems (present in Muybridge and Anschütz's work) as well as the superimpositions in Marey's single plate chronophotographic method. Kohlrausch's technique, while ingenious, was nevertheless part of a strand of pioneering efforts which could produce a very limited number of images, making it possible therefore only to record and analyse extremely brief movements. (For years Marey had chosen the main route: that of a camera with a single lens and a photographic strip moving intermittently, that is to say film). Owing to its great weight and the space it took up, not to mention the cost of the twenty-four cameras (each with its own lens and plate), Kohlrausch's machine could not, and probably did not, have applications beyond those undertaken by its inventor. Partly to try and get past these limitations, he subsequently built a second model that made use of four lenses. With this new machine Kohlrausch filmed some pathological cases (nervous illnesses) of human locomotion.[396]

Another teacher, also German, is among the pioneers whose work has only in recent years come to light: Professor Ludwig Münch of Darmstadt, many of whose films on mathematics, made around 1911, have now been discovered. Münch produced these works as animations based on thousands of drawings on paper. The quality of these works, apart from the deterioration in the physical and chemical state of the films themselves, is excellent. Also discovered were some flip-books probably derived from his films, which were sold as teaching aids.[397]

It is necessary to add to what has been said on that important sector of scientific cinematography, the fields of medical, surgical and biological films. The Cinemateca Argentina has made available two surgical films produced in 1900, but only re-discovered in 1971 and 1987, reprinting them from originals which were on inflammable stock and restoring deteriorated sections. They are films of two operations (CISTI IDATIDEA POLMONARE and ERNIA) undertaken by the Argentinean surgeon Dr Alejandro Posadas, who for the first operation devised an extremely fast operating technique (the film and the operation last about three and a half minutes). Since at the time there was no means to assist a patient's breathing, who was under general anaesthetic through toxic chloroform, the speed of the operation was fundamental. Dr Posadas had his operations filmed to present them at conventions, seminars and conferences, including some held in Europe. The filming was carried out, using Pathé cameras, by the first Argentinean cameraman Eugenio Py (actually a Frenchman, Eugène Py), and took place on the hospital patio, to make best use of the strong southern sun and achieve acceptable photographic results given the low sensitivity of the film stock.

These two films were important because they made possible the transmission of scientific information and techniques beyond the restricted circle of those present at Posadas' operations. Today they constitute notable documents in the history of surgery and anaesthesiology. Even in terms of the history of cinema it should be pointed out that the film of the removal of a pulmonary cyst is not made up of a single stationary shot – as was the norm in the earliest days of cinema – but of two successive angles: an overall wide shot and a closer shot for the most crucial parts of the operation. To the best of our knowledge these constitute the two oldest surviving surgical films.[398] There is always the hope, however, that through further research in who knows which country, we may be able to find films produced before Dr Posadas'.

As demonstration of such hopes, after the publication of the first edition of this book, we found two microcinematographic films by Dr Jean Comandon, in excellent state of repair. One of these is SPIROCHETA PALLIDA (DE LA SYPHILIS), which was presented to the Académie des Sciences in Paris in 1909 and which had been thought lost. The history of the recovery of this title is a curious one and is worth describing in some detail. On the occasion of the 35th Congress of the International Scientific Film Association held in 1982 at the Friedrich Schiller University in Jena, German Democratic Republic (DDR), we had the opportunity, thanks to the interest of Dr Manfred Gerbing, vice-chancellor of the Hochschule für Film und Fernsehen of Potsdam-Babelsberg, to consult the catalogue of the archive of scientific cinema of the DDR. Despite the fact that we were unable to view the material, given that these were original nitrate copies, we were able to ascertain that these were films by Dr Comandon, produced by Pathé in Paris.

To get hold of these two films to use extracts in the third film of the ORIGINS OF SCIENTIFIC CINEMATOGRAPHY series, there were two difficult problems to overcome, both tied to the Cold War political situation and two German states which did not recognise each other's sovereignty. The first was the financing of safety prints of Comandon's films. The main producer of the films (IWF) was prepared to meet the duplicating costs, but the corresponding institutions in East Germany could not accept this financing. This impasse seemed insurmountable, until – with the help of many people of good will – an ingenious solution was found. The International Scientific Film Association, which had offices in Paris, through its help in organising the Jena Congress, had the right to make use of delegates' subscription fees. This sum consisted of DDR marks which could not be converted into any Western currency and which were therefore frozen in a bank account in East Berlin. The decision was made to use these funds to duplicate the films, thus resolving the first problem. The second problem was a typically formal one, almost Byzantine in the subtlety of its meanings. The official representative of the Association for Scientific Film of the DDR could not send the duplicated material to an institution in the Federal Republic. Therefore it was decided that the roll of safety film containing the dupe negatives would be brought to Paris in a briefcase (that is, without export documents) from the then General Secretary of the International Scientific Film Association (Kurt Eifert, of the DDR) and delivered in person to the Italian author of the film THE ORIGINS OF SCIENTIFIC CINEMATOGRAPHY, then being prepared. A few minutes later the roll of 35mm film was, by the same author, handed over *brevi manu* to the director of the IWF, who was staying in the same hotel. Today all of this might seem ridiculous, but it illustrates well the political situation which still existed in the mid 1980s.[399]

Even after the making of the three ORIGINS OF SCIENTIFIC CINEMA-TOGRAPHY films, research work has continued, with the centenary of cinema providing a further incentive. FIAF (Fédération Internationale des Archives du Film – International Federation of Film Archives) invited all its affiliated film archives to take part in the celebrations with a variety of initiatives aimed at helping to generate a fuller appreciation of the importance of the origins of cinema, and to track down films made on inflammable stock from those early years. For example, the cinematheque of the UNAM (Universidad Nacional Autónoma de México) published a Spanish language edition of this book in 1993 as its scientific contribution to the anniversary of cinema, distributing it to all archives; while the Cinémathèque Royale de Belgique decided to catalogue all Belgian films. This led to the discovery, after decades in oblivion, of a number of scientific films made during the first years of cinema, which now constitute some of the earliest titles held by the archive in Brussels. These films, now identified and transferred to safety stock, deal with neurology and were made between 1905 and 1914 for teaching and research purposes by Professor Arthur Van Gehuchten (1861–1914) of the Catholic University of Louvain. These films are currently being analysed and will once again be used for teaching purposes. The quality of those films that have been made available to view so far is very good and they must certainly be considered as pioneering contributions to the very first uses of cinema in the field of neurological science. They illustrate a number of neurological complaints, their spontaneous evolution and functional recovery after surgery. In 1895 Van Gehuchten was an active member of the Association Belge de Photographie; alongside his activities as a researcher and lecturer at the university, he had a strong interest in photo-cinematographic techniques and their scientific application. He not only shot the film but developed it and edited it, occasionally with help from one of his sons.[400]

In 1999 there was another discovery of a film important in the history of the origins of scientific cinema. José Manuel Costa, of the Cinemateca Portuguesa, informed us that among its still uncatalogued nitrate archive holdings there were films of surgical operations which might be by Dr Doyen and hitherto considered lost. A detailed check of catalogues from 1911 and 1922 allowed us to make some conclusions with a reasonable degree of certainty. The five reels of film deposited at the Cinemateca Portuguesa had been brought to Lisbon by Doyen as part of a presentation at the International Congress of Medicine held in the Portuguese capital in 1911. Probably at the request of a colleague, Doyen subsequently decided to leave the films at the end of the congress. A detailed and comparative analysis of these materials might establish if they contain his first surgical film, CRANIECTOMIE TEMPORALE SUIVANT LA MÉTHODE DU DR. DOYEN. Similar titles in Spanish and Portuguese appear among titles found in the Cinemateca Portuguesa. According to statements made by Doyen and his cameraman Clément-Maurice, a film with that same title was presented for the first time by the French surgeon at the sixty-sixth meeting of the British Medical Society, held in Edinburgh in July 1898.

Regarding the scientific applications of cinema to ethnography we can also add some important updates to the information in previous chapters. Not long before this book was first due to go to press we learned of the discovery of hundreds of short chronophotographic films made by Marey and his collaborators. This was a discovery of enormous importance: Lucien Bull had deposited those films in the Cinémathèque founded by Henri Langlois. Unfortunately some time later other precious materials from the Institut Marey were lost. However, Bull's films were not immediately identified and catalogued. When we had the opportunity to examine them, we urgently recommended not just their cataloguing but their restoration and their complete photographic duplication. Many of the small rolls were in an alarming state of physical-chemical decomposition, with the partial detachment of the emulsion leading inevitably to irretrievable loss of the materials. Fortunately the suggestion was accepted, and we were no longer able to access the materials until the restoration work was complete. Subsequently it was possible to establish that many of the films could be attributed with certainty to the ethnologist Félix Regnault, whose collaboration with Marey was already known. Up to this point all that was known about these films were references to them and the reproduction in print of a few frames in Regnault's scientific publications.[401]

Some European and Australian archives hold important films on the origins of ethnographic film. There are films showing ritual dances and details of starting fires made as part of the 1898 Cambridge Anthropological Expedition, organised by Alfred Cort Haddon (1855–1940), into the region of the Torres Strait.

To these one should add the numerous films made by Sir Baldwin Spencer in 1901 and 1912 during his expeditions among the Aborigines in Australia. It is interesting to note that, among Spencer's films, there are dances which the native Australians still consider to be sacred and secret and to which they thus oppose access. The sacredness and secrecy is due, it would appear, to the fact that some of the male dances are not meant to be seen by women. Therefore, following agreements between Aboriginal organisations for the preservation of native traditions and the Australian authorities, these films have only limited distribution.

The Austrian professor, Rudolf Pöch, made important contributions to scientific cinematography in the field of ethnography, especially with films he made in New Guinea starting in 1904. It is worth stressing that Pöch was dedicated to the use of audio-visual techniques (then still in embryonic stages), integrating observations made in the field with photographic, cinematographic and phonographic documentation. Among Pöch's films one curious example of scientific documentation is the sound film BUSCHMANN (KALAHARI) SPRICHT IN DEN PHONOGRAPHEN. This is actually a modern version on 16mm of a film Pöch made in 1908 on 35mm with simultaneous recording on an Edison cylinder of a tale told by a native African. The scene shows in close up a bushman named Kubi speak and gesture while keeping his mouth near the gramophone horn, also visible in the shot. After the discovery some years ago of the phonographic recording, sound and image were synchronised in 1984.[402] However, we have now discovered that this creation of an audio-visual document for scientific research in the field of ethnography was

Frame still from A.C. Haddon's films of the Torres Straits islanders, 1898.

preceded by Haddon, who in 1906 is recorded as having exhibited his 1898 films of the Torres Strait islanders alongside Phonograph recordings made on the same expedition.[403]

In Italy, as already noted, the physiologist Professor Osvaldo Polimanti undertook research work of considerable interest. While making the films on the origins of scientific cinematography we attempted a reconstruction of two sequences on the pathologic locomotion of a dog recorded by Polimanti in 1905. Of the original films there is no trace; the only image source remains a few plates in a German physiological journal.[404] For the two sequences we only had access to a few dozen photographic frames reproduced on coated paper. Filming each of the images twice with special registration techniques to avoid juddering, we were able to reproduce brief sequences that were certainly similar to corresponding sections of the lost films: the latter in fact had been shot at eighteen frames per second, whereas today images are shown at twenty-four or twenty-five frames per second. While looking for details among Polimanti's scientific articles on how the films were originally made, we came across a name guaranteed to make any historian of the origins of cinema jump, especially if Italian. Filoteo Alberini, the Italian film pioneer, was apparently the camera operator on Polimanti's films. This piece of information is highlighted for at least two reasons. Firstly, by the time Alberini was collaborating with Polimanti on his films, he was already a cinema owner and was already producing the well-known film LA PRESA DI ROMA (1905), considered by historians to be the first Italian film in the spectacle genre. This tells us the value Alberini placed on working with a university professor – beyond any probably meagre financial recompense – who was a convinced proponent of applying the new language of moving images to scientific research. Secondly, it means that one can now say that two of the most important pioneers of Italian cinema (the other is Roberto Omegna) were both, at the start of their careers, participants in these first experiments in the field of scientific cinematography.

When this book first came out in 1984, historical research on cinema was focused mainly on the upcoming centenary of the birth of entertainment cinema. The celebrations of this event, especially in Europe, acquired connotations not so much to do with the first film shows, but rather related to the fact that, in the course of the twentieth century, film had become the most widely disseminated and popular entertainment in the whole world. The attitude was, one might say, one of vindication in character as it once again gave prominence to a phenomenon which faced various crises towards the end of the twentieth century through the massive and unstoppable effect caused by television and new technologies.

The publication of this book (and its subsequent Spanish language edition in 1993) therefore took on the character of a clarion call, one outside of the chorus of celebrations for the centenary of entertainment cinema. A call to look at the true birth of cinema, understood as a language of moving images, a call to examine the scientific roots of cinema as an instrument of communication, research, discovery and documentation. In the years that have followed one has been able to see, internationally, a distinct development in historical studies regarding the period of so-called pre-cinema, not to mention works on scientific cinema pioneers such as Muybridge and especially Marey.

The year 2004, centenary of the deaths of both Marey and Muybridge, was the occasion for some celebratory events which led to new publications in this field. In the same year there was an astronomical occurence which had a specific link to an important date in the origins of scientific cinematography. On 8 June 2004 we saw the planet Venus go past the sun. This same event, when it occurred in 1874, led the astronomer Janssen to build and use his photographic revolver, the first step in the development of scientific cinematography.

Bibliography

Books and exhibition catalogues only are cited here. Titles marked with an asterisk either appeared after the publication of the first edition of this book (1984), or are earlier titles which we have only discovered since then.

Aérodynes: Les débuts de l'aviation, catalogue of an exhibition held by the Musée Marey, Beaune, 1999*

Animal Locomotion: The Muybridge Work at the University of Pennsylvania (reprint, New York: Arno Press, 1973) [originally published Philadelphia, 1888]

Barnes, John, *The Beginnings of Cinema in England* (London: David & Charles, 1976)

Bernardini, Aldo, *Cinema muto italiano, Vol. 1: Ambiente, spettacoli e spettatori, 1896/1904* (Rome/Bari: Editori Laterza, 1980)

Bessy, Maurice and Lo Duca, *Louis Lumière inventeur* (Paris: Prisma, 1948)

Boleslaw Matuszewski I jego pionierska mysl filmowa (Warsaw: Filmoteka Polska, 1980)

Braun, Marta, *Picturing Time: The Work of Étienne-Jules Marey (1830–1904)* (Chicago/London: University of Chicago Press, 1992)*

Breuil, Henri and Hugo Obermaier, *Las cuevas de Altamira a Santillana del Mar* (Madrid: Topografías de Archivos, 1935)

Buhot, René, *La voix de Marey, histoire de l'invention du cinématographe, première partie* (Boulogne-sur-Seine: René Buhot, 1937)

Bull, Lucien, *La cinématographie* (Paris, 1928)

Cartwright, Lisa, *Screening the Body: Tracing Medicine's Visual Culture* (Minneapolis/London: University of Minnesota Press, 1995)*

Catalogue du Musée du Conservatoire National des Arts et Métiers, Section L (Paris, 1949)

Ceram, C.W., *Eine Archäologie des Kinos* (Reinbek bei Hamburg: Rowohlt, 1965), translated as *Archaeology of the Cinema* (London: Thames and Hudson, 1965)

Cine qua non, exhibition catalogue (Florence: Valleecchi, 1979)

Coe, Brian, *Muybridge & the Chronophotographers* (London: British Film Institute, 1992)*

Coissac, G.-Michel, *Histoire du cinématographe de ses origines à nos jours* (Paris: Cinéopse/Gauthier-Villars, 1925)

Cuenca, Carlos Fernandez, *Historia del cinema* (Madrid: Aguado, 1948)

Dagognet, François, *Etienne-Jules Marey: La passion de la trace* (Paris: Hazon, 1987)*

Delimata, Joyce (ed.), *Marey/Muybridge, pionniers du cinema: rencontre Beaune/ Stanford* (Beaune: Conseil Régional de Bourgogne, 1996)*

Demeny, Georges, *Les origines du cinématographe* (Paris: Henry Paulin, 1909)

Deslandes, Jacques, *Histoire comparée du cinéma* (Tournai: Casterman, 1966 and 1968)

Dorikens, Maurice (ed.), *Joseph Plateau 1801–1883: Living Between Art and Science* (Gent: Provincie Oost-Vlaanderen, 2001), exhibition catalogue*

Doyen, E.L., *Invatarea tehnicii operatorii prin proiectiuni vii* (Bucharest, 1914)

Doyen, E.L., *L'Enseignement de la technique opératoire par les projections animées* (Paris: Société Générale des Cinématographes Eclipse, 1911)

Ducom, Jacques, *Le cinématographe scientifique et industriel, son évolution intellectuelle, sa puissance educative et morale* (Paris, 1923), second edition

E.J. Marey, sa vie, son œuvre: Communications présentées au Congrès 'Marey' de l'Association bourguignonne des Sociétés Savantes (Beaune, 1974)

E.J. Muybridge (1830–1904) – E.J. Marey (1830–1904) Histoires parallèles, catalogue of an exhibition organised by the Musée Marey of Beaune, 2000*

En Hommage à Etienne-Jules Marey (Paris: DD Productions, c.1995)*

Fescourt, Henri (ed.), *Le cinéma des origines à nos jours* (Paris: Editions du Cygne, 1932)

Fescourt, Henri, *La foi et les montagnes (ou le 7ème art au passé)* (Paris: Paul Montel, 1959)

Frizot, Michel (ed.), *E.J. Marey, 1830/1904: La photographie du mouvement* (Paris: Centre Georges Pompidou/Musée National d'Art Moderne, 1977)

Frizot, Michel (ed.), *Etienne-Jules Marey* (Paris: Photo Poche, 1983)*

Frizot, Michel (ed.), *La chronophotographie* (Beaune: Association des Amis de Marey and Ministère de la Culture, 1984)*

Fulton, Albert R., *Motion Pictures: The development of an art from silent films to the age of television* (Norman: University of Oklahoma Press, 1960)

Gernsheim, Helmut and Alison, *Storia della fotografia* (Milan: Frassinelli, 1966)

Ghirardini, Lino, *Storia generale del cinema, 1895–1959, con problematica introduttiva* (Milan: Marzorati, 1959)

Gilardi, Ando, *Muybridge, il magnifico voyeur* (Milan: Mazzotta, 1980)

Gilardi, Ando, *Storia sociale della fotografia* (Milan: Feltrinelli, 1976)

Grazzini, Giovanni, *La memoria negli occhi: Boleslaw Matuszewski: un pioniere del cinema* (Rome: Carocci, 1999)*

Griffiths, Alison, *Wondrous Difference: Cinema, Anthropology and Turn-of-the-Century Visual Culture* (New York: Columbia University Press, 2002)*

Gubern, Roman, *Storia del cinema* (Naples: Marotta, 1972)

Guinea, Miguel Angel Garcia, *Altamira principio del arte* (Madrid: Silex, 1980)

Haas, Robert Bartlett, *Muybridge, Man in Motion* (Berkeley/Los Angeles: University of California Press, 1976)

Hampton, Benjamin, *History of the Movies* (New York: Covici-Friede, 1931)

Hecht, Hermann (ed. Ann Hecht), *Pre-Cinema History: An Encyclopaedia and Annotated Bibliography of the Moving Image before 1896* (London: Bowker-Saur/British Film Institute, 1993)*

Hendricks, Gordon, *Beginnings of the Biograph* (New York, 1964)

Hendricks, Gordon, *Eadweard Muybridge, The Father of the Motion Picture* (New York: Viking, 1975)

Hendricks, Gordon, *The Edison Motion Picture Myth* (Berkeley: University of California Press, 1961)

Hendricks, Gordon, *The Kinetoscope* (New York, 1966)

Hendricks, Gordon, *Thomas Eakins: His Photographic Works* (Philadelphia: Pennsylvania Academy of the Fine Arts, 1969)*

Herbert, Stephen (ed.), *Eadweard Muybridge: The Kingston Museum Bequest* (Hastings: The Projection Box, 2004)*

Herbert, Stephen (ed.), *A History of Pre-Cinema* [three volumes] (London: Routledge, 2000)*

Herbert, Stephen and Luke McKernan (eds.), *Who's Who of Victorian Cinema: A Worldwide Survey* (London: British Film Institute, 1996)*

Hoffmann, Hilmar, and Walter Schobert (eds.), *Perspektiven: Zur Geschichte der filmischen Wahrnehmung* (Frankfurt am Main: Deutsches Filmmuseum, 1986–1987)*

Hopwood, Henry V., *Living Pictures: Their History, Photo-Production and Practical Working* (London: Optician & Photographic Trades Review, 1899; reprinted New York: Arno Press, 1970)

Janssen, Jules, *Oeuvres scientifiques complètes* (Paris, 1929)

Jean Comandon [Les pionniers du cinéma scientifique] (Brussels: Hayez, 1967)

Keeping Track: A Runners's Log, illustrated with photographs from *Animal Locomotion* by Eadweard Muybridge (New York: The Metropolitan Museum of Art, 1983)*

Knight, Arthur, *The Liveliest Art: A panoramic history of the movies* (New York: Macmillan, 1957)

La passion du mouvement au XIXe siècle: hommage à E.-J. Marey, catalogue of the exhibition of the Association des Amis de Marey (Beaune, 1991)*

Lefebvre, Thierry, Jacques Malthête, Laurent Mannoni (eds.), *Lettres d' Étienne-Jules Marey à Georges Demenÿ, 1880–1894* (Paris: Association française de recherche sur l'histoire du cinéma, 1999)*[405]

Leish, Kenneth W., *Cinema* (New York: Newsweek Books, 1974)

Leyda, Jay, *Kino: A History of the Russian and Soviet Film* (London: George Allen and Unwin, 1960)

Liesegang, F.P., *Die Begründung der Reihenphotographie durch Eadweard Muybridge, Ein Beitrag zur Geschichte der Kinematographie* (1940)

Liesegang, F.P., *Das lebende Lichtbild* (Leipzig, 1910)

Liesegang, F.P., in collaboration with Dr K. Kieser and Professor O. Polimanti, *Wissenschaftliche Kinematographie* (Leipzig, 1920)

Liesegang, F.P., *Zahlen und Quellen zur Geschicte der Projektionskunst und Kinematographie* (Berlin, 1926), translated and edited by Hermann Hecht as *Dates and Sources – A contribution to the history of the art of projection and to cinematography* (London: The Magic Lantern Society of Great Britain, 1986)*

Londe, Albert, *La photographie moderne* (Paris: G. Masson, 1888)

Lucien Bull [Les pionniers du cinéma scientifique] (Brussels: Hayez, 1967)

Macdonnell, Kevin, *Eadweard Muybridge: The Man who Invented the Moving Picture* (London: Weidenfeld & Nicholson, 1972)

MacGowan, Kenneth, *Behind the Screen: The History and Techniques of the Motion Picture* (New York: Delacorte Press, 1965)

Mach, Ernst, *Die Optische-akustische Versuche* (Prague, 1873)

Maffei, Lamberto and Luciano Mecacci, *La visione* (Milan: Edizioni Scientifiche e Tecniche Mondadori, 1979)

Mannoni, Laurent, *Le grand art de la lumière et de l'ombre: archéologie du cinéma* (Paris: Nathan, 1995). English edition (trans. Richard Crangle), *The Grand Art of Light and Shadow: Archaeology of the Cinema* (Exeter: University of Exeter Press, 2000)*

Mannoni, Laurent, *Étienne-Jules Marey, la mémoire de l'oeil* (Milan/Paris: Mazzotta/Cinémathèque Française, 1999)*

Mannoni, Laurent, M. de Ferrière le Vayer, P. Demeny (eds.), *Georges Demenÿ pionnier du cinema* (Douai: Pagine, 1997)*

Manvell, Roger (ed.), *Experiment in the Film* (London: The Grey Walls Press, 1949)

Marey pionnier de la synthèse du mouvement, catalogue of the exhibition held by the Musée Marey, Beaune, 1995*

Marey, E.J., *La chronophotographie* (Paris: Gauthier-Villars, 1899)

Marey, E.J., *Développement de la méthode graphique par l'emploi de la photographie* (Paris: Masson, 1884)

Marey, E.J., *Du mouvement dans les fonctions de la vie* (Paris: Ballière, 1868)

Marey, E.J., *La machine animale: Locomotion terrestre et aérienne* (Paris: Ballière, 1873)

Marey, E.J., *La méthode graphique dans les sciences expérimentales, et principalement en physiologie et en me´decine* (Paris: Masson, 1878)

Marey, E.J., *Le mouvement* (Paris: Masson, 1894)

Marey, E.J., *Le mouvement* (Nîmes: Éditions J. Chambon, 1994, reprint)*

Marey, E.J., *Physiologie du mouvment: Le vol des oiseaux* (Paris: Masson, 1890)

Marey, E.J., *Physiologie médicale de la circulation du sang, basée sur l'étude graphique des mouvements du coeur et du pouls artériel, avec application aux maladies de l'appareil circulatoire* (Paris: Delahaye, 1863)

Mendelssohn, Kurt, *Science and Western Domination* (London: Thames and Hudson, 1976)

Messter, Oskar, *Mein Weg mit dem Film* (Berlin: Max Hesses Verlag, 1936)

Michaelis, Anthony R., *Research Films in Biology, Anthropology, Psychology, and Medicine* (New York: Academic Press, 1955)

Mitry, Jean, *Histoire du cinéma: art et industrie* (Paris, 1967)

Mozley, Anita Ventura, Robert Bartlett Haas and Françoise Forster-Hahn, *Eadweard Muybridge, The Stanford Years, 1872–1882*, catalogue of an exhibition at the Museum of Art of Stanford University, San Francisco, 1972

Muybridge, Eadweard, *Animal Locomotion, Males (nude)*, vol. I (New York: Da Capo, 1969), with a facsimile of *Prospectus and Catalogue of Plates* (Philadelphia, 1887)

Muybridge, Eadweard, *Animals in Motion* (New York: Dover, 1957)

Muybridge, Eadweard, *The Human Figure in Motion: An Electro-Photographic Investigation of Consecutive Phases of Muscular Actions* (London: Chapman & Hall, 1901)

Muybridge, Eadweard, *The Human Figure in Motion* (New York: Dover, 1955)

Newhall, Beaumont, *The History of Photography, from 1839 to the present day* [revised and enlarged edition] (New York: Museum of Modern Art, 1964)

Paolella, Roberto, *Storia del cinema muto* (Naples: Gianini, 1956)

Pesenti Campagnoni, Donata, *Verso il cinema – Macchine spettacoli e mirabili visioni* (Turin: UTET, 1995)*

Physiologie expérimentale, Ecole pratique des Hautes études, travaux du laboratoire du prof. Marey (Paris, 1876–1880, four volumes)

Potonniée, Georges, *Les origines du cinématographe* (Paris: Paul Montel, 1928)

Prodger, Philip, *Time Stands Still: Eadweard Muybridge and the Instantaneous Photography Movement* (New York: Oxford University Press, 2003)*

Raffaelli, Sergio, *Cinema film regia* (Rome: Bulzoni, 1978)

Ramsaye, Terry, *A Million and One Nights: A history of the movies* (New York: Simon and Schuster, 1926)

Rhode, Eric, *A History of Cinema from its Origins to 1970* (London: Allen Lane, 1970)

Rieger, František Ladislav (ed.), *Riegruv slovník naucný* (Prague, 1865)

Rivista di fisica, matematica e scienze naturali (Pavia, 1901)

Rognoni, Luigi, *Cinema muto dalle origini al 1930* (Rome: Edizioni di Bianco e Nero, 1952)

Rossell, Deac, *Living Pictures: The Origins of the Movies* (New York: State University of New York Press, 1998)*

Roux-Parassac, E., *...et l'image s'anima, ou la merveilleuse et véridique histoire d'une grande invention* (Paris: Editions du Monde Moderne, 1930)

Sadoul, Georges, *Histoire du cinéma mondial des origines à nos jours* (Paris: Flammarion, 1964)

Sadoul, Georges, *Histoire générale du cinéma: Part 1 – L'invention du cinéma, 1832–1897* (Paris : Editions Denoel, 1946)

Sadoul, Georges, *Storia generale del cinema: Le origini e i pionieri (1832–1909)* (Turin: Einaudi, 1965)

Santuola, M., *Breves apuntes sobre algunos objetos prehistóricos de la provincia de Santander* (Santander: 1880)

Sauvage, Léo, *L'affaire Lumière du mythe à l'histoire: enquête sur les origines du cinéma* (Paris: Lherminier, 1985)*

Scharf, Aaron, *Art and Photography* (London: Allen Lane, 1968)

Solnit, Rebecca, *Motion Studies: Time, Space and Eadweard Muybridge* (London: Bloomsbury, 2003)*

Stampfer, Simon R. von, *Die Stroboscopischen oder optischen Zauberscheiben. Deren Theorie und wissenschaftliche Anwendung, erklärt von dem Erfinder* (Vienna/ Leipzig: Trentsensky and Vieweg, 1833)

Storia universale illustrata (Milan: Sonzogno, 1907)

Taylor, Deems, *A Pictorial History of the Movies* (New York: Simon and Schuster, 1943)

Thévenard, Pierre, and G. Tassel, *Le cinéma scientifique français* (Paris: La Jeune Parque, 1948)

Thomas, D.B., *The Origins of the Motion Picture* (London: HMSO, 1964)

Tichonov, Michail, *Kino na služ be nauki* (Moscow: Iskusstvo, 1954)

Traub, Hans, *Als Man Anfing zu Filmen* (Berlin: UFA Buchverlag GmbH, 1940)

Trutaut, Eugène, *La photographie animée* (Paris: Gauthier-Villars, 1899)

Vincent, Carl, *Storia del cinema* (Milan: Garzanti, 1949)

Vivié, Jean, *Traité général de technique du cinéma, vol. 1: Historique et développement de la technique cinématographique* (Paris: Editions BPI, 1946)

Von Leyden, E. and E. Pfeiffer (eds.), *Verhandlungen des Congresses für Innere Medicin* (Wiesbaden, 1898)

Von Zglinicki, Friedrich, *Der Weg des Films, Die Geschichte der Kinematographie und ihrer Vorläufer* (Berlin: Rembrandt Verlag, 1956)

Wright, Basil, *The Use of the Film* (London: Bodley Head, 1948)

Wrigley, Maurice Jackson and E. Leyland, *The Cinema: Historical, Technical and Bibliographical* (London: Grafton, 1939)

Zguridi, Alexsandr, *Ekran, Nauka, žizn'* (Moscow: Iskusstvo, 1983)

Notes

PART I

Chapter 1

1. Roberto Paolella, *Storia del cinema muto* (Naples: Gianini, 1956), p. 16.
2. Roman Gubern, *Storia del cinema* (Naples: Marotta, 1972), p. 23.
3. M. Santuola, *Breves apuntes sobre algunos objetos prehistóricos de la provincia de Santander* (Santander: 1880). The sketch can also be found in Miguel Angel Garcia Guinea, *Altamira principio del Arte* (Madrid: Silex, 1980), plates 4-5.
4. Henri Breuil and Hugo Obermaier, *Las cuevas de Altamira a Santillana del Mar* (Madrid: Topografías de Archivos, 1935). Also cited in Carlos Fernandez Cuenca, Historia del cinema (Madrid: Aguado, 1948), footnote 5, p. 23.
5. Cuenca, *Historia del cinema*.
6. Cuenca, *Historia del cinema*, p. 45.
7. Deems Taylor, *A Pictorial History of the Movies* (New York: Simon and Schuster, 1943), p. 8.

Chapter 2

8. Terry Ramsaye, *A Million and One Nights: A history of the movies* (New York: Simon and Schuster, 1926).
9. Jacques Deslandes, *Histoire comparée du cinéma* (Tournai: Casterman, 1966 and 1968). The second volume *Du cinématographe au cinéma* was written in collaboration with Jacques Richard.
10. For Britain, see Maurice Jackson Wrigley and E. Leyland, *The Cinema: Historical, Technical and Bibliographical* (London: Grafton, 1939). Subsequently other British writers have put Friese-Greene's achievements into its broader context: Brian Coe 'William Friese-Greene and the Origins of Cinematography' in *Photographic Journal* (March-April, 1962) and John Barnes, *The Beginnings of Cinema in England* (London: David & Charles, 1976). For America, see Benjamin B. Hampton, *History of the Movies* (New York: Covici-Friede, 1931, reprinted in New York 1970); Kenneth W. Leish, Cinema (New York: Newsweek Books, 1974). In some cases, the Lumières are mentioned merely as followers of the invention.
11. Lino Ghirardini, *Storia generale del cinema, 1895-1959, con problematica introduttiva* (Milan: Marzorati, 1959), p. 164.
12. E. Roux-Parassac, *...et l'image s'anima, ou la merveilleuse et véridique histoire d'une grande invention* (Paris: Editions du Monde Moderne, 1930).

Chapter 3

13. Albert R. Fulton, *Motion Picture: The development of an art from silent films to the age of television* (Norman: University of Oklahoma Press, 1960), p. 5.

14. Paolella, *Storia del Cinema muto*, p. 17.
15. André Bazin, 'Invenzione e mito del cinema', *Sequenza no. 8* (1950), p. 5. Edition dedicated to the birth of cinema.
16. Carl Vincent, *Storia del cinema* (Milan: Garzanti, 1949), pp. 3-4.
17. Vincent, *Storia del cinema*, pp. 11-15.
18. Luigi Rognoni, *Cinema muto dalle origini al 1930* (Rome: Edizioni di Bianco e Nero, 1952), p. 16.
19. Arthur Knight, *The Liveliest Art: A panoramic history of the movies* (New York: Macmillan, 1957), p. 4; Eric Rhode, *A History of Cinema from its Origins to 1970* (London: Allen Lane, 1970), pp. 4-15; Basil Wright, *The Use of the Film* (London: Bodley Head, 1948), pp. 11-34; A. Angelini has consulted dozens of histories of the cinema in the ambit of my courses on documentary and scientific film at the Centro sperimentale di cinematografia of Rome. See his essay 'Il fattore tecnico-scientifico nella nascita del cinema: un confronto tra i testi', *Bollettino dell'Associazionene Italiana di Cinematografia Scientifica* (December 1979), p. 21 and in the same issue 'Influenza della rivoluzione industriale sulle origini del cinema.'

Chapter 4

20. Henry V. Hopwood, *Living Pictures: Their History, Photo-Production and Practical Working* (London: Optician & Photographic Trades Review, 1899, reprinted New York: Arno Press, 1970).
21. Hopwood, *Living Pictures*, p. 48.
22. G.-Michel Coissac, *Histoire du cinématographe de ses origines a nos jours* (Paris : Cinéopse/Gauthier-Villars, 1925).
23. Georges Potonniée, *Les origines du cinématographe* (Paris : Paul Montel, 1928).
24. Georges Sadoul, *Histoire générale du cinéma: Part 1 – L'invention du cinéma, 1832-1897* (Paris: Editions Denoel, 1946), p. 29.
25. Coissac, *Histoire du cinématographe*, p. 224. Taken from the transcripts of the Société Française de Photographie when supporters of Lumière and Marey were debating the text of a memorial to commemorate the thirtieth anniversary of the first film show.
26. G.-Michel Coissac, 'Précisions sur l'histoire du Cinematographe', in Henri Frescourt (ed.), *Le Cinéma des origines à nos jours* (Paris : Editions du Cygne, 1932), p. 61. In any event, Sadoul himself in the second edition of the first volume of his *Histoire générale* reiterates in good faith his lack of nationalistic pride, notes that for him Lumière was not the sole inventor of cinema, underlines the importance of Edison's contribution, and states that in the first edition (due to the war, secretiveness, the difficulty of getting documentary evidence) he had perhaps underestimated the importance of foreign contributors especially the British and German ones, but then again falls prey to false information when he writes that Skladanowsky 'during the war 1939-1945 travelled through Central Europe at the expense of the Hitlerian Propaganda Ministry.' Skladanowsky actually died in 1939.
27. Sadoul, *Histoire générale du cinéma: Part 1 – L'invention du cinéma, 1832-1897*; Georges Sadoul, *Histoire du cinéma mondial des origines à nos jours* (Paris: Flammarion, 1964).
28. Sadoul, *Histoire du cinéma mondial des origines à nos jours*, p. 338.
29. Sadoul, *Histoire du cinéma mondial des origines à nos jours*, p. 23 (Italian edition).
30. Friedrich Von Zglinicki, *Der Weg des Films, Die geschichte der kinematographie und ihrer vorläufer* (Berlin: Rembrandt Verlag, 1956). Gordon Hendricks, in *Film Culture*, November 1957, wrote a critical review of Von Zglinicki's book, listings its errors on American pioneers.

31. Deslandes, *Histoire comparée du cinéma*, p. 7.
32. Jean Mitry, *Histoire du cinéma: art et industrie* (Paris, 1967).
33. Mitry, *Histoire du cinéma*, pp. 42-43.
34. Jean Mitry (ed.), *Le cinéma des origins*, special issue of *Le Cinéma d'aujourd'hui* (Autumn 1976).
35. Roger Manvell (ed.), *Experiment in the Film* (London: The Grey Walls Press, 1949).
36. Kenneth MacGowan, *Behind the Screen: The History and Techniques of the Motion Picture* (New York: Delacorte Press, 1965).
37. Sadoul, writing his general history well before the publication of Hendricks' research and MacGowan's book, reproduced the flyer and, believing it to be authentic, refers to the occurrence as an historical event. Sergio Raffaelli in *Cinema, Film, Regia* (Rome: Bulzoni, 1978), citing Sadoul as his source, refers to what he believed to be a linguistic 'anomaly' in the text of the flyer since it uses the French word 'Cinématographe' instead of 'Cinématograph' as used by LeRoy. From this point of view, one might see this as further proof of the falsity of the document.
38. C.W. Ceram, *Eine Archäologie des Kinos* (Reinbek bei Hamburg: Rowohlt, 1965), translated as *Archaeology of the Cinema* (London: Thames and Hudson, 1965).
39. The illustrations were collected by Olive Cook, who had a much wider view of the subject than Ceram (*Editor's note*).
40. Hans Traub, *Als Man Anfing zu Filmen* (Berlin: UFA Buchverlag GmbH, 1940).
41. D.B. Thomas, *The Origins of the Motion Picture* (London: HMSO, 1964).
42. Jean Vivié, *Traité général de technique du cinéma, vol. 1, historique et développement de la technique cinématographique* (Paris: Editions BPI, 1946).
43. Vivié, *Traité général de technique du cinéma*, p. 98.

Chapter 5

44. Jacques Ducom, *Le cinématographe scientifique et industriel, son évolution intellectuelle, sa puissance educative et morale* (Paris, 1923), second edition, p. 8.
45. Ducom, *Le cinématographe scientifique et industriel*, pp. 33-54.
46. F.P. Liesegang, in collaboration with Dr K. Kieser and Professor O. Polimanti, *Wissenschaftliche Kinematographie* (Leipzig, 1920).
47. From the scientific writings of Professor Polimanti it is clear that in the field of physiology, filming was already taking place by 1907. Some series of frames have been reproduced as figures 141 and 142 in the book referred to in the previous note.
48. It should be noted that the International Association of Scientific Film was structured along these three fundamental applications.
49. Liesegang would return to the subject of the history of the birth of cinema with a highly specialised work as the title itself would tend to indicate: *Zahlen und Quellen zur Geschicte der Projektionskunst und Kinematographie* (Berlin, 1926). It is a detailed series of annotated chronologies with rich and detailed bibliographies on the history of luminous projection starting with G.B. Della Porta and Kircher; the development of serial photography, and the birth of cinema. It remains an important reference work although it has been made incomplete by more recent research and discoveries. [The Magic Lantern Society of Great Britain published Liesegang's work in an English translation by Hermann Hecht in 1986, entitled *Dates and Sources on the History of Projection and Cinematographic Technique* (*Editor's note*).]
50. Liesegang, *Wissenschaftliche Kinematographie*, p. 259. In 1910 in Leipzig under the title *Das lebende Lichtbild*, Liesegang published a curious little volume in which he tried to explain to those that had been to the cinema at least once what it was and how the

'luminous living image' worked and who invented it. In the book there were plates that could be cut out to make a 'magic disc' (Thaumatrope); a Phenakistiscope (with a series of images of a rider on a horse taken by Muybridge) and a functioning model of a 'Maltese Cross', for intermittent movement of the film. In addition to this on the top right hand corner of the odd-numbered pages were reproduced twenty-six square images of Muybridge's rider on a horse in various phases of movement. Flicking through these quickly one would have an example of the so-called 'pocket-size cinematograph.' Polimanti took from this text his view on the merits of the contribution of the Lumières (see p. 16 of Liesegang's 1910 book), while Liesegang himself entitled one short chapter 'Marey, the founder of modern cinematography.'

51. Lucien Bull, *La cinématographie* (Paris, 1928).
52. Bull, *La cinématographie*, p. 158.
53. *Rivista Ciba*, Italian edition, no. 18, III, June 1949.
54. *Rivista Ciba*, p. 573.
55. *Rivista Ciba*.
56. Pierre Thévenard, and G. Tassel, *Le cinéma scientifique français*, preface by Jean Painlevé (Paris: La Jeune Parque, 1948).
57. Thévenard and Tassel, *Le cinéma scientifique français*, p. xv.
58. Thévenard and Tassel, *Le cinéma scientifique français*, p. 8.
59. Anthony R. Michaelis, *Research Films in Biology, Anthropology, Psychology, and Medicine* (New York: Academic Press, 1955). A second volume by the same author on research films in other sciences was announced but appears to have never been published.
60. Michaelis, *Research Films in Biology, Anthropology, Psychology, and Medicine*, p. 85.
61. An update on the author's research since 1984 is given in the Coda chapter. A number of books relating to the origins of scientific cinematography published since 1984 are given in the bibliography (*Editor's note*).

PART II

62. Both Sadoul, *Histoire générale*, and Ceram are in absolute and categorical agreement. The former has the year 1832 in his book 'The invention of cinema' in the *Histoire générale*. Ceram writes that 'the prehistory of cinematography begins at a perfectly specific time, the year 1832', *Eine Archäologie des Kinos*, p. 17.
63. Sadoul, *Histoire générale*, p. 7.

Chapter 6

64. Peter Mark Roget, 'Explanation of an optical deception in the appearance of the spokes of a wheel through vertical apertures', *Philosophical Transactions of the Royal Society*, 1825, p. 121.
65. See Deslandes, *Histoire comparée du cinéma*, p. 30 and the catalogue *Kinematografické museum, Vystava 50 let cs. Filmu* (Prague, 1948), p. 13.
66. Sadoul, *Histoire générale*, p. 10. [These various examples relate to different visual phenomena, indicating a growing interest in visual perception experiments, each of which played its part in the development of motion pictures, by stimulating enquiry. None by itself, however, explain how we see pictures in motion. For example, Roget's observation of the convexity of the curved images of spokes refers to anorthoscopic distortion, which is a persistence of vision phenomenon, but not in any sense part of why we see motion pictures; and Newton's disc relates to colour fusion (*Editor's note*).]

67. Deslandes, *Histoire comparée du cinéma*, p. 31.

68. Sadoul, *Histoire générale*, p. 11. Sadoul however seems over emphatic in expressing his opinion on the matter: 'In this experimental, very primitive, mechanism one can see the very beginnings, in very rough form, of the essential elements of today's cinema' (ivi, p. 11) In the first edition of Sadoul's book there are two figures meant to show the similarity between Roget's experimental diagram and a diagram on the functioning of the cinema. His passion and enthusiasm in unearthing the scientific inventors of cinematic equipment push him too far however: we do not think that one can compare Roget's mobile strip with parallel bands (perpendicular to the movement) to the frame lines that separate the various frames on a strip of film. In the case of the former, the parallel bands are the element which create the optical illusion, while there is no doubt that it is the actual picture on the frame and not the separation line which creates the moving film image.

69. The classic example of this is that of a bird and its cage drawn on separate faces of the disc. With rapid rotation one will see the bird inside the cage.

70. Ceram, *Eine Archäologie des Kinos*, p. 17.

71. See Deslandes, *Histoire comparée du cinéma*, p. 26 and also Liesegang, *Zahlen und Quellen*, p. 30.

72. One should note that the Thaumatrope, before ending up as a children's toy, was the subject of interest and conversation in society and could be purchased at the Royal Institution.

73. The title of Faraday's publication is: 'On a peculiar class of optical deceptions', *The Journal of the Royal Institution of Great Britain*, 1831, vol. 1, p. 205; the report had been presented on 10 December 1830.

74. It is interesting to note that, in his speculative fervour, Faraday dedicated the last four pages of the cited work on optical illusions to the biological issues surrounding the microscopic 'animalculae', which had only just been identified and described and which would later be known as rotifers. At that time there was a debate between those that believed that these organisms were furnished with actual wheels to move water and gather food and those (like Faraday) who thought that it was an optical illusion caused by a crown of brows vibrating in rapid alternating movements.

Chapter 7

75. Plateau's blindness is now thought to have been caused by infection or hereditary tendency (*Editor's note*).

76. MONSIEUR PLATEAU, 16mm. The documentary won an award at the Cannes Film Festival and a diploma at the 19th Congress and Festival of the International Association of Scientific Film.

77. Deslandes, *Histoire comparée du cinéma*, p. 32. This research was undertaken by Plateau between 1826 and 1828 and published before he finished his degree.

78. Sadoul, *Histoire générale*, p. 16. [It is now recognised by most authorities, including the author, that the notion of a 'persistence of vision' does not explain why it is that we are able to see moving pictures. We do not 'see' motion pictures because of any persistence of each image on the retina. At sufficient frequency of presentation, our eye-brain combination is unable to detect the gaps between the images, and fuses the individual images into one continuous image which we perceive, psychologically, as a moving picture (*Editor's note*).]

79. Cited by Marey in *La meìthode graphique dans les sciences expeìrimentales, et principalement en physiologie et en meìdecine* (Paris, 1878), p. 422 (1885 edition), who

took it from Ernst Mach, *Die Optische-akustische Verusche* (Prague, 1873). It is probably a paper written by Plateau in 1836 and published in the Brussels *Bulletin de l'Académie Royale des Sciences* (no. 13, p. 364-369) and cited by Liesegang, *Zahlen und Quellen*, p. 38.

80. *Annales de Chimie et de Physique*, Brussels 1833.

81. Plateau published this paper in the seventh volume of the *Correspondance Mathématique et Physique de l'Observatoire de Bruxelles*, 1832, p. 365. His text however, is entitled *Sur un nouveau genre d'illusions d'optique*, bearing the date 20 January 1833. In the opening Plateau cleared up the misunderstanding that was created with Faraday since, while Plateau knew and cited Faraday's works, the English scientist had ignored in his publication the previous works by Plateau. The latter recognised that Faraday, as soon as he became aware of this, wrote to him 'admitting, in the most flattering terms towards me, the priority of my observations.' Plateau's text compares Faraday's experiments with his own, pointing out their differences, and describes in details the manufacturing and functioning of the first disc of what would later be called the Phenakistiscope.

82. Potonniée, *Les origines du Cinématographe*, pp. 14-19 records the strange story of one Dr. Sinsteden, a German, who in 1851 who accused Plateau of having copied the Phenakistiscope from Lucretius. Among other things, Sinsteden presented an altered and mutilated version of the quotation from *De Rerum Natura*. One should add that the very serious Plateau took the trouble of answering his detractor, demonstrating through an analysis of the text that Lucretius was in fact referring to dreams and spiritual visions and certainly was not referring to either the effect of the persistence of vision on the retina or even to a physics apparatus. He modestly concluded by writing: 'I hope that this note will be sufficient in removing me from any doubts over plagiarism.'

Chapter 8

83. Simon R. von Stampfer, *Die Stroboscopischen oder optischen Zauberscheiben. Deren Theorie und wissenschaftliche Anwendung, erklärt von dem Erfinder* (Vienna/Leipzig: Trentsensky and Vieweg, 1833). In their preface the publishers confirm that Stampfer began his experiments in December 1832 and that he presented his first six stroboscopic discs to friends and peers in February 1833. The text, without the illustrations, was reprinted in *Jahrbücher des k.k. Polytechnischen Institutes*, Vienna 1834, t 18, pp. 237-258 under the title 'Ueber die optischen Täuschungs-Phänomene, welche durch die stroboskopischen Scheiben (optischen Zauberscheiben) hervorgebracht werden.' The variant spellings Stroboscopischen/ Stroboskopischen are in the original text. The quote is taken from the Polytechnic's annals, p. 243. The references to the cylinder, the apparatus made up of two discs and the small matte in the shape of a stage can be found in pages 244-247.

84. Sadoul, *Histoire générale*, p. 34.

85. Sadoul, *Histoire générale*, p. 36. The final allusion refers to Marey and Stanford.

86. Deslandes, *Histoire comparée du cinéma*. He went so far as to dedicate a short chapter to it: 'La dispute d'antériorité entre Plateau et Stampfer', pp. 40-41; see also Sadoul, *Histoire générale*, pp. 17-18.

87. Sadoul, *Histoire générale*, pp. 12-13; also Marey, *La méthode graphique*, note 17, p. 423 and Liesegang, *Zahlen und Quellen*, p. 38 which cites a work by Savart in the *Annales de Chimie et de Physique*, 53, 1833, p. 335.

88. Catalogue of the Kinematografické Museum, Prague, p. 14; Liesegang, *Zahlen und Quellen*, p. 39 which cites the work by Müller in *Poggendorffs Annalen*, 67, 1846, p. 271.

Chapter 9

89. W.G. Horner, 'On the properties of the Daedaleum, a new instrument of optical illusion', *The London and Edinburgh Philosophical Magazine and Journal of Science*, January 1834, pp. 36-41. Deslandes, *Histoire Comparée du Cinéma*, pp. 37-39 reproduces the quotation; Liesegang, *Zahlen und Quellen*, p. 36 makes reference to the difficulties that King Jr, a Bristol optician, had in precisely making the strips of drawings sent by Horner to be used in the cylinder.

90. Sadoul, *Histoire générale*, p. 19.

91. MacGowan, *Behind the Screen*, p. 39. Over a century after it first appeared, the word 'Zoetrope' came to the fore again as the name as Francis Ford Coppola's production company, American Zoetrope. It was perhaps chosen as a reminder of his studies at UCLA where there has been renewed interest in the birth of cinema and in Eadweard Muybridge in particular.

Chapter 10

92. Purkyně's contribution to the birth of cinema has only been mentioned in a few items published in Czechoslovakia; it has also been noted in Liesegang, *Zahlen und Quellen*, p. 38. The title of Purkyneě's doctoral dissertation was *Beiträge zur Kenntnis des Sehens in subjectiver Hinsicht* [Contributions to the knowledge of vision in its subjective aspects]. It was such a success that it was republished after a year. The Bohemian physiologist is also remembered for his descriptions of the so-called 'Purkyně effect', the change in apparent luminosity of colours depending on the brightness of light. See, for example, Lamberto Maffei and Luciano Mecacci, *La Visione* (Milan: Edizioni Scientifiche e Tecniche Mondadori, 1979).

93. According to Sadoul, who does not mention Purkyně, Phenakistiscopes with two separate disks only appeared in Europe after 1850.

94. This is a good example of a scientific use of photography cited as a precursor of the invention of cinema. But in fact, as in many other cases, this is a mistaken inference. In 1865 the Frenchman E. Onimus in collaboration with the photographer A. Martin managed to record with one exposure on a photographic plate the two extreme positions, in the ambit of a circulatory cycle, of the beating heart of a tortoise. The heart had been exposed by surgical operation. Owing to the poor sensitivity of the emulsion, one made use of the fact that the muscular movement was slightly slowed down in the two culminating phases of the contraction and expansion; therefore on the plate the major and minor outlines of the volume of the heart were sharper, while the intermediate phases were more blurred. Liesegang, *Wissenschaftliche*, p. 11; Marey, *La méthode graphique*, p. 123; Vivié, *Traité général de technique du cinéma*, p. 19.

Chapter 12

95. If one wishes to do further research in this vast and important subject, there are a large number of books on the subject. A starting point, even relating to later points, would be Beaumont Newhall, *The History of Photography, from 1839 to the present day* [revised and enlarged edition] (New York: Museum of Modern Art, 1964).

96. In 'Troisième note sur des applications curieuses de la persistence des impressions de la rétine', *Bulletin de l'Académie Royale des Sciences*, no. 7, 1847, quoted in Deslandes, *Histoire comparée du cinéma*, p. 73. See also Liesegang, *Zahlen und Quellen*, pp. 39-64.

97. For further research one should consult the texts already referred to written by Sadoul, Deslandes, Vivié and Ceram. It is possible that the first attempt to use a series of photographs in such a machine was in 1851-52 by the Frenchman Jules Duboscq (1817-

1860), who built a 'Stéréofantascope' or bioscope with thirty pairs of images. It seems though that it did not work very well and did not find a distributor. To get his series of images, Duboscq photographed, for a example, the successive stages of an apparatus in motion one at a time so as to reconstruct its movement, rather than record actual movement. Potonniée, *Les origines du cinématographe*, pp. 23-25; Liesegang, *Zahlen und Quellen*, pp. 36, 40, 42.

98. Sadoul, *Histoire générale*, p. 32 and Deslandes, *Histoire comparée du cinéma*, pp. 81-82.

99. The utopian side to projects that were impossible to realise and technically taken to the limits of the absurd like those by Ducos de Hauron does not mean that one cannot give him his due for the positive and concrete results he obtained in some fields of photography such as the first colour reproductions. Newhall, *The History of Photography*, pp. 162 and 193; Mitry, *Le cinéma des origins*, p. 38 et seq.; Liesegang, *Zahlen und Quellen*, p. 102 et seq.

100. Deslandes, *Histoire comparée du cinéma*, p. 72. The speech has been attributed to Claudet and is said to be from 1865. See Potonniée, *Les origines du cinématographe*, p. 22. It refers to the photographer and author of books on photography Antoine F.-J. Claudet (1797-1867), a Frenchman living in Britain. In 1853 he built a stroboscope with dual images to create stereoscopic effects.

101. Newhall, *The History of Photography*, p. 83.

Part III

Chapter 13

102. Janssen was accepted on 7 April 1876, on the occasion of the presentation of his photographic revolver; the membership of the King of Portugal to the Society was accepted at the same session.

103. In Jules Janssen, *Oeuvres scientifiques complètes* (Paris, 1929), p. 50, we found a textual quotation which reads: 'La couche sensible photographique est la véritable rétine du savant' (Janssen made this remark at a conference in 1887 at the Congress of the French Association for the Advancement of the Sciences, but referred it to one of his earlier declarations in 1882). Another quotation reads: 'La plaque photographique est la rétine du savant, mais une rétine bien supérieure à l'oeil humain car, d'une part elle garde trace du phénomène qu'elle a perçu, et de l'autre, dans certains cas, elle voit plus que celui ci.' We find one on page 88 of the same volume of the complete works and another on page 166: 'Avais-je tort, Messieurs, de dire que la pellicule photographique est la vraie rétine du savant?' (conference on photography of 17 August 1889 at the conclusion of the International Photography Congress). Two days later, on the fiftieth anniversary of the dissemination of photography, speaking of when the centenary would be celebrated, he said: 'La photographie sera devenue l'oeil universel.'

104. 'Comptes rendus des séances de l'Académie des Sciences', Paris, volume LXXIX, séance du 6 juillet 1874, given by Deslandes, *Histoire comparée du cinéma*, pp. 111-112.

105. Camille Flammarion, 'Le passage de Vénus', *La Nature*, 8 May 1875, p. 356.

106. Janssen, *Oeuvres scientifiques complètes*, I, pp. 304-5.

107. Flammarion, 'Le passage de Vénus'; also in *Catalogue du Musée du Conservatoire National des Arts e Métiers, Section L* (Paris, 1949).

108. Jules Janssen, *Bulletin de la Société Française de Photographie*, April 1876, p. 101.

109. E.J. Marey, *Développement de la méthode graphique par l'emploi de la photographie* (Paris, 1885), p. 7.

110. G. Turpin, in *Société Française de Photographie*, January-February 1977, p. 155, writes: 'It is curious that the father of chrono-photography did not think for a moment that the fact of recording consecutive frames at more than a minute of interval from each other in no way required the invention of such a complex and precise apparatus as the photographic revolver.'

111. Bull, *La cinématographie*, p. 16; Albert Londe, *La photographie moderne* (Paris: G. Masson, 1888), p. 254; Potoniée, *Les origines du cinématographe*, p. 32); Vivié, *Traité général de technique du cinéma*, p. 20; Thomas, *The Origins of the Motion Picture*, p. 20; Henri Fescourt (ed.), *Le cinéma des origines à nos jours* (Paris: Editions du Cygne, 1932), p. 44.

112. Liesegang, *Wissenschaftliche*, p. 25. The reference to Wolf is taken from his report to the Académie des Sciences reported in *Bulletin de la Société Française de Photographie*, 1895, p. 28. In Liesegang, *Zahlen und Quellen*, I, p.70, it is repeated that the shots took place at intervals of approximately one second for a series of forty-eight pictures.

113. Janssen, *Oeuvres scientifiques complètes*, I, p. 304.

114. Janssen, *Oeuvres scientifiques complètes*, I, pp. 305 and 338. Flammarion, 'Le passage de Vénus', p. 358, writes: 'Mr Janssen preferred the Daguerre procedure to photography on paper, because of its better incising of the picture on the silvered plate.'

115. Janssen, *Bulletin de la Société Française de Photographie*, April 1876, p. 105. And further forward, he adds in a note: 'The English Commission appointed to observe the full eclipse of 5 April 1875 on the Andamane islands, brought revolvers with the intention of photographing the different phases of that eclipse. Unfortunately time did not permit use of the instrument for this new and important purpose.' Also Liesegang, *Wissenschaftliche*, p. 26, speaks of the English team who took fifty and sixty plates of images at intervals of a half and one second.

116. From the G. Turpin article cited above, we can deduce that the plate attributed to Janssen and shown at the Science Museum in London (deriving from the National Maritime Museum at Greenwich) was however obtained with one of the *Janssen Apparatuses* of the English astronomers. It contains sixty images and bears the inscription: $J^1 - 12h\,27m\,30^s - 12h\,28m\,50^s\,20$. This leads to the belief that the sixty takes were carried out over a period of eighty seconds with an exposure time per frame of considerably less than a second, given that the necessary time had to be calculated for the rotation of the plate and the shutter carried out by the handle.

117. Janssen, *Bulletin de la Société Française de Photographie*, April 1876, p. 103. He added: 'nevertheless, afterwards, still during our stay, we obtained numerous plates that were very incisive' and presented some to the participants at the session.

118. MacGowan, *Behind the Screen*, p. 56, is also of this opinion.

119. Janssen, *Oeuvres scientifiques complètes*, I, p. 313. D'Almeida was a Brazilian photographer who 'at the request of the Emperor of Brazil took part in my mission', p. 330.

120. E.J. Marey, *Le mouvement* (Paris: Masson, 1894), p. 102.

Chapter 14

121. Janssen, *Bulletin de la Société Française de Photographie*, April 1876, pp. 105-6.

122. Janssen, *Bulletin de la Société Française de Photographie*, April 1876.

123. In *Bulletin de la Société Française de Photographie*, 1895, p. 423, referred to in Deslandes, *Histoire comparée du cinéma*, p. 227; also in Janssen, *Oeuvres Scientifiques complètes*, II, p. 381.

Chapter 15

124. Concerning the first photographers, Gisèle Freund wrote: 'Many of the first photographers left the circles usually referred to as Bohemian – in brief all sorts of average and small talents that, for the most part, had not managed to make their mark, and turned to this new activity that promised a better life. At the beginning of the second half of the century, photographic technique was sufficiently developed not to require special knowledge from its professionals.' *Fotografia e Società,* 1976, p. 31.

125. Her son grew up in an orphanage. Although not recognizing him as his son, Muybridge did not make him change his name; he also contributed to his upkeep until he reached his majority.

126. Eadweard Muybridge, *The Human Figure in Motion* (New York: Dover, 1955); Eadweard Muybridge, *Animals in Motion* (New York: Dover, 1957).

127. Eadweard Muybridge, *Animal Locomotion, Males (nude),* vol. I (New York: Da Capo, 1969), with a facsimile of *Prospectus and Catalogue of Plates* (Philadelphia, 1887).

128. Aaron Scharf, 'Painting, Photography, and the Image of Movement', *Burlington Magazine,* May 1962; Aaron Scharf, *Art and Photography* (London: Allen Lane, 1968).

129. Anita Ventura Mozley, Robert Barlett Haas and Françoise Forster-Hahn, *Eadweard Muybridge, The Stanford Years, 1872-1882,* exhibition catalogue at the Museum of Art of Stanford University, San Francisco 1972.

130. Kevin Macdonnell, *Eadweard Muybridge: The Man Who Invented The Moving Picture* (London: Weidenfeld & Nicholson, 1972).

131. Gordon Hendricks, *Eadweard Muybridge, The Father of the Motion Picture* (New York: Viking, 1975); Robert Bartlett Haas, *Muybridge, Man in Motion* (Berkeley/Los Angeles: University of California Press, 1976). [Our understanding of Muybridge's work has been extended since by a number of recent studies, including Marta Braun, *Picturing Time: The Work of Étienne-Jules Marey (1830-1904)* (Chicago/London: University of Chicago Press, 1992), which has crucial observations on Muybridge's work; Rebecca Solnit, *Motion Studies: Time, Space and Eadweard Muybridge* (London: Bloomsbury, 2003); Philip Prodger, *Time Stands Still: Eadweard Muybridge and the Instantaneous Photography Movement* (New York: Oxford University Press, 2003); and Stephen Herbert (ed.), *Eadweard Muybridge: The Kingston Museum Bequest* (Hastings: The Projection Box, 2004) *(Editor's note).*]

132. Gordon Hendricks, *The Edison Motion Picture Myth* (Berkeley: University of California Press, 1961); *Beginnings of the Biograph* (New York, 1964); *The Kinetoscope* (New York, 1966).

133. Thom Andersen, EADWEARD MUYBRIDGE, ZOOPRAXOGRAPHER, 16mm film, 60 mins., colour, 1975; produced by Animation Workshop, Motion Picture Division, Department of Theater Arts, University of California, Los Angeles, in partial fulfilment of the requirements for the degree of Master of Fine Arts.

134. In 1976 the Biennale di Venezia used for its poster on the cinema sector some strips of photographs by Muybridge, with a semi-nude woman moving to pick up a veil, taken from different angles. The name of Muybridge was not cited. In the same year, Ando Gilardi, in *Storia sociale della fotografia* (Milan: Feltrinelli, 1976), evaluated Muybridge's contribution as a proto-photographer and precursor of cinema and divulged the influence that his photographs had on the figurative arts. Subsequently, Gilard also published *Muybridge, il magnifico voyeur* (Milan: Mazzotta, 1980), an album of reproductions with a wide choice of the plates on human and animal movement, preceded by an essay in which the author developed a hypothesis of the possible homosexuality (if only latent) of Muybridge, as well as deducing strong evidence for his

voyeurism and exhibitionism. All this in the framework of an even excessive appreciation of the work of Muybridge (he compared him to Leonardo da Vinci and Michelangelo) and, unfortunately, including numerous errors. In 1983, it was possible to consult the manuscript of historical research on Muybridge (approximately 160 typed pages) of the previously quoted German scholar and technician, F.P. Liesegang, *Die Begründung der Reihenphotographie durch Eadweard Muybridge, Ein Beitrag zur Geschichte der Kinematographie* (1940). The text was ready for publication, but was probably blocked by the events of the Second World War.

135. Mozley, Haas and Forster-Hahn, *Eadweard Muybridge, The Stanford Years, 1872-1882*, p. 33.

136. Haas, *Muybridge, Man in Motion*, p. 45 et seq.

137. Muybridge, in the preface to the original edition of *Animals in Motion*, dated December 1898 and reproduced in the 1957 edition, p. 13.

138. Mozley, Haas and Forster-Hahn, *Eadweard Muybridge, The Stanford Years, 1872-1882*, p. 8.

139. Haas, *Muybridge, Man in Motion*, p. 46. For all details relating to the reconstruction of these historical events references will be from Haas and his essay in *Eadweard Muybridge, The Stanford Years, 1872-1882*.

140. After the arguments and lawsuits between Muybridge and Stanford were over, Muybridge (referring to this event and without referring to ex-governor Stanford) had a journalist write: 'Mr Muybridge was called in as referee, and he promptly decided that instantaneous photography would furnish the desired evidence' (in *The Evening Bulletin*, 5 November 1887, newspaper cutting from Muybridge's *Scrapbook*, held at the Kingston-upon-Thames Museum, p. 169).

141. O.G. Rejlander, 'On Photographing Horses', *British Journal Photographic Almanac* (London 1872-1873), p. 115.

142. *Photographic News*, 11 May 1869, quoted in Haas, *Muybridge, Man in Motion*, p 47.

143. Haas, *Muybridge, Man in Motion*, p. 93.

144. Letter by Muybridge published in *Alta California*, 3 August 1877, reproduced in Haas, *Muybridge, Man in Motion*, pp. 93-94 and by Hendricks, *Eadweard Muybridge*, p. 99. Some newspapers expressed doubts over the results, either suggesting that they were fakes or refusing to take the matter seriously.

145. One should note that Muybridge in his original letter to the paper referred to a speed of 'less than 1/1000th of a second', while the caption for the photographic reproduction reads 'less than 1/2000th of a second.'

146. For more information on this episode, see also Haas, *Muybridge, Man in Motion*, p. 95; Mozley, Haas and Forster-Hahn, *Eadweard Muybridge, The Stanford Years, 1872-1882*, pp. 19 and 63; Hendricks, *Eadweard Muybridge*, p. 99 et seq.

Chapter 16

147. The role played by these technicians in the development of the shutter mechanism would in later years, after the success and fame obtained by Muybridge, lead to disputes over the rights, especially from Isaacs; there were no concrete results however.

148. There is no doubt that the artifice of the string interfered with the dynamics of the experiment; according to Hendricks, *Eadweard Muybridge*, p. 104, the breaking of the threads did not guarantee the regularity of the intervals between the clicks of the shutter; in addition to which, the threads frequently frightened the horses and broke their stride.

149. *Resources of California*, August 1878, cited in Haas, *Muybridge, Man in Motion*, p. 111.

Muybridge himself stated on several occasions that it was Stanford who had the original idea ('He originally suggested the idea', he wrote, for instance, in March 1879 in *The Philadelphia Photographer*).

150. Over a century later one writer observed: 'the photographs of a horse's gallop were more amazing than those of the hidden side of the moon, or of our own planet seen from space. The cinema and its inventions prepared the masses for these images; the drawing and painting of animals on the other hand had left open an "interval" in time and in space of a movement that had interested everyone for thousands of years' (Gilardi, *Muybridge*, p. 15). 'Muybridge had brought about a change in human consciousness. In much the same way as the telescope and the microscope, his sequences opened up a world to the eye that the eye formerly had been unable to see.' Rhode, *A History of Cinema from its Origins to 1970*, p. 10.

151. *Scientific American*, 8 October 1878, cited in Haas, *Muybridge, Man in Motion*, p. 116.

152. 'The Motion of a Wagon Wheel', *Scientific American*, 16 November 1878, clipping from the *Scrapbook*, p. 32.

153. Perhaps even thirty; see a news item from the London *Times* of 28 March 1879 which was copied out by Muybridge himself on page 47 of his *Scrapbook*. Of course it may just have been an idea.

154. It was initially demonstrated as the Zoögyroscope, but this soon changed to Zoöpraxiscope. One of the original machines is still in existence and held at the Kingston-upon-Thames Museum. In 1946 it proved to be in perfect working order for a show in London, even for eight hours a day during the six-week run of the exhibition. Haas, *Muybridge, Man in Motion*, p. 120.

155. Muybridge, in his preface to the original edition of *Animals in Motion*, p. 15 in the 1957 edition.

156. Muybridge, in his introduction to the original edition of *The Human Figure in Motion*, p. 7.

157. Muybridge also wrote: 'The anecdote may not be without interest, especially to the constructors of the many different instruments which, at the present day, have taken the place of their prototype.' Muybridge, *The Human Figure in Motion*, pp. 6-7.

158. Hendricks, *Eadweard Muybridge*, p. 115.

159. Haas has calculated that Stanford must have spent at least $42,000; *Muybridge, Man in Motion*, p. 114.

160. The publicity blurb relating to his photographic activities, from 1877 onwards, apart from using such phrases as 'official photographer of the United States Government', also included 'horses photographed as they run or trot at full speed.'

161. 'Hon. Leland Stanford: Sir, Herewith please find the photographs illustrating the attitudes of Animals in Motion executed by me according to your instruction ...' In 1880 Muybridge had published, through his editor G.D. Morse, a few photographs of a solar eclipse, with the caption 'photographed for the honorable Leland Stanford, at Palo Alto, California, by Muybridge.'

162. Hendricks, *Eadweard Muybridge*, p. 133.

163. It is said that the painter had a special vehicle constructed on tracks so that he could sketch horses while racing.

164. Haas, *Muybridge, Man in Motion*, p. 128.

165. See photograph number 96 in Hendricks, *Eadweard Muybridge*.

166. From the text one learns among other things that the wife of the editor of the newspaper provided the food for the evening (Marey was a bachelor).

167. The 'revelations' in Muybridge's photographs induced Meissonnier to modify the

position of the legs on horses in at least one of his paintings. Scharf, *Art and Photography*, pp. 222 and 387; Hendricks, *Eadweard Muybridge*, p. 201.

168. Cutting from the edition of 29 November 1881 in the *Scrapbook*, p. 69.

169. *La Nature*, 1 April 1882.

170. Letters dated 28 November 1881 and 23 December 1881; see the Documents section of Mozley, Haas and Forster-Hahn, *Eadweard Muybridge, The Stanford Years, 1872-1882*, p. 123 et seq.

171. According to Anita Ventura Mozley, for 'dispositions' one should read 'additional financing'; Mozley, Haas and Forster-Hahn, *Eadweard Muybridge, The Stanford Years, 1872-1882*, p. 133, note 51.

172. Mozley, Haas and Forster-Hahn, *Eadweard Muybridge, The Stanford Years, 1872-1882*, Documents section, p. 124; and letter from Muybridge to Frank Shay, 23 December 1881, reproduced in Documents section, p. 125.

173. Cutting dated 9 April 1882 from the *Scrapbook*, p. 81.

174. Even the summary of his presentation to the Royal Institution was published, under the title: *Syllabus of a Course of Two Lectures on the Science of Animal Locomotion in Its Relation to Design in Art*.

175. Before leaving England, Muybridge stated that there was another financier in San Francisco interested in backing the enterprise, but nothing came of it. (Hendricks, *Eadweard Muybridge*, p. 141).

176. His new house in San Francisco had a 'Pompeiian room' and the house was decked out with a large collection of paintings as well as many classical and neo-classical sculptures.

177. They can be found among the plates in his 1881 album.

178. From Stillman's deposition for the subsequent trial, quoted in Document section of Mozley, Haas and Forster-Hahn, *Eadweard Muybridge, The Stanford Years, 1872-1882*, p. 119. In this catalogue there is also an unattributed article published by the San Francisco *Examiner* (6 February 1881) which may have been written by Muybridge. Although the fact that Muybridge is referred to in the third person might make one think otherwise (and despite a few inaccuracies), it is clear from the level of detail that he must have either written it or got someone to write it for him. The article itself is written in a somewhat pompous style and was entitled: *The gift by Leland Stanford to the Arts and Sciences – The invention by Mr Eadweard Muybridge of the instantaneous photograph and the marvellous Zoogyroscope*. The article overflows with praise for the 'builder of the railway' and the artist that fulfilled his hopes by taking his art to the pinnacle of perfection.

179. From the first draft of a letter that Muybridge would send to Stanford many years later (2 May 1892) and in which he went over the details of their affairs together, it appears that the book's title should have read: *The Horse in Motion, as demonstrated by a series of photographs by Muybridge, With an attempt to elucidate the theory of Animal Locomotion by J.D.B. Stillman MD, Published under the auspices of Leland Stanford*. Mozley, Haas and Forster-Hahn, *Eadweard Muybridge, The Stanford Years, 1872-1882*, p. 128.

180. 'I think that the fame that we have brought him has gone to his head': Stanford to Stillman, 23 October 1882. Mozley, Haas and Forster-Hahn, *Eadweard Muybridge, The Stanford Years, 1872-1882*, p. 127.

181. *The Horse in Motion, As Shown by Instantaneous Photography, With a Study on Animal Mechanics, Founded on Anatomy and the revelations of the Camera, in which is Demonstrated the Theory of Quadrupedal Locomotion, by J.D.B. Stillman, A.M., M.D., Executed and Published under the Auspices of Leland Stanford*.

182. *Evening Transcript*, 27 October 1882, cited in Haas, *Muybridge, Man in Motion*, p. 137.
183. *The Evening Transcript*, 21 and 27 October 1882.
184. At one point these were handled by a talent agency.

Chapter 17
185. According to Professor R. Taft of the University of Kansas, author of the preface to the 1955 edition of *The Human Figure in Motion*, Eakins was the greatest American painter of the nineteenth century.
186. Leland Stanford Jr died through illness in Rome, Italy on 13 March 1884, during a family holiday in Europe.
187. *British Journal of Photography*, 8 May 1891, p. 677, cited in Newhall, *The History of Photography*, p. 86.
188. 'The Zootrope', *The Art Interchange*, 9 July 1879, cutting from the *Scrapbook*, p. 55.
189. This was the same company that had supplied the cameras for his experiments at Palo Alto. The original document is in the Muybridge *Scrapbook* at Kingston Museum.
190. The photographs taken some two years later however only reached a maximum speed of 1/5000th of a second.
191. Note the poisonous reference to the Stillman-Stanford book.
192. According to Macdonnell, *Eadweard Muybridge, the Man who Invented the Moving Picture*, p. 152, the size of these small negatives was 24 x 33 mm. Liesegang's 1940 manuscript (pp. 45-148-155) instead claimed that the Pennsylvania negatives were, for each camera, 3 inches by 3 inches (7.6 x 7.6 cm), all placed together on three contiguous plates 3 inches square each. According to him, however, the negatives used for the twenty-four cameras at Palo Alto were 24 x 36 mm. [It is probable that Macdonnell confused small post-production glass images with original negatives (*Editor's note*).]
193. Scharf, *Art and Photography*, p. 168.
194. Haas, *Muybridge, Man in Motion*, p. 157, quotes criticisms made in the *New York Times* on 5 March 1888 of Eakins (referred to simply as 'a painter from Philadelphia') for his 'completely absurd' position of the horses' feet pulling a carriage. Hendricks (*Bulletin of the Philadelphia Museum of Art*, Spring 1965, p. 58) also cites this but does not mention that Muybridge was its author.

Chapter 18
195. Auguste Rodin, one of the subscribers to Muybridge's plates, expressed himself thus: 'It is the artist that tells the truth and the photographer who lies because in reality time does not stop, and if the artist is able to give the impression of a movement that requires other movements to be accomplished, his work is certainly less conventional than the scientific image, where time is brusquely suspended.' He also said: 'Here lies the sentence for those modern painters who, when they wish to show horses at the gallop, reproduce the poses provided by instantaneous photographs.' Whereas for those painters who did not concern themselves with scientific reality, he added: 'I believe that Géricault is right, not the camera, because his horses *seem* to be running.' See Scharf, *Art and Photography*, pp. 173-174.
196. See for example the films on animal locomotion from the catalogue of the Institut für den Wissenschaftlichen Film (IWF).
197. One should keep in mind that in the period of the silent cinema the usual speed of filming and projection to reproduce natural looking movement was approximately sixteen frames per second.
198. Scharf, *Art and Photography*, p. 169.

199. Beginning in the 1950s Bacon painted a number of pictures derived from human and animal subjects in photographs by Muybridge.

200. According to Hendricks, *Eadweard Muybridge*, p. 168, the hands being photographed were Eakins'. Scharf, *Art and Photography*, p. 230, thinks that these close-up images of hands by Muybridge may have influenced similar sculptures by Rodin.

201. Hendricks, *Eadweard Muybridge*, p. 168. The level of ingenuity in the filming technique is notable; not having at his disposal a film or moving plate which would allow him to record the phases of the beating of the heart, Muybridge obtained his result by moving the whole tortoise beneath all twelve lenses.

Chapter 19

202. From the notes held in the University of Pennsylvania archives, as reported in Hendricks, *Eadweard Muybridge*, p. 70 and by Haas, *Muybridge, Man in Motion*, p. 167.

203. In the preface to the original edition of *Animals in Motion* dated December 1898, p. 15 in the 1957 edition. The meeting with Edison came two days after a conference-demonstration that Muybridge held in Orange (NJ), not far from the Edison laboratories. On that occasion Edison made out a subscription for 100 plates from *Animal Locomotion*.

204. Edison had also hoped to take part in the fair with his Kinetoscope, as it could have served as the occasion to launch this new invention in fine style. He had to pass on this idea, however, owing to a number of technical problems that had to be solved before it could be offered for sale; this instead occurred in 1894.

205. In the Chicago Fair pavilion Muybridge also exhibited a number of Phenakistiscope series discs showing various animals running. The discs could be purchased for ornamental as well as scientific purposes: mounted on to a bamboo handle one could be used as a Japanese fan.

206. It was the description of the equipment and work methods used for the experiments in Pennsylvania first published in the 1887 *Prospectus and Catalogue of Plates*.

207. Muybridge ignored the fact that in 1890 Professor Marey had published his treatise *Le vol des oiseaux* which incorporated all his results based on chronophotographic observations.

Chapter 20

208. B. Carter, 'The Genesis of the Moving Picture', *The Bioscope*, 20 March 1913, pp. 845, 847, 849.

209. L.F. Rondinella, 'Muybridge's Pictures', *The Camera*, October 1929, pp. 252-254.

210. Haas, *Muybridge, Man in Motion*, p. 201.

Chapter 21

211. In Rome in 1882, the number of subscribers did not even reach 300.

212. E.J. Marey, *La meìthode graphique dans les sciences expeìrimentales, et principalement en physiologie et en meìdecine* (Paris: Masson, 1878), p. 9. But in *Du mouvement dans les fonctions de la vie* (Paris: Ballière, 1868) he had already insisted at length on the insufficiency of our senses for the perception of many physical and biological phenomena.

Chapter 22

213. Quoted by L. Escoube, in *La Revue du cinema*, no. 25 (1931), p. 70.

214. E.J., Marey, *Physiologie médicale de la circulation du sang, basée sur l'étude graphique des mouvements du coeur et du pouls artériel, avec application aux maladies de l'appareil circulatoire* (Paris: Delahaye, 1863).

215. A physiologist from Lyon, professor Chauveau, so described this 'curious and picturesque installation' as follows: 'The surface of the floor of this one large room, which constituted both the stage and the seating area for the spectators, was subdivided into various sections depending on their destination. Pride of place was given to the actual laboratory where of particular note was the first "exploratory drum" which was used for the study of birds. Then followed the laboratory of mechanics and the professor's study. Next to that was the dining room, the lounge with its piano.' Quoted by H. Savonnet, in *E.J. Marey, sa vie, son œuvre, communications présentées au Congrès 'Marey' de l'Association bourguignonne des Sociétés Savantes* (Beaune, 1974), p. 13.

216. His series of lectures were later published in a book, *Du mouvement dans les functions de la vie* (Paris: Ballière, 1868).

217. *Physiologie expérimentale, Ecole pratique des Hautes études, travaux du laboratoire du prof. Marey* (Paris, 1876-1880, four volumes).

218. Marey referred to himself as 'ingénieur de la médecine' (and also as 'bibeloteur' and 'physiologiste en chambre'); Savonnet, in *E.J. Marey, sa vie, son œuvre*.

219. Marey, *La meìthode graphique*.

220. Marey, *La méthode graphique*, p. 9 (1885 edition).

221. Escoube, in *La Revue du cinéma*, no. 25 (1931), p. 71.

222. Marey, *La méthode graphique*, p. 18 (1885 edition).

223. In fact Marey was the first to record the electric potential from the charge of a torpedo fish (see session of the Académie des Sciences of 22 January 1877).

224. Marey, *La méthode graphique*, pp. 153-154.

225. At a conference in 1899, Marey recalled those years thus: 'I had a part in the idea that drove those experiences. For many years I had been studying via mechanical means the movements of horses at the gallop and trotting ... Using these methods I was able to demonstrate that a galloping horse does rest on *one* hoof ... Colonel Duhousset, who combines great equestrian experience with real talent as a sketch artist, kindly made some drawings which represented the positions of the horse derived from that *chronophotograph*. These images ended up being seen by a rich American, Mr Stanford, ex-governor of California, who did not want to believe such results, such as the fact of the momentary resting of the quadruped on a single posterior hoof. To verify my observation he asked Muybridge to make a counter-experiment photographically.' E.J. Marey, *La chronophotographie* (Paris: Gauthier-Villars, 1899), p. 6.

226. E.J. Marey, *La machine animale: Locomotion terrestre et aérienne* (Paris: Ballière, 1873), pp. 142-3 (1891 edition).

227. E.J. Marey, *Le mouvement* (Paris: Masson, 1894), p. 300; Marey, *La méthode graphique*, pp. 425-426.

228. Marey, *La machine animale*, in the appendix to the 1883 edition. In *La Nature*, 24 April 1882, p. 327, Marey acknowledged that Muybridge's photographs had proved to him that some of the drawings on the position of joints in midair were incorrect.

229. Letter by Marey to the editor of *La Nature*,18 December 1878.

230. Letter dated 17 February 1879 published in *La Nature*, 22 March 1879.

231. Michel Frizot (ed.), *E.J. Marey, 1830/1904. La photographie du mouvement* (Paris: Centre Georges Pompidou/Musée National d'Art Moderne, 1977), p. 16: catalogue for the exhibition of the same name held at the Pompidou Centre in Paris.

232. There is something resembling romantic fiction about this eighteenth century affair: it

appears that the surname given to his natural daughter was that of a Neapolitan doctor, a friend of Marey's who looked after the girl during her infancy. The woman with whom he had the daughter may have been a Parisian nurse from an unfortunate marriage whom he met during the 1870 war. The religious principles of Marey's mother seem to have blocked any attempt to shed any further light on the real situation. She lived into old age and spent long periods with her son and with her 'adopted niece', who as a young woman looked after the running of house in Paris. While revising the 1984 version of this text some 400 letters (for the most part new), written by Marey while in Naples to Demeny between 1881 and 1894, were found at the Cinémathèque Française. Although often hard to read and given that we were only able to look at the material briefly, we have added some of the empirical data to the main text or in the notes, but plan on giving the material its due in a monograph on their contents. Among other things, the letters confirm that Marey's long stays at Posillipo were connected to his relationship with one Mme Vilbort, whose health then and in the years that followed was always precarious when not grave. [Post-scriptum 2005: the projected monograph could not be undertaken since the Marey-Demeny correspondence was made unavailable to researchers for many years while a compilation of the work was being prepared (*Author's note*).]

Chapter 23

233. E.J. Marey, *Développement de la méthode graphique par l'emploi de la photographie* (Paris: Masson, 1884), p. 12.
234. Marey wrote: 'So, over the question of bird flight, I was thinking of a sort of photographic gun which could capture a bird in a position or better still a series of positions, recording the successive phases of the movements of its wings.' Letter of 18 December 1878 to *La Nature*.
235. In a note at a conference in 1891, published in the *Revue Génerale des Sciences*, Paris 15 November 1891, Marey wrote: 'We first gave our method the name "Photochrono-graphy"; but the International Congress of photography held in Paris, in 1889, decided … to adopt the name "Chronophotography". We will abide by this decision.'
236. Marey, *La chronophotographie*, p. 11.
237. Marey, *Le mouvement*, p. 102.
238. Here, as on other occasions, Janssen did not demonstrate the grace and serenity exhibited so often by Marey in acknowledging the efforts of others. After reading the paper sent by Marey on the photographic gun, Janssen stood up (during the session of 13 March 1882 at the Académie des Sciences) to present some 'remarks' in which, after a few formal niceties, he made a point of underlining the fact that he had previously said that such a machine could be constructed and that Marey had written to him to ask for details on the revolver. 'I do not know yet to what extent the characteristics of the revolver may have been used by M. Marey, but without a doubt the principle of this apparatus …can give good results …' ('Comptes rendus de l'Académie des Sciences', no. 94, p. 684; also in Janssen, *Ouevres scientifique*, pp. 456-457). A few weeks later, 3 April 1882, he presented to the Academy a 'note on the principles of a new photographic revolver' for use in exactly the same area as Marey's, that is to say, the flight of insects. It did not have any practical repercussions however; instead, at just that time (May 1882), an English scientist wrote to Marey to ask how much it would cost to buy his photographic revolver, saying that he had been sent to him by Janssen, whom he had initially approached. This document is reproduced in René Buhot, *La voix de Marey, histoire de l'invention du cinématographe, premières partie* (Boulogne-sur-Seine: René

Buhot, 1937), p. 196. When in 1894 Janssen passed the presidency of the Société Française de Photographie over to Marey, he was fairly ungenerous in the remarks that accompanied the transfer (Janssen, *Ouevres scientifique*, p. 336); in the already quoted lecture given at Lyon on 15 June 1895, he confirmed punctiliously once again that: 'It is well-known that the eminent incumbent President of the Académie des Sciences and the Société Française de Photographie successfully took possession of the principles of the instrument [the photographic revolver] which in any event he completely transformed.' Janssen, *Ouevres scientifique*, p. 381.

239. *La Nature*, 22 April 1882, p. 327. The description of the photographic gun was also published in the *Bulletin de la Société Française de Photographie*, May 1882, vol. XXVIII, p. 127.

240. E.J. Marey, *Physiologie du mouvment: Le vol des oiseaux* (Paris: Masson, 1890), p. 138. In *La Nature*, 18 January 1890, Albert Londe noted that 12/750th of a second were used overall for the twelve exposures while 738/750th (that is to say 98.4%) were needed to move the plate (as quoted in Vivié, *Traité général de technique du cinéma*, p. 25).

241. Marey, *Développement de la méthode graphique*, p. 15.

242. Marey, *Le vol des oiseaux*, p. 138.

243. *La Nature*, 22 April 1882, p. 330.

244. Marey, *Le vol des oiseaux*, p. 138. According to a note, after 1882 Marey did go back and use a single shot photographic gun. He wrote: 'I recently constructed a single image rifle, but one with a fairly powerful lens so that the posing time can be reduced to a minimum.' He did this to study a few details of birds in flight. This piece of equipment does not seem to have survived.

245. Lucien Bull, 'Quelques souvenirs personnels de mon maître Et.-J. Marey', *Bulletin de l'AFITEC* (1954, special issue), p. 6.

246. Marey, *Le mouvement*, preface.

247. Bull, 'Quelques souvenirs personnels de mon maître Et.-J. Marey.'

248. One should note that a similar system is still used in one of the methods for high-speed cinematography.

249. E.J. Marey, conference at the Collège de France, July 1891, in *Revue Générale des Sciences*, Paris, no. 21, 15 November 1891, p. 693.

250. Presentation to the Académie des Sciences of 3 July 1882.

251. In fact, in the presentation to the Academy cited above, he pointed to the fact that these plates produced images similar to those drawn by the Weber brothers to explain theoretically the progress of man through a series of partially overlapping progressive silhouettes.

252. Presentation to the Académie des Sciences of 25 June 1883.

253. See, for example, Scharf, *Art and Photography*, bibliography; see also the catalogue *E.J. Marey, 1830/1904* for the Marey exhibition at the Pompidou Centre.

254. Marey, *Développement de la méthode graphique*, p. 26.

Chapter 24

255. Presented 1 September 1885.

256. See the report by Dr R. Masson, 'Marey, médecin', in *E.J. Marey, sa vie, son œuvre*.

257. Marey, *Le vol des oiseaux*, p. 168.

258. Marey, *Le vol des oiseaux*, pp. 175-176. According to the Science Museum, London, the plastic figures were made in 1885 in collaboration with Paul Nadar, but Marey's recently discovered letters to Demeny confirm that the work was done in Naples by a local sculptor.

259. Scharf, *Art and Photography*, p. 276.
260. Marey, *Le mouvement*, pp. 171-172.
261. Marey, *Le vol des oiseaux*, p. 165. Already in 1882, when presenting his photographic rifle, Marey had anticipated the use of the Phenakistiscope in reproducing the appearance of movement, but was worried that he had too few images for each beat of the wing (*La Nature*, 22 April 1882, p. 350).
262. Marey, *Le vol des oiseaux*, p. 182.
263. Max Ernst, untitled collage from *Rêve d'une petite fille qui voulut entrer au Carmel* (Paris, 1930), reproduced in *Marey pionnier de la synthèse du mouvement*, catalogue of the exhibition held by the Musée Marey, Beaune, 1995, illustration no. 56.

Chapter 25
264. Marey, *Le vol des oiseaux*, p. 183.
265. Translation: 'Deconstruction of the phases of a movement by means of photographic images collected on a strip of sensitive paper which unrolls.'
266. Marey, *La chronophotographie*, p. 18.
267. These measurements were probably chosen because they corresponded to the size (9 x 9 cm) of the photographic plates that were then used for the projection lanterns used at conferences (Marey, *Le mouvement*, p. 123).

Chapter 26
268. Sadoul, *Histoire génerale*, p. 87.
269. Sadoul, *Histoire génerale*, p. 195.
270. E.J. Marey, 'Noveaux Développements de la Chronophotographie', *Revue des Travaux Scientifiques*, 1892; cited in Deslandes, *Histoire comparée du cinéma* p. 188.
271. Hendricks' *The Edison Motion Picture Myth*, is an important work on Edison in terms of historical research, and as a critical reassessment of his role in the birth of entertainment cinema (Hendricks is also the author of one of the most important works on Muybridge). Among other things, in his book Hendricks shows the importance of the meeting between Edison and Marey in Paris. Used as he was to the secretive nature of industrial research, Edison was taken by surprise by the European tradition of the scientific community making public its findings and its methodologies. He was thus able to use all of Marey's inventions and developments. Hendricks also shows that in November of that year (1889), well before making his new patent request, Edison thanked Marey for having sent him his new book *Le vol des oiseaux* (which actually carries 1890 as its official publication date), which describes in detail his various chronophotographic techniques. The letter from Edison to Marey was exhibited in Paris in 1963 as part of the 'Hommage à J.E. Marey' at the Langlois Musée du Cinéma.
272. Frizot, *E.J. Marey, 1830/1904*, p. 66.
273. In the letters that Marey wrote from Naples to his assistant, there are many references to shortages of film stock, to the differing quality of types of negative, to the search for new suppliers when neither Balagny nor Eastman (through the photographer Nadar) were able to supply him. On 18 June 1891 he wrote: 'I am without film. Balagny is coming up with all sorts of excuses for the failed delivery ... You can imagine how put out I am. I have a good eight days of work to do before leaving Naples, which means about thirty metres of film. Can you get it for me ... by sending some as a recommended sample?' A few days later (26 June 1891): 'If I'd had some film in this period I could have done a lot of work.' On 16 August 1891 (from Paris): 'I have no 9 cm film and my work has stalled ... I would even make do with Balagny's blotchy ones.'

274. Marey, *Le vol des oiseaux*, p. 155. As we have already seen, *Le vol des oiseaux* had been printed and distributed during the autumn of 1889; Marey therefore was referring to experiments undertaken with the first filmstrip chronophotography, still imperfect in its use of an electromagnet to pause the film.

275. Marey's letters have provided much useful information on the chronophotographic projector. On 1 December 1891 he wrote to Demeny: 'Print me some positive strips of the wave [LA VAGUE, filmed by Marey that year at Posillipo]. I need it to be 1.5 metres in length for trials on the projection of movement ... I have made designs for equipment to project movements; it is still just on paper, but it looks as though it should work. It will take between eight and ten days to build it quickly.' A few months later (20 March 1892): 'I had to scrap the projector, I will take it up again, it looks promising.' On 6 July 1892: 'I haven't been able to work on the projector since I had to give the time I had set aside for it to adjust the chronophotographe to get regular intervals.' Finally on 12 July 1892: 'I'm putting off my follow-up work on my studies for a projector until a quieter period. I was hoping to obtain completely equal intervals between images by transforming the chronophotographe. But the intervals are still not exact. In addition to which I have also undertaken some physiological experiments on the movements of the heart and muscles.' From the same letters of July 1892 one also learns that Marey had decided not to present (as he had previously planned) a model of the projector in a photographic exhibition in Paris, in a display dedicated to chronophotography, and instead suggested other items to take its place.

276. Marey, *Le mouvement*, p. 310. In 1899 (therefore after his break up with Demeny) Marey recounted the episode again, but in a more caustic tone: 'While I continued with this research, I learned that my assistant, who knew my chronophotograph very well having used it many times at the Station Physiologique, had patented this piece of equipment under his name. To do this, he added a modification to it that was well known in my laboratory, but which I had not used.' Marey, *La chronophotographie*, p. 26.

Chapter 27

277. Marey, *La chronophotographie*, p. 33.

278. The images detailing the fall of the cat are (as far as is currently known) twelve from one session and fourteen in another, while over thirty were taken on another occasion; fifteen for those of the rabbit. One of the sessions was taken from an axial angle (the cat was photographed from behind), while the others show the fall laterally. The photographs must have been taken at a speed of sixty images per second (see *Comptes rendus de l'Académie des Sciences*, session of 29 October 1894, and *Paris Photographe*, 30 November 1894). Given that the Zoetrope presentation of the event could be at a speed of ten images per second, Marey obtained a notable slowing down of real time. For some of these details I am indebted to M. Frizot, curator of the catalogue for Marey exhibition at the Pompidou Centre. During the preparation of this book I was able to rediscover and consult in the holdings of the Cinémathèque Française many of the chronophotograph films made by Marey (and his colleagues) which were previously unknown, some of which were dated pre-1895 by Lucien Bull and some after. These include photographs of falling cats, rabbits (even blindfolded) and of a hen as well as subjects hitherto not known to have been photographed by them.

Chapter 28

279. Marey, *La machine animale*, p. 288.

280. *Storia universale* (Milan: Sonzogno, 1907), p. 92.

281. Otto Lilienthal, in *Prometheus*, no. 6, 1895, p. 7. Lilienthal also refers to Anschütz.
282. Marey, *La chronophotographie*, p. 15.
283. The phrase is related by Noguès, Marey's collaborator and then deputy director of the Institut Marey, who said 'I well remember Wilbur Wright who exclaimed out loud at Mme Lazare Weiller's reception' (the quoted phrase follows). P. Sabon, 'Ralenti et accéléré – une visite à l'Institut Marey', *La Revue du Cinéma*, June 1930, p. 28.

Chapter 29

284. Marey, *Le mouvement*, p. 296.
285. The first meeting of the 'Association Internationale de l'Institut Marey' was held in 1902. Headed by Marey until his death, the Institut Marey was then run by his pupils from both France and overseas. Among the directors and deputy directors there were Pierre Noguès, Lucien Bull, Ion Athanasiu, Charles Richet and G. Weiss. After the Second World War, the Institut was absorbed within the Collège de France, which was already looking after the Station Physiologique. The last honorary director was Professor A. Fessard. Recently the Collège de France – following pressure from the Ministry of Sport – let Parc des Princes be turned into tennis courts, breaking up the equipment and library collections of the Institut and the Station.

Chapter 30

286. *Catalogue du 'Musée Centennal' de la classe 12 (Photographie) à l'Exposition Universelle Internationale de 1900 à Paris, Métrophotographie & Chronophotographie, Deuxième Partie*, pp. 22-35. From the last phrase of the text ('...depuis la clotûre de l'Exposition...') one can deduce that it was published at the end of the exhibition.
287. E.N. Bouton claims that Louis Lumière was part of Marey's entourage (in *E.J. Marey, sa vie, son oeuvre*, p. 22). Bouton was Marey's nephew, the son of his 'adopted' daughter. Sadoul, *Histoire générale*, p. 149, confirmed that the Lumières 'knew Marey personally'; in a note on the same page, Sadoul reported that Lumière, in old age, wrote to him that: 'At that time I was ignorant of Marey's research', but this is clearly a memory lapse since he was speaking of Edison's Kinetoscope.
288. Marey, *Le chronophotograpie*, pp. 26-7. However, that same year, 1899 (in the preface to Eugène Trutaut's *La photographie animée*) Marey wrote: 'Chronophotography was born of necessity to science ... but if it has gained in popularity it is not due to its true value; it had the good fortune to interest the public through the attractive illusions it provides ... But no matter how perfect the reproduction of scenes which are familiar to us, we begin to tire of seeing them ... Already there is searching for unusual subjects; one looks for spectacles in foreign lands, but soon even these will not be enough to maintain interest. Then chronophotography, returning to its origins, will become scientific again.'
289. Auguste and Louis Lumière, *Notice sur le cinématographe*, cited in Vivié, *Traité général de technique du cinéma*, p. 37.
290. *Revue du Siècle*, May 1897, reproduced in Auguste and Louis Lumière, *Résumé des travaux scientifiques, 1887-1914* (Lyons/Paris: Union photographique industrielle, établissements Lumière et Jouglas réunis, 1914), p. 11.
291. The text of the letter dated 22 March 1900 was reprinted in Frizot, *E.J. Marey, 1830/1904*, p. 88.
292. One can get a taste of them in the many pages dedicated to the subject in Coissac, *Histoire du cinématographe*.
293. Like Solomon, the Société Française de Photographie deliberated and 'without wishing not to recognise the eminent role played by its venerated ex-president' it approved the

text of the plaque proposed by the Vieux Paris Committee (favourable to Lumière), but then also voted for another one to glorify Marey, 'true creator and uncontested master of chronophotography.' (Coissac, *Histoire du cinématographe*, p. 225). This did in fact take place and one can still find at Boulevard Delessert 11 a plaque inscribed 'Ici habita de 1881 à 1904 ... un des fondateurs de la physiologie expérimentale et de la science de l'aviation, créateur de la chronophotographie base technique de la cinématographie.'

294. Buhot, *La voix de Marey*. This booklet also contained some documents published for the first time, probably obtained from the Institut Marey (the Parc des Princes establishment was on land belonging to the local authorities of the Paris *banlieu* of Boulogne-sur-Seine). We do not know if the second part of the work was actually ever published.

295. Roux-Parassac, *...et l'image s'anima, ou la merveilleuse et véridique histoire d'une grande invention*, p. 23.

296. Among the signatories to the document (printed in Boulogne-sur-Seine, probably around 1928), apart from the ex students and collaborators of Marey, one finds Professor R. Anthony of the Muséum d'Histoire Naturelle, Professor E. Gley of the Collège de France and Vice President of the Académie de Médecine, Professor R. Marage of the Sorbonne and the anthropologist Félix Regnault.

297. P. Sabon, 'Visite à l'Institut Marey', second part, in *La Revue du Cinéma*, 1930, p. 779 (in the 'reprint' edition of the magazine).

298. G.M. Coissac, in Fescourt, *Le cinéma des origines à nos jours*.

299. See Frizot, *E.J. Marey, 1830/1904*.

300. It is known, though, that in 1945 when yet another plaque was placed on Boulevard des Capucines for the fiftieth anniversary of the first public screening of the 'cinématographe', the Lumières complained that the inscription mixed their names together with other Frenchmen considered to be 'pioneers' of the cinema, 'To Reynaud, Marey, Demeny, Lumière, Méliès ....' Quoted by Maurice Bessy and Lo Duca, *Louis Lumière inventeur* (Paris: Prisma, 1948), p. 43.

301. In 1979 in parallel with an exhibition in Florence dedicated to experimental and avant-garde cinema, a small show was set up under the title 'The Immobility of Movement', which had a section devoted to Marey. In the catalogue for the event (*Cine qua non*, Florence: Vallechi, 1979) E. Fulchignoni writes: 'If someone were to ask me one day which among the scientists of the nineteenth century had contributed the most to changing the world, I would answer without hesitation: Marey.' He later adds: 'I cite Galileo's name because Marey's is ... the one that, in my opinion, is the closest to him.' 'With Marey we are at the triumph of empirical experimentation' (p. 159).

Chapter 31

302. According to Liesegang, *Die Begründung der Reihenphotographie durch Eadweard Muybridge*, p. 19, Anschütz' first series photographs date from July 1885 and were then made available commercially in November of that year.

303 Marey, *Le mouvement*, p. 107.

304. General Sébert analysed the trajectory of bullets with a multi-lens camera. Marey refers to him in his chronological survey of the developments of chronophotography prepared for the exposition of 1900. Potonniée gives a date of 1890 for Sebert's studies on the speed of bullet using chronophotography; Liesegang (*Wissenschatliche*, pp. 34-35) includes two images of Sebert's machine.

305. The first hypothesis is from Ceram, *Eine Archäologie des Kinos*, p. 89, the second from Marey, *La chronophotographie*, p. 8.

306. Traub, *Als Man Anfing zu Filmen*, p. 33, says that between 1892 and 1895 the company manufactured seventy-eight examples of the Elektrischen Schnellseher after Anschütz received the support of the Deutsche Automaten Gesellschaft Stollwerck und Cie of Cologne. Some of these machines were demonstrated in London and Vienna in 1892; according to Traub, in that same year in Berlin the number of spectators who came to watch the projection of animated images using the Anschütz machine numbered 16,618 in June and 17, 271 in July.

307. Sadoul, *Histoire générale*, p. 75.

308. A number of historians who refer to this 'film show' have accepted uncritically the contents of Dickson's memoirs and Ramsaye's book.

309. Interesting details on this can be found in Liesegang, *Die Begründung der Reihenphotographie durch Eadweard Muybridge*, pp. 14, 98-100, 114 and *passim*. In passing one should note that while Muybridge's series of plates were created to analyse movement and used to reconstruct its synthesis purely for demonstration purposes, Anschütz' images were created above all to reproduce the synthesis of the phases of the photographed movements.

310. Among the spectators at these brief shows was Oskar Messter (1866-1943) who would become one of the first makers of cinema projectors, a film producer and manager of cinemas in Germany. He is worth remembering here because in 1897-98, in collaboration with professors Lubasch and Spiess, he repeated the film of the cat being dropped upside down in front of a black backing which had already been undertaken by Marey in 1894. In the frame, apart from the cat falling, one can see a chronometer and two balls (one made of iron, the other of cork) which fell at the same time as the cat in front of a metric scale. Examining the images, photographed at a speed of sixty-six frames per second, one can clearly see that the animal rights itself in less than a tenth of a second. (Oskar Messter, *Mein Weg mit dem Film* (Berlin: Max Hesses Verlag, 1936), p. 81, fig. no. 80.

Chapter 32

311. It appears that it was Londe's work which made Marey construct and experiment with a Chronophotographe prototype with a fixed plate and six lenses grouped in a crown shape, but which was later abandoned. Londe had for his part looked at the parallax problem in similar types of equipment, but considered it to be of marginal importance as his images were only used for medical documentation.

312. In *Le Chasseur Français*, May 1896, cited in part both by Sadoul in *Histoire générale*, pp. 156-57 and Deslandes, *Histoire comparée du cinéma*, pp. 232-33.

313. Sadoul, *Histoire générale*, p. 163.

Chapter 33

314. In some sources the name has a final umlaut on the letter 'y' which would seem to attest to the Hungarian origins of his family. However in most texts, even the French ones and in the letters written to him by Marey, the name is given simple as Demeny.

315. Sadoul, *Histoire générale*, p. 119. In a letter to Demeny from Naples dated 4 August 1892, Marey wrote: 'Given the facial expressions, it would be more pleasant to have women to look at.'

316. Georges Demeny, *Les origines du cinématographe* (Paris: Henry Paulin, 1909), p. 21.

317. An article in *Phono-Ciné-Gazette* from 1905, quoted in Coissac, *Histoire du cinématographe*, p. 127, claimed that 1,200 people attended Demeny's conference.

318. Letter from Marey to Demeny dated 10 July 1892.

Chapter 34

319. Deslandes (*Histoire comparée du cinéma*, p. 176) bemoaned the impossibility of throwing light on many aspects of their relationship until all the documentation came to light. We still lack the letters from Demeny to Marey which perhaps the latter did not keep, but the information offered by the hundreds of letters by Marey is already significant.

320. Among Demeny's commercial experiments one should also remember the 'turning portrait' which he described thus: 'I put the person being photographed on a piano stool and during a single rotation of this I took fifty separate shots ... I then placed these images in a picture in which the same person was seated some fifty times around a circular table, but with differing expressions.' (Demeny, *Les origines du cinématographe*, p. 25). One should compare this idea with Marey's notion of 'photosculpture' (see Chapter 24).

321. Quoted in Sadoul, *Histoire générale*, p. 301. The last sentence clearly anticipates similar thinking experienced half a century later by theoreticians and filmmakers of the Italian 'neo-realism' such as Cesare Zavattini.

322. The text of the conference (*Les origines du cinématographe*) was published by Demeny with extracts of letters by him and Marey. As it so often happens in these cases, either through lapses in memory or more or less conscious alterations to recorded fact, some of the claims and references to dates made by Demeny are incorrect.

Chapter 35

323. Friedrich Engels may have been of the first, if not the very first, to define the process of English industrialisation in this manner.

324. See Kurt Mendelssohn, *Science and Western Domination* (London: Thames and Hudson, 1976), especially chapter five.

325. Marey, *La méthode graphique*, pp. XVI-XVII of the 1885 edition.

326. Thomas, *The Origins of the Motion Picture*, p. 8.

327. Potonniée, *Les origines du cinématographe*, p. 39.

328. Newhall, *The History of Photography*, p. 88.

329. Newhall, *The History of Photography*, p. 89.

330. There is a photograph of the tablet in Gilardi, *Storia sociale della fotografia*, p. 430.

331. Gilardi, *Storia sociale della fotografia*, pp. 430-431; Helmut and Alison Gernsheim, *Storia della fotografia* (Milan: Frassinelli, 1966), pp. 35-36.

Chapter 36

332. When Edison's collaborator, W.K.L. Dickson, first asked Eastman for a roll of film, he asked for a width of 3/4 of an inch, i.e. approximately 19 millimetres. But Vivié, *Traité général de technique du cinéma*, p. 57, holds that this measurement was that of the sensitive surface, while the film was 35 mm wide (including the space for the perforations). Hendricks, *The Edison Motion Picture Myth*, points out, however, that that first request for film did not concern the Kinetoscope, but had to do with otherwise non-specified astronomic experiments.

333. Muybridge, *The Human Figure in Motion*, p. 6.

334. Demeny, *Les origines du cinématographe*, p. 21.

335. Mitry, *Le cinema des origins*, p. 87.

336. Sadoul, *Histoire générale*, p. 152 (Italian edition).

337. Recorded by Deslandes, *Histoire comparée du cinéma*, p. 234.

338. Referred to by Potonniée in an article he wrote in 1936 and quoted by Deslandes, *Histoire comparée du cinéma* , vol. II, pp. 260-261.

339. Translated from the French in Deslandes, *Histoire comparée du cinéma*, vol. I, p. 268.
340. Armat's declaration is recorded by Deslandes, *Histoire comparée du cinéma*, vol. II, p. 271.
341. It is well-known that Edison was self-taught; his attendance at regular schools did not last more than a few months.
342. Sadoul, in *Histoire général*, dedicates several pages to the question of this withdrawal of the Lumière brothers.
343. See also Angelini, 'Il fattore tecnico-scientifico nella nascita del cinema.'

Chapter 37

344. The management of the Cinématographe Lumière published announcements in the newspapers, declaring that they used only electric lights for their projectors.
345. 'After the earliest years of enthusiasm and curiosity, people only considered it [the cinematograph] one of the many para-scientific eccentricities that had invaded places of entertainment everywhere at the end of the nineteenth century.' A. Bernardini, G. Cereda, in Aldo Bernardini, *Cinema muto italiano, Vol. 1: Ambiente, spettacoli e spettatori, 1896/1904* (Rome: Editori Laterza, 1980), p. xv.
346. These were the famous L'ARRIVÉE DU TRAIN, SORTIE DE L'USINE, L'ARROSEUR ARROSÉ, LE DÉJEUNER DE BÉBÉ, etc.
347. Gorky's article was published in the *Nizhegorodski listok* newspaper of 4 July 1896, under the pseudonym I.M. Pacatus, and it concludes with all the violence of the writer, not yet thirty years old, who proposed something that was 'not exactly piquant, but quite edifying': impaling some parasite dandy to a gate, in the way of the Turks, filming it and then giving a screening. The text of the article (in English) was re-published in an appendix to Jay Leyda, *Kino: A History of the Russian and Soviet Film,* London: George Allen and Unwin, 1960), pp. 407-409.
348. Félix Regnault, 'La Chronophotographie dans l'Ethnographie', in *Bull. Soc. Anthrop.,* 1900, p. 421, cited by Michaelis, *Research Films in Biology, Anthropology, Psychology, and Medicine,* pp. 193 and 443, which mentions the various works. Osvaldo Polimanti, in Liesegang, *Wissenschaftliche,* p. 262, recalls the work of Regnault and other researchers who used the Marey method.
349. Regnault would be one of the signatories to the protest manifesto published by a group of scientists to affirm the role of Marey in the invention of cinema (see Chapter 30).
350. *Catalogue du 'Musée Centennal',* p. 33.
351. Polimanti, in Liesegang, *Wissenschaftliche.* p.307 and F. Rodolfi, 'Il cinematografo', in *Rivista di fisica, matematica e scienze naturali* (Pavia, 1901), p. 330.
352. Marey, *La chronophotographie,* pp. 29-30. Sergio Raffaelli, *Cinema film regia* (Rome: Bulzoni, 1978), p. 31, quotes an Italian preceding Matuszewski in proposing the use the cinematograph for police purposes: in 1896 C. Nasi wrote an article for a Turin newspaper illustrating the idea of giving police officers cine-cameras to film demonstrators in the squares.
353. The Filmoteka Polska published a book, *Boleslaw Matuszewski I jego pionierska mysl filmowa* (Warsaw: Filmoteka Polska, 1980), in which the two texts quoted are reproduced with an essay on Matuszewski, 'first theoretician of cinema', by Z. Czeczot-Gawrak. It should be borne in mind that while some re-prints of the first booklet are known (for example, in a UNESCO review, *Cultures,* II, 1, 1974); as far as the text of *La photographie animée* is concerned, no copy has yet been found of the original publication, but only a 'typographical print proof', which, furthermore, is not quite accurate.

Chapter 38

354. Apart from the priority claim already quoted on the part of Matuszewski (who, moreover, spoke with enthusiasm of both Doyen and his operator), there are other claimants to the role of first user of cinema in the medical field: for example, the Berlin surgeon, Ernst von Bergmann, who apparently had one or more operations (including the amputation of a leg) filmed in the same year, 1898, by the pioneer of German cinema, Oskar Messter ('Il film nell'insegnamento della medicina', in *Rivista Ciba*, p. 597). The French doctor, M. Badouin published an article 'Le cinématographe appliqué aux sciences médicales' in the *Gazette Médicale de Paris* (no. 69, p. 371 – referred to by Michaelis, *Research Films in Biology, Anthropology, Psychology, and Medicine*, pp. 270 and 382) and considered himself to have been the one to suggest the use of cinema to Doyen. Henri Fescourt, *La foi et les montagnes (ou le 7ème art au passé* (Paris: Paul Montel, 1959), p. 123.

355. Matuszewski referred to the summary of the statement of Doyen published by *La Semaine Médicale*, 17 August 1898 (in *La photographie animée*, pp. 76-77).

356. E.L. Doyen, 'Le Cinématographe et l'Énseignement de la Chirurgie' in *Les Nouvelles Scientifiques et Photographiques*, 15 September 1899, p. 99, quoted in Mitry, *Le cinéma des origins*, p. 103.

357. In *Revue Critique de Médicine et Chirurgie*, 15 August 1899, Doyen refers to another technician, Ambroise-François Parnaland, who carried out some of his films with an apparatus 'invented by himself', while Clément-Maurice used a Lumière cine camera.

358. From the summary of the *La Semaine Médicale*, 17 August 1898.

359. E.L. Doyen, in *Revue Critique de Médicine et Chirurgie*, 15 August 1899.

360. Referred to by Professor Polimanti and quoted by N. Kaufmann in *Rivista Ciba*, p. 595; the same observations were also referred to in 1911 by R. Kutner (see Michaelis, *Research Films in Biology, Anthropology, Psychology, and Medicine*, pp. 270, 421).

361. Letter of a reader to the daily newspaper *Paese sera* of Rome, 28 March 1972.

362. Referred to by Mitry, *Le cinéma des origins*, p. 104.

363. Mitry, *Le cinéma des origins*, p. 105.

364. Doyen's cameraman, Clément-Maurice confirmed the theft of some of their negatives (see his letter in *La Revue de Cinéma*, March 1930, p. 19). The French scientific cineaste Jean Painlevé wrote: 'So-called "serious" people held the cinema in low esteem due to its exploitation as a sideshow attraction … In fact the surgical films of Dr Doyen were shown in fairgrounds: in 1911 at Chartres, at the age of nine, I watched … a Caesarean birth, coupled with an actuality film.' *Jean Comandon* [Les pionniers de cinéma scientifique] (Brussels: Hayez, 1967).

365. E.L. Doyen, *L'Enseignement de la technique opératoire par les projections animées* (Paris: Société Générale des Cinématographes Eclipse, 1911) and E.L. Doyen, *Invatarea tehnicii operatorii prin proiectiuni vii* (Bucharest, 1914).

366. Gheorghe Marinescu, 'Les troubles de la marche dans l'hémiplégie organique étudiés à l'aide du cinématographe', *La Semaine Médicale*, 5 July 1899.

367. In *Nouvelle Iconographie de la Salpêtrière*, no. 2, 1900.

368. Gheorghe Marinescu, 'Les applications du cinématographe dans les sciences biologiques et dans l'art', *Revue génerale des sciences pures et appliqués*, 15 February 1900.

369. For Marinescu and Bolintineanu see I. Cantacuzino and G. Bratescu, 'Date noi privitoare la primele utilizari ale cinematografului în cercetarea stiintifica', *Neurologia Psihiatria Neurochirurgia*, July-August 1971. In 1965 the Rumanian scientific documentary filmmaker Ion Bostan made the short film PE URMELE UNUI FILM DISPARUT [Searching for a lost film], in which Marinescu's first films were carefully reconstructed

by patiently re-photographing every single one of the drawings derived from his original frames. In 1973 another Rumanian filmmaker, A. Gaspar, having found some of Marinescu's original films, presented them in another documentary, A 'PREMIERE' AFTER 75 YEARS. In Bostan's film there is a reference to the possibility that Marinescu had started dealing with the problems of locomotive pathology as early as 1889, in Paris at Marey's laboratory.

Chapter 39

370. Owing to their fascinating facility for show the invisible, for a while X-rays became a paying 'scientific attraction.' It did not last for long however.
371. Carvallo published his results in the annals of the Institut (*Travaux de l'Association de l'Institut Marey*, 1910) under the significant title 'Méthode radiochronophotographique.'
372. The difficulty refers to the size of the field being explored, but also the high cost of the equipment needed for developing and printing large format films.
373. According to Liesegang in *Wissenschaftliche*, p. 144, at the 1909 international photographic show in Dresden the Germans Biesalski and Kohler presented serial images of the movements of articulated bone movements shot using the indirect roentgencinematographic method, but essentially these were a series of successive photographs, obtained with long pauses between each exposure. Both Liesegang and Michaelis dedicate much space to this and provide interesting technical descriptions relating to the birth and development of X-ray photography.

Chapter 40

374. Some of Pfeffer's films have been preserved and can be found in the catalogues of the Institut für Wissenschaflichen Film.
375. Mach's idea is recounted by Marey in *Le mouvement*, p. 305. Without prior knowledge of this precedent, in 1950 the Italian cinema technician Carlo Rambaldi (who later became famous for his special effects which were rewarded with Academy Awards) began a similar experiment with his own children; we do not know however if he continued this work with any regularity.
376. A curious system was used to get an exact measure of the length of the filming: the same shot included lead balls falling from a given height. Von Lendenfeld started his work with single photographs analysing rapid movement back in 1880.

Chapter 41

377. Bull, 'Quelques souvenirs personnels de mon maître Et.-J. Marey.'
378. Bull, 'Quelques souvenirs personnels de mon maître Et.-J. Marey.' In the same article Bull describes having stayed with Marey in his villa at Posillipo in Naples for three months during the winter, and that they made some films together at the aquarium, which was then under the direction of its founder (and Marey's friend), the German biologist A. Dohrn.
379. Jean Painlevé in *Lucien Bull* [Les pionniers de cinema scientifique] (Brussels: Hayez, 1967, p. 5: 'Lucien Bull removed the mortgage of time; he gave us the possibility to penetrate intimately the evolution of the subject, inventing the technical means to control the rhythm of the observation of phenomena. Beyond linear dimensions, a new dimension, vague until then, offered new challenges.'
380. Lucien Bull, 'Dispositif optique pour la réception des images cinématographiques à haute fréquence', *Comptes-rendus de l'Académie des Sciences*, 1952, no. 235, p. 1210; see also *Research Film*, 1952, no. 1, p. 11.

381. One must mention two of Bull's articles: 'The origin and early development of high speed cinematography', *Science and Film*, June 1958, p. 26; and 'La technique cinématographique au temps de pionniers', *Bulletin de l'Institut de Cinématographie Scientifique*, 1961, no. 2. These were written in his later years, which may explain a few inaccuracies in the texts, but do contain a number of interesting points of view. An interview film on Bull by the Frenchman A. Dyja entitled MONSIEUR BULL was completed in the year of his death (1972).

Chapter 42

382. Ion Athanasiu, 'La Chronophotographie', *Travaux de l'Association de l'Institut Marey*, 1905.
383. Generally speaking these various techniques could generate only a limited number of images, frequently small in size and nearly always only directly usable for analysing images one frame at a time, and not for normal projection.
384. Bull, 'The origin and early development of high speed cinematography'; see also Liesegang, *Wissenschaftliche.*
385. Michaelis, *Research Films in Biology, Anthropology, Psychology, and Medicine*, refers to at least seven works by François-Franck published in the first ten years of the twentieth century, based on results obtained from film.
386. Unfortunately, when business started to go badly after the end of the first world war, the Pathé company abandoned Comandon's laboratory. Comandon to continue his work, first turned to a banker as sponsor and then took a position at the Institut Pasteur at Garches. For further details on Comandon's films, see the 1967 monograph produced by the Brussels Cinémathèque Scientifique Internationale as part of their series *Les pionniers du cinéma scientifique.*

Chapter 43

387. Liesegang, *Wissenschaftliche*, p. 285.
388. Their first scientific presentation on the sea urchin was to the Paris Academy of Science in 1909 (149, 806). Von Ries' work was published in German in 1909 (*Arch. Mikr. Anat.*, 74, 1) and in French the following year (*Travaux de l'Association de l'Institut Marey*, II, 225). Chevroton subsequently became the wife of Professor François-Franck and published under her married name, returning once again during the 1920s to the topic of the sea urchin egg with a new film.
389. Sadoul, *Histoire générale*, p. 470. The subjects being filmed were partly on a macroscopic level; the microcinematographs were presented in the Urban catalogue as 'The Urban-Duncan Micro-Bioscope'; it advertised films between twenty and twenty-five feet long (approximately 20-25 seconds in duration when projected), but there is also one listed as seventy-five feet long with enlargement sizes from 25x to 850x (one page of *The Unseen World* catalogue is reproduced in MacGowan, *Behind the Screen*, p. 93). Ceram (*Eine Archäologie des Kinos*, p. 192) published a frame from THE ANATOMY OF A WATERFLEA, dating it as 'towards the end of the last century.' Urban, however, only started making such films in 1903.
390. Michail Tichonov, *Kino na slu be nauki* (Moscow: Iskusstvo, 1954), which among other things also provides a detailed description of Makarov's experiment; Alexsandr Zguridi, *Ekran, Nauka, izn'* (Moscow: Iskusstvo, 1983).
391. *Gazzetta del Popolo*, 18 February 1908.
392. Many of Omegna's films, including some from the first decade of the twentieth century (for example NEVROPATOLOGIA [Neuropathology], LA VITA DELLE FARFALLE

[The life of butterflies], CACCIA AL LEOPARDO [Hunting the leopard]) have been preserved either complete or as fragments at the Museo nazionale del cinema di Torino, the cinema archive of Istituto Luce and the Cineteca Nazionale of Rome. There is also a biographical anthology film on Omegna made by Virgilio Tosi (Istituto Luce, 1974). See also Virgilio Tosi,, 'Il pioniere Roberto Omegna (1876-1948)', *Bianco e Nero*, no. 3, 1979.

Chapter 44

393. Reynaud died in a hospice in 1918. Some years earlier in frustration he had taken a hammer to his last 'Théâtre Optique' equipment and had thrown practically all his animated drawing strips into the Seine.
394. Sadoul, in *Storia del cinema mondiale* (Milan: Fektrinelli, 1964), p. 141, refers to many founders of the great Hollywood production companies such as Fox, Laemmle, Mayer, Warner, Zukor etc as: 'base second hand dealers, clowns, traffickers in fake jewellery, rabbit's fur or herring, travelling salesmen without credit.'

CODA

395. Author and director Virgilio Tosi, executive producer Dr Hans-Karl Galle. The films were produced by the Intitut für den Wissenschaftlichen Film, Göttingen, co-produced with CNRS Audio-Visuel, Paris and Istituto LUCE, Rome, with the collaboration of the British Universities Film & Video Council (BUFVC), London. The original version is in English. The films are also available in German, French, Italian and Spanish language versions. In addition to the version available on film (35mm or 16mm depending on the language version), the three films are available on VHS. The Italian version is also available on DVD from Instituo Luce.
396. Kohlrausch's first machine, albeit incomplete, is exhibited at the Deutsches Filmmuseum of Frankfurt am Main (Germany): to the curators of this cinema museum goes the credit for having put in its proper proportion the contribution made by this German pioneer of scientific cinematography. See Ernst Kohlrausch, 'Beschreibung des photographischen Apparates für Serien-Aufnahmen', *Photographische Mitteilungen*, no. 432, February 1891, pp. 306-309; Ernst Kohlrausch, 'Demonstrations-Vortrag über photographische Reihen-Aufnahmen vom Gange nervenkranker Personen und deren lebendiger Wiedergabe durch Projection', in E. von Leyden and E. Pfeiffer (eds.), *Verhandlungen des Congresses für Innere Medicin* (Wiesbaden, 1898).
397. Münch's films on mathematics, the original drawings and some of the flip-books are held at the Deutsches Filmmuseum of Frankfurt am Main (Germany).
398. See interview with Dr F. Sanguinetti (who discovered the film of the removal of the pulmonary cyst) in *Primera Plana*, no. 456, 26 October 1971, pp. 40-43; also the typescript (unpublished) *Origenes del cine en Buenos Aires (1894-1910)* (1971) at the Cineteca Argentina. Our thanks to Ivan Trujillo Bolio, director of cinematographic activities at the Filmoteca of the Universidad Nacional Autonoma in Mexico City, for his help to us in this research.
399. We would like to take the opportunity once again to thank all those people who contributed to the solution to these problems, underlining the role played by the International Scientific Film Association, which (using otherwise inaccessible funds) made it possible to overcome a stalled situation.
400. The identification and recent acclaim for Van Gehuchten's films is the work of Geneviève Aubert, professor of the Department of Neurology of the Catholic University

of Louvain, who made a brief documentary (9 mins) entitled ARTHUR VAN GEHUCHTEN - PIONEER OF CINEMATOGRAPHY IN CLINICAL NEUROLOGY, produced by the Cinémathèque Royale de Belgique and the Audiovisual Centre of Louvain, Brussels, 1998. See also Geneviève Aubert, 'Arthur Van Gehuchten takes neurology to the movies', *Neurology,* no. 59 (November 2002), pp. 1612-1618.

401. Our thanks to Dr Jean-Dominique Lajoux, scientific cineaste and ethnologist of the CNRS, Paris, for his collaboration in identifying Regnault's chronophotographic films and for his important technical contribution to the production of THE ORIGINS OF SCIENTIFIC CINEMATOGRAPHY, particularly for his work transferring the images to 35mm film and for the reanimation of Marey's chronophotographic films and those of other pioneers of scientific cinema.

402. An anthology of Pöch's earliest films was released in 1958 in the previously cited *Encyclopaedia Cinematographica* by Göttingen under the title NEU-GUINEA 1904-1906 – IN MEMORIAM PROF. DR RUDOLPH PÖCH. The sound edition of the film from 1908 was released in 1987 by the Österreichisches Bundesinstitut für den Wissenschaftlichen Film of Vienna.

403. The exhibition was reported as follows: 'A phonograph record was played simultaneously with the exhibition of a dance by means of a cinematograph, and the result was a very successful and vivid representation of a custom of savagery. With life-like fidelity three natives in palm leaf costumes, and disguised with hideous marks, were seen gyrating amid a luxuriant tropical growth, while the other machine supplied the rhythmic sinister sounds that seemed to be the fitting accompaniment of the menacing disguise with which the dancers had disfigured themselves. Dr Haddon said the dances were of a severe character, and were good training in athletics for young men.' 'The Cinematograph and the Phonograph', *Optical Lantern and Cinematograph Journal,* January 1906, p. 64. With thanks to Luke McKernan for bringing this reference to our attention.

404. Osvaldo Polimanti, 'Neue physiologische Beiträge über die Beziehungen zwischen den Stirnlappen und dem Kleinhirn', *Archiv für Anatomie und Physiologie – Physiologische Abteilung,* 1908, pp. 83-102; Osvaldo Polimanti, 'Über Ataxie cerebralen und cerebellaren Ursprungs', *Archiv für Anatomie und Physiologie – Physiologische Abteilung,* 1909, pp. 123-136.

BIBLIOGRAPHY

405. In the introduction to this important volume which collects a few hundred letters by Marey, Mannoni writes: 'Ce n'est que durant les années 1980 que la correspondance refait surface à la Cinémathèque. Elle est alors mise à la disposition des chercheurs (Marta Braun, Michel Frizot ou moi-même).' In truth, the day after the discovery of this precious document in 1983, the author of this book (who was in Paris) was alerted to the fact by the Cinémathèque Française itself and was the first scholar (together with the then director of the Museum and the Library, Noëlle Giret) to open the packets of letters and to begin deciphering Marey's difficult handwriting.

Index

The Origins of Scientific Cinematography

THE ORIGINS OF SCIENTIFIC CINEMATOGRAPHY is a documentary film series directed by Virgilio Tosi, and produced by Dr Hans-Karl Galle for the Institut für den Wissenschaftlichen Film. The films complement Tosi's book *Cinema Before Cinema*, using archive film and original equipment to show how cinematography had its origins not in the music hall or the fairground, but in the laboratory, as scientists of the 19th and early 20th centuries attempted to find new ways of seeing and measuring the natural world. The English-language version of the films is distributed by the British Universities Film & Video Council.

Part 1: The pioneers

Jules Janssen's 'photographic revolver' (1873–4), Eadweard Muybridge's development of serial photography of human and animal locomotion (1878–87); and Étienne-Jules Marey's 'photographic gun' (1882), and his models of the Chronophotographe (1882–93), along with his first research films.

Part 2: Technical developments at the turn of the century

Technical advancements of scientific cinematography between 1883 and 1914 and in different countries, by scientists, photographers, teachers, and officers such as Londe, Sébert, Anschütz, Kohlrausch, Demeny, Bull, von Lendenfeld and Noguès.

Part 3: Early applications

A compilation of sequences from twenty scientific films, made between 1895 and 1911. The subjects include biology (Pfeffer, Ries, Comandon, Polimanti, Carvallo), medicine (Marinescu, Posadas, Doyen, von Bergmann, Negro, Macintyre, Lomon), technical sciences (Cranz) mathematics (Münch), and ethnology (Regnault, Haddon, Spencer, Krämer, Pöch).

97 mins, col/bw, in English. Available on VHS or DVD.
To order a copy, please visit www.bufvc.ac.uk/publications, or contact the BUFVC at 77 Wells Street, London W1T 3QJ,
☎ *020 7393 1503 email: services@bufvc.ac.uk.*